About My Life
and the
Kept Woman

Also by John Rechy

Novels
City of Night
Numbers
This Day's Death
The Vampires
The Fourth Angel
Rushes
Bodies and Souls
Marilyn's Daughter
Our Lady of Babylon
The Miraculous Day of Amalia Gómez
The Coming of the Night
The Life and Adventures of Lyle Clemens

Nonfiction
The Sexual Outlaw: A Documentary
Beneath the Skin: Collected Essays

Plays
Tigers Wild (The Fourth Angel)
Rushes
Momma as She Became—But Not as She Was

About My Life

and the

Kept Woman

A Memoir

JOHN RECHY

Grove Press
New York

Published simultaneously in Canada
Printed in the United States of America

FIRST EDITION

ISBN-10: 0-8021-1861-5
ISBN-13: 978-0-8021-1861-5

Grove Press
an imprint of Grove/Atlantic, Inc.
841 Broadway
New York, NY 10003

Distributed by Publishers Group West

www.groveatlantic.com

08 09 10 11 12   10 9 8 7 6 5 4 3 2 1

FOR THE MEMORY OF MY MOTHER

High school graduation, El Paso, Texas

I THANK MICHAEL EARL SNYDER
FOR HIS STEADFAST ENCOURAGEMENT
IN THE WRITING OF THIS BOOK

New York City, late sixties

THIS IS NOT WHAT HAPPENED; IT IS WHAT IS REMEMBERED.
ITS SEQUENCE IS THE SEQUENCE OF RECOLLECTION.

About My Life
and the
Kept Woman

1

I was twelve, and my sister was about to marry her football-captain sweetheart. She was sixteen, he was seventeen, and the approaching union was fraught with dangers whose effects, many years later, would multiply and spread into the core of San Francisco society and would, more years later, help to define my life.

But now it was 1945 in El Paso, Texas, and plans for my sister's wedding had aroused the wrath of the groom's father. A twig of a man, Señor Antonio Guzman, referred to only as "Señor," "Sir,"—bedridden for years and partially paralyzed—had sworn to stop the wedding "by whatever means may become necessary." His anger was meant to punish his son, who had, he declared, "strayed beyond decent bounds by intending to marry so young, a breach of decorum I will not condone." Being underage, the teenagers required permission of their respective parents. They had my parents' permission for a reason that Señor did not know.

Now, to understand the enormity of Señor's wrath at his son, and my mother and father's escalating anxiety that my sister's wedding proceed immediately, one must know that these implications of danger were swirling on the border of two juxtaposed cities—Juárez in Mexico and El Paso in Texas—cities separated only by a stretch of the Rio Grande, most often a bed of dry sand along whose banks lazy spiders spun their webs.

That geographical proximity had created in Texas a class of unique immigrants—men and women of education and means who had fled Mexico during the revolution of 1910, when Porfirio Díaz, the president turned dictator, was forced into exile, throwing the country into a chaos of shifting factions and loyalties. That class of formerly privileged Mexican immigrants often claimed ancestral lineage to "someone noble in Spain."

Displaced and impoverished by the revolution, they were drained once again by the Great Depression. They grasped onto a societal hierarchy, disdaining those Mexicans of Indian ancestry, a fact revealed, they staunchly claimed, by darker skin, by their "chicanismos"—crude mannerisms, the designation "chicano" being relegated then to a lower class of Mexicans—and by coarse down-tilted eyelashes. Not until years later did I understand why my mother so diligently and gently guided me, five or six years old at the time, to lie on her lap while we sat during stifling Texas nights on the unscreened porch of our dilapidated house as she curled my already long curly eyelashes with a saliva-moistened finger.

The two groups of Mexican immigrants had this in common: Spanish was the language of communication; English was practiced only as necessary among older Mexicans, though increasingly among the younger ones. My mother, like others of her generation and by announced choice, never learned English, considering speaking it to be a betrayal of the country her family had been forced by turmoil and circumstances to flee. At home, we spoke only Spanish.

During World War II, just recently ended, Mexican families with sons in the military had made a notable exception to their clinging fealty to Mexico. They were swept into patriotic fervor. Square signs—red, white, and blue—sprouted in windows: "Our Son is Serving America."

My mother went to church almost daily to recite tearful rosaries for the safety of my brothers: Robert, the older of the two, in the South Pacific; and Yvan, the younger, in Germany. Both would be returning soon, a fact that made me lament that that would not occur sooner so they might use their military skills to thwart the growing menace of Señor.

Through tumultuous times in El Paso, the class of once privileged immigrants, however poor they increasingly became like other Mexicans in the foreign state of Texas, retained from their previous culture, unbudging attitudes toward social propriety and morality. Those included a staunch belief in the Catholic church and in the sacred virginity of the Holy Mother, considered the Mother of God, not only of Christ. They held an equally staunch belief in the virginity of unwed women.

Señor's initial threat to stop the marriage of my sister Olga and his son Luis soon escalated into an overt declaration of war conveyed by his tiny wife in a second visit to my family—the first visit had announced his fierce opposition.

Señor's wife was a woman so small, so like a buzzing hummingbird, that it was difficult to believe what was generally known, that she daily dressed Señor in suit, tie, and shoes, and then carried him, coaxing, pushing him a little, and finally shoving him—gently—to a reclining couch, where, propped up, he glowered through a window and denounced the modern world's immorality. What she probably suspected and what had coaxed my father and mother to grant permission for the union was that my sister was pregnant by Señor's burly son and might very soon begin to swell.

Whether knowing of the pregnancy would have caused Señor to relent—or to fall dead—was something his wife and son preferred not to chance. "Any more revelations," the fluttery woman said after she had delivered Señor's emphasis on his earlier warning, "will enrage him to the point that we will all be in mortal danger, God help us!"

"Over my dead body he'll stop the wedding," my father proclaimed, launching a war of tyrants—he would not allow another tyrant to impose his will on his own daughter, and therefore on him. He, like Señor, ruled rigidly over his family; he did not permit anyone else to even question our conduct. (Once, he confronted a truant officer who had captured me leaving the Texas Grand Theater by the exit door that I used to squeeze in free—I had gone to see Claire Trevor and John Wayne in *Dark Command* during Revival Week, my favorite period, which came, too infrequently, once every three months or so and featured movies that, even then, had become "old." "Don't dare punish my son; only I can do that," my father warned the truant officer, who was already backing away from the short, red-faced Scotsman's fists, prepared to stress his words.)

Adding to the burgeoning dangers indicated in the alerts from Señor via his spindly wife was this equally grave one: The groom's sister, older than he by eight years, had conveyed her intention to travel from Mexico City and return to El Paso to attend her younger brother's wedding, thus challenging Señor, who had banished her years ago. That banishment had been accompanied by his vow that if she ever again crossed his path, or entered its environs, he would exile her not only from the city but from life. He had added to his harsh admonition one of his most emphatic curses—"a father's righteous curse"—because, he said, "of her vile association that my dignity will not allow me to clarify." He also demanded that she never again use his name as her surname.

Her banishment and the "vile association" had resulted from the fact that she was the kept woman of one of Mexico's most powerful and richest men (the "invisible president"). Marisa Guzman was often referred to only as "the kept woman of Augusto de Leon."

The kept woman! What did it mean to be kept? Not a wife, but belonging to—"the kept woman of!"—de Leon, a powerful man, a rich man whose wealth allowed him to choose among all others. To be kept meant—had to mean—that the kept woman was beautiful, didn't it? Being kept was special—and scandalous enough to enrage Señor so fiercely. Banished and cursed! Yet if the rumors were true, she was also brave to challenge the wizened little man who ruled like a despot from his couch. The enormity of it all sent my imagination spinning into vague but exciting conjectures.

All this acquired the fascinating taint of thrilling things forbidden, a matter underscored by my mother's despondent sighs and the loud epithets from my father each time a further message promising to block the marriage was issued by Señor through his frightened wife, who came next to gasp only this:

"What more? What more? *Ay, Dios mio!*"

The answer to "What more?" came in *El Continental,* the daily Spanish-language newspaper published in El Paso. Framed in an ominous black border, like a warning of obituaries, an advertisement, four inches by two columns, appeared in its pages, formally announcing Señor's grave displeasure.

> I, Señor Antonio Guzman, formally oppose the union of my son to a girl whose name I shall not mention in deference to her gender. I will banish from my esteem anyone who sanctions such a union, which will be stopped.

Since Señor's wife and my mother had once exchanged visits, I had seen the wizened mustachioed dictator on his couch as he shrank daily while his curses on the world and his uncannily dark mustache grew in fierce opposite proportion. When he barely glanced at me that day, I ran away, terrified, although I knew he was restricted to his couch.

"They'll have to marry immediately because God knows what Señor is planning and Olga looked plump to me today," my beautiful Mexican mother said as she conferred with my father in the dingy kitchen that defined his fall from grace. A gifted musician and orchestra conductor, my father had lived a privileged life in Mexico, the son of a Scottish father and a snobbish mother who proclaimed insistently that she was of "pure Spanish blood." The family had been regular guests at dinner with President Porfirio Díaz before his fall, sharing his vacation mansion in Guadalajara. My father had gone on to excel at the University of Mexico, to learn how to play "every musical instrument," and eventually to conduct his own orchestra, his own opera company. From the heights of artistic accomplishment and of Mexican society—and through the vicissitudes of disasters and poverty that the Depression had wrought in Texas—he had fallen to the rank of occasional musical tutor to untalented, grudging Texan children.

"We'll take them to Juárez, and they'll be married in a civil ceremony, but they'll have to agree not to live together until they marry in church, in a Catholic ceremony; and I will write the music," my father said, asserting his own moral qualifier to the wedding of the two teenagers, as well as his artistic participation in the nuptials.

Whether my mother thought that strategy was appropriate or not, she never dared challenge him. "Yes, you're right, Roberto."

We traipsed—there was no one to leave me with—my mother, my father, my sister, and her fiancé, across the border to Juárez, where any marriage or divorce might be obtained for a fee. A dowdy Mexican magistrate in a gray suit took a few hard-earned dollars from my father and pronounced the couple legally wed. They agreed not to live together until a church wedding could take place—quickly. Such a church wedding had now become possible without Señor's consent because the marriage was technically legal.

Another advertisement, even larger, appeared in *El Continental:*

The claimed union of my son, and a young woman I will not name in consideration of her gender, is illegitimate, not sanctioned by the Holy Catholic Church, or by me. If this canard proceeds into the Holy Church, I shall appear at the sacred altar to proclaim the fraudulence of such a union.

"Does he intend to crawl to the altar?" my father said with a nasty chuckle, while my mother shivered at the prospect of Señor's carrying out his vow. "We'll see how he intends to interfere." My father's tone indicated that he was more than ready to meet the challenge in this escalating war. I envisioned the two tyrants entangled, exchanging blows at the entrance to the church, a sight that caused me to double over with laughter, which would have earned me a vicious smack from my father if I had not learned, though not always successfully, to dodge.

Rehearsals for the wedding ceremony proceeded in a private home, the address withheld as long as possible. Apprehensive bridesmaids and nervous awkward ushers gathered there, my future brother-in-law's fellow football players proclaiming their manliness by emphasizing their clumsiness. The stoutest among them was stationed at the door to make sure no invasion occurred. The wedding would take place next weekend in the Church of the Sacred Heart.

The tense silence that prevailed in our house was broken by a shrill little voice. Señor's wife had escaped from her husband's tightening scrutiny to appear again and warn us: "Señor intends to rise like Lazarus to stop the wedding!"

Whatever he did intend, I was sure that the man I had once retreated from in fear was capable of horrors, horrors that included my mother's and his wife's instant speculation that he would set fire to the church.

What's more—my mother expounded on added perils—if he learned that his daughter Marisa was indeed expected, then he would surely have someone carry him into the church on a stretcher to fulfill his terrible promise.

"Might your daughter be coaxed not to come?" my mother asked the trembling little woman, who gasped, "Oh, she's coming all right, nothing can keep her away, and she refuses to change her name, as he demanded—it's still his *and* hers!—and it will infuriate Señor to the limit of endurance because everyone knows she's the kept woman of Augusto de Leon."

The kept woman! Those words resonated from what I overheard. I tried to envision her, shape her. Nothing I could conjure satisfied the extravagant title. I knew only that being a kept woman had created scandal; and so I imbued all the secrecy and whispers about her with a glow of glamorous wickedness. I begged God:

Please let the kept woman come.

The time of the ceremony arrived. The church had been adorned with as much opulence as limited funds allowed, including paper flowers intermixed with real flowers gathered that very morning from outlying fields. In the balcony in back of the church, my father was directing his small band of enduring musicians playing the special music he had arranged with enormous care to further affront his adversary in this battle of wills.

Wearing a suit jacket that one of my brothers had outgrown and that draped over me like a cape, I sat in the front pew nearest the altar with my mother, who clutched her rosary as if it was a weapon she might hurl if the tyrant invaded. I had noticed that two hideous aunts—my mother's older sisters, whom I did not remember having ever said a kind word about anyone during their frequent unwelcome and unannounced visits to our house—were stationed like evil sentries by the entrance to the church, anticipating, I was sure, that Señor would somehow appear and that they would be able to egg him on to do his worst while they pretended to ask for God's succor for us all.

I was jolted by something else, strangely unexpected. I saw my sister entering the church wearing a white veil, while the groom, visibly uncomfortable out of his football uniform and in his rented tuxedo, awaited her at the altar. My sister? That was my sister Olga?

My friend who had been a gangly tomboy who chewed her hair when she was anxious? Had I been so overwhelmed by the spiraling dangers, and so capable of ignoring my mother sewing into the late night on yards of white lustrous material—how purchased, only she and God knew—that I hadn't realized my sister was the cause of the main danger? *She* was being married?

How was that possible?—leaving me, her friend? Hadn't she given me my greatest moment of victory in baseball when, as a moony child of eight—she was twelve—I had been relegated to the "outfield" of a vacant weed-claimed lot to daydream while a neighborhood baseball game proceeded? As I had been imagining what lay behind the sheet of blue Texas sky, I heard her shout at me across the lot: "Jump and catch it!" Responding to her command, I jumped, my hand up, and I made the catch that won the game.

In church now, seeing her like a ghostly ship gliding away from my life, only then did I realize that my sister, who was not gangly anymore and was very pretty—would never again play games with me. I felt a sense of betrayal, deepened when she passed by in the procession of bridesmaids flouncing like lavender butterflies and she did not glance at me. Was she embarrassed by what she was doing?—there in white, getting married?

My mother, weeping, kept looking toward the back of the church, nervously, and then fretting with her rosary so absently that her fingers did not advance along its beads.

"God protect us!" my mother exhaled loud enough to be heard by those seated several rows away. They and others, stirred by her reaction, turned to locate the object of her shock at the entrance to the church.

Agitated whispers!

Señor! He had done it. He had been carried to the church on a stretcher, and then, with all the force of his meanness, he had pushed himself up. There he stood at the entrance to the church, the morning sun carving a threatening shadow along the main aisle as he paused, ready to unleash on us all whatever horrors he had plotted.

But it wasn't the tyrant that had cast such an imposing shadow. It was—

"The kept woman of Augusto de Leon!" my mother gasped.

2

My mother nudged me to coax my attention back to what was occurring before the altar. To ensure that, she placed her hand with the rosary on my head so that the crucifix dangled before me like a warning.

But she could not yank my thoughts away from the excitement created by the kept woman. What would she look like when she emerged out of the shadows of the church?

I tried borrowing characteristics from the women in my father's troupe of players, a lingering hint of his former life, that motley crew he recruited to play in his local productions, under the sponsorship of the parish priest, who offered him the school auditorium for his makeshift operas, which, nonetheless, my father tinted with a desperate splendor that dazzled the poverty-ridden population, some of whom, plucked by him to be his stars, learned under his tutelage to perform a pavan in the style of the court of Marie Antoinette. Their resplendent wigs were molded from the same cotton some of them picked from nearby fields, and then sprinkled with crumbled tinsel.

During my short life, I had already seen what I had once thought were beautiful women in my father's troupe. Beautiful to me then, and dressed in what seemed to me opulent costumes, those women, recalled in subsequent memories and adjusted into their time of deprivation, were not grand at all; they wore clothes that were attempts at camouflage, costumes edged in crinkled colored paper because good material was too expensive.

Now, in the Church of the Sacred Heart, I stealthily pushed away from my eyes the crucifix dangling from my mother's rosary, her hand firmed on my shoulder. I needed to clear away any possible intrusion from my conjuring of the kept woman.

I evoked the most beautiful woman I had ever seen—the most beautiful next to my mother and my older, married sister, Blanca, not yet Olga, silly at the altar. I had seen that most beautiful woman when I was a performer in the traveling company of the renowned Mexican actress Virginia Fabrigas, an associate of my father from his days of grandeur in Mexico. At age seven, I had played an allegorical boy Jesus in a production of *El Monje Blanco,* by a Catalan poet, Eduardo Marquina. It featured fine costumes, carefully kept by a wardrobe mistress. In the play, my mother was played by Magda Holler, a luminous, beautiful blonde actress; and my father was the movie actor Manolin, almost as pretty as she. The climax of the drama came when I, wearing an abbreviated toga and sandals, leaned against two abandoned boards of wood, and with my arms linked over them, converted them into a cross, whereupon my father in the play lamented: "Look! He is already crucified!" I could hear the sobs of women and men, in the audience, and that encouraged me, when my scene was over, to run out into the audience, to be kissed and hugged by the tearful spectators—until someone was put in charge of me, to make sure I didn't court the wonderful embraces.

During the play, smitten, I would take every opportunity to situate myself close to Magda Holler, to the point that I was relocated during our scenes together after she noticeably nudged me away onstage, almost causing me to trip on my sandals.

Would the kept woman look like her? No. Remembering her nudging rejection, I dismissed her as a contender.

Always fascinated by beauty, I had even coaxed my sister Olga, then still gangly, to enter a "worldwide search" for a woman to play a modern Salome in the western *Salome, Where She Danced*. I posed her in what I assumed—after many false attempts—made her look glamorous, a formidable feat, since she had not yet blossomed into the girl in a wedding dress. Constantly gnawing on a strand of her dark hair, she had grumbled as I snapped the small box camera I had acquired by saving bubble-gum wrappers. I mailed the pictures to the studio involved. Yvonne DeCarlo got the role. (Despondent about the fact that my sister was not the means to get us to Hollywood and into the movies, I wrote to Shirley Temple at her studio, asking whether she wanted me as a dance partner; she never answered.)

Would the kept woman look like Yvonne DeCarlo?

No, movie stars were unreal people who existed only on a flat screen, or in black-and-white photographs.

Would she look like Gloria Garcia, who had been Madama Butterfly in my father's staging? No, no, no, pale and wispy—and strange looking.

Would she look like Gloria Patiño, who had played Carmen wearing a fiery dress my mother had stayed up nights to sew? Carmen's eyes were blackened with mascara and slanted wickedly; black, black hair cascaded over her forehead; huge earrings swayed with her hips; her lips exploded with lipstick. Certainly formidable.

Carmen! Yes, she might look like Carmen!

No, no, a kept woman looking like a decorated gypsy?

Like any kind of gypsy?

That thought made me shudder so obviously that my mother strengthened her grasp on my shoulders, thinking I would once again turn toward the back of the church in an attempt to locate the forbidden presence.

Certainly the kept woman would not look like the gypsies I had seen when a ragged band of them had invaded El Paso.

They had appeared overnight and camped in a trash-littered vacant lot; their makeshift wagon-trailer was a large boxlike contraption within which they all lived. How they had hauled it there was a puzzle. I saw a run-down car nearby, propped up on bricks, but it seemed incapable of lugging the trailer. Three or four children roamed in and out, never straying from the area of the wagon or from a swarthy older man and woman. These two—she with a headband, he with a pipe whose embers gleamed on and off like disturbed spirits—sat on makeshift steps in the late evening when the Texas sun turned bloody on the desert horizon.

Pondering what, plotting what? Behind a barricade of giant tumbleweeds abandoned by a recent windstorm, I studied them, fascinated, for what seemed like hours.

They all wore beads, somewhere, about their heads, their hands, their necks, glittery beads that I recognized as powerful amulets, sinister amulets capable of . . . anything! Everything!

Gauzy lights from candle lamps inside the wagon cast a mothy glow within the darkened interior of the trailer, openings into the dark cavern of the gypsies' world. That world contained all that I feared then, dangers and mysteries, all that was alien, not yet understood, just felt, just feared.

Where had they come from? Why were they in Texas—in El Paso? What did they keep hidden inside the trailer?

The busiest in their band was a little girl, about twelve, very dark brown, dressed in a skirt made out of patches, all colors. She would run around in nervous spurts. As if there was an invisible wall that the man and the woman had constructed, she would halt, not stepping beyond what I assumed was a warning circle.

Once, when she stopped at that undrawn demarcation, she stared at the pile of weeds behind which I was hiding, penetrating it, I knew, and spotting me. I ran breathlessly away—and stumbled on a rock. When a threatening haze cleared, I looked up. There she stood, the brown gypsy girl, over me.

I jumped up, to resume my escape. She grabbed me. I struggled to release myself from her grip. She held on. I fought her more. She put her spangled arms around me and clutched me tightly against her.

Her darkening face was only inches from mine, her mouth so close that I could breathe what I was sure was an evil vapor to hold me until the others would come and trap me, take me away with them, make me a gypsy. My mother would never know where I had gone. Before the brown girl could press her lips to mine, to inject me with a foul potion—but why was she smiling?—I managed to pull away.

Then the gypsies were gone, all the secrets I had attributed to them left intact, relinquishing no answers.

That, eventually, was more than right, because now, when I was age twelve, mysteries were not about vague fears; no, I was now dealing with actual mysteries, vaster mysteries, the mysteries of the world of adults, of scandals. I was now roaming their landscape like a spy, gathering evidence for conclusions I would draw much later, all whirling, not yet shaped, about my sister's marriage, Señor's threats, and about the kept woman whose image still remained elusive.

In the Church of the Sacred Heart with my sister Olga and her soon-to-be husband Luis kneeling before the altar like uncomfortable children, along with bridesmaids and ushers equally uncomfortable—and my older sister, Blanca, standing in her position as matron of honor, the only adult in the wedding party—I strained away from my mother's hold to stare back at the mysterious woman. Instead, I noticed that my two miserable aunts in the back had been thrown into a state of agitation by the kept woman, their heads swirling around. My attention filtered them out, along with any other distraction, as I saw *her!*

She moved slowly—glided—out of the slash of light that had created the menacing shadow, which mellowed as she moved into the clearer light of the church. A conspiracy of multi-tinted light filtered through the colored mosaic of stained windows, creating a magical light that followed her; or rather, she seemed to entice it to come along with her, to a back pew, where she sat, kneeling and performing a reverential sign of the cross.

My mother poked me with the cross on her rosary, so insistently that I thought she had pinched me—a rare occurrence, since she never menaced us in any way. When my head resisted being turned away from the kept woman, my mother's hands directed it back to the nuptials, but not before I knew that my life had been invaded by an awesome presence.

Hearing the urgent admonitions that my mother was whispering to me—so close to the altar—my sister glanced back and saw me squirming in the floppy jacket not entirely successfully taken in by my mother for the occasion. The girl I had played baseball with, the tomboy who somehow had found her way to the altar with a white veil—did she see herself in it for the first time?—returned. Her gleeful stare still on me, she tried to suppress a giggle that I echoed, causing hers to increase into laughter.

Then the football captain turned around, saw me, heard her— and tried unsuccessfully to stifle his own giggling. At the altar, one by one as if some immediate virus was running through them, the bridesmaids became convulsed with laughter, laughter raised to an even higher level by the ushers as they all turned back into the children they still were. My sister Blanca moved futilely about, randomly shaking those who were laughing, and then, surrendering, issued what would have been a loud guffaw if the tittering had not risen so formidably. The priest looked on in horror for only a few seconds before he turned away, to face the martyred Christ on the altar, but also—his quivering body informed us—to suppress his own choked giggles.

My father's soaring music smothered the laughter before the contagion could spread into the congregation.

The ceremony was over.

Taking advantage of the fact that the bridal party was now marching out—the participants still like strangely attired children playing parts in a high school play—I wrenched myself away from my mother's clutch and turned to locate the startling woman.

Where had she gone?

Had she evaporated, a vision of my imagination? Or had she come in secret to El Paso only for the ceremony—and with a changed name, fearing Señor's threats? If so, she wasn't courageous, as I had imagined—she had fled immediately. I felt profoundly betrayed. So I would never see her again, never *see* her.

The tyrant Señor did not appear. The groom's mother had even managed to step out of the range of Señor's radar to peek in on the ceremony and provide a secret benediction with fingers dipped in holy water at the door.

As we walked out of the church, my mother's face bathed in tears, my father's music surging wondrously, I still searched forlornly for the magical presence, hoping that I was wrong, that she hadn't fled, afraid. Only the hideous aunts were there. I never could decide which of the two was the uglier; they were like homely twins. I assumed my mother had been given all the beauty allowed the daughters in the family. Now I heard them hiss loudly to each other:

"Can you believe that that woman—"

"—that *immoral* woman—"

"—that she would dare disgrace the holy church of God—"

"—and defy her father's warnings!"

3

In Mexico at the time, among Mexican gamblers, politicians, businessmen, gangsters—a tentative "upper class" collectively called "*los políticos*"—mistresses seemed to be required. A few of the mistresses might surface from the streets and alleys along which they strolled like painted phantoms in and out of the smoky light that squeezed out of bars. Some of the mistresses might come from houses, a stratum a few steps higher than that of the alleys. The lucky ones, not many, graduated to become madams, and, chosen, lived in the peripheries of their keepers' lives. A very few, the most fortunate, became wives, but they could erase only some of the stain of scandal; they were never accepted in the desirable echelons of Mexican high society. Their practiced veneer of sophistication did not camouflage the tough, rough women they were as they battled to retain their positions before a young mistress might shove them out of their relatively comfortable lives in miniature mansions, gaudy imitations of the homes populated by the most powerful men and their wives.

My mother's brother, Carlos, who had accrued some amount of wealth from sources unknown and who still lived in Juárez, had such a woman. According to gossip, she had been a house prostitute who had worked her way up to being a madam. Now she was married to my uncle, set up in a flimsily opulent home, with Indian maids in constant attendance.

I had gone to Juárez with my mother once, to buy papaya that I had learned was good for developing muscles, which I wanted badly before my ten-year-old body made that possible. My mother decided to drop in on my uncle. That's what we did then, dropped in—not everyone had a telephone, and we could not afford one.

We were led into the large house by an Indian maid, a silent woman who seemed to be in a defensive trance. My uncle was not in. But our presence was announced. We were abandoned inside a hall glittering with several—yes, several—glassy chandeliers, tinkling mysteriously.

We followed loud voices into another room, voices so loud that they must have accounted for the nervous chandeliers. There sat Carmen, my uncle's wife, at a round table, playing poker, with four other hefty women who resembled her remarkably, all dressed like her in expensive clothes that still looked tawdry, altered to create deep cleavage to display abundant breasts, which one or another of the women occasionally hoisted, a formidable shove upward to expose more haughty flesh.

A large bottle of whiskey ruled the middle of the table, a bottle lifted frequently by each of the women for yet another long shot into their glasses, or, hurriedly, into their mouths. From Carmen's lips, a cigarette dangled. All the other women were smoking, puffing relentlessly after swallows of the liquor and between noisy epithets at the vagaries of luck. The stench of smoke filled the air. The Indian woman waited against a wall to be summoned for any urgent necessity—more liquor.

Carmen only glanced at us and nodded in acknowledgment of our presence, an attempted smile thwarted by the precariousness of her cigarette. Involved in a tense moment in the game of poker, she dropped a card with such a triumphant thud that it stilled the other voices. "There!"

Another woman dropped her own card, even more triumphantly. "I win!" she said and reached for the pile of pesos.

Carmen glowered at the exposed cards. "I say you cheated, *cabróna,*" she accused.

"I say you're a liar," spat the offended woman, "and you're the *cabróna,* a bitch—and worse, a sore loser." She stood up to leave, wobbling, with the spoils of the game.

Carmen's body shot up, just as shakily—both women propped themselves up by holding onto the table—and out came a small revolver that Carmen had hidden somewhere out of sight, perhaps in her lap. She pointed it at the other woman.

The women at the table prepared to dodge, since the pointed gun was wavering dizzily in Carmen's hand and her eyes squinted as if to verify her aim. The Indian maid fled.

"Put that gun down and I'll take you on, *mano a mano,*" the accused woman bargained. "We'll settle this with our fists."

My uncle's wife narrowed her squint to the point that her eyes closed, and she seemed about to fall asleep standing; still, her lips clung to the mere butt of a cigarette that was making its way into her mouth. Her eyes shot wide open.

"Sit down, *desgraciada,*" she commanded the other woman, and underscored her order by firming the revolver with the aid of her other hand.

"*Estás judida, maldita,*" the other woman held her ground, claiming that Carmen was fucked and cursed.

"Well, then—" Carmen cocked her revolver with a loud click and pointed it somewhat unequivocally.

"Well, *then!*" the other woman echoed. She fished into her purse, and out came her own revolver.

The dueling revolvers were pointed so unsteadily that the other women ducked under the table, sending the offending cards cascading to the floor.

My mother hurried us out of the house, pushing me along because I kept looking back, hoping to see a scene that would rival the ones I saw in old movies during Revival Week at the Texas Grand Theater.

Since we didn't hear shots, I assumed the matter had been settled without murder.

That was the rung of Mexican society occupied by the women of the *políticos*.

But that was not the world that the kept woman of Augusto de Leon occupied, as I would learn only later because the future still waited to illuminate the present, and I was hoarding the pieces of a puzzle that I would try to fit subsequently into my life, when memories would assume whatever meaning they would ever assume.

The kept woman of Augusto de Leon existed in the tradition of the great mistresses—du Barry, Pompadour, Barbara Palmer, Emma Hamilton before the fall. She was not ostracized by Mexican society; nor did she live in secrecy—her keeper was much too powerful and aristocratic to permit that.

Although she would not attend state dinners at which the powerful man was in dutiful attendance with his wife, she lived not far from them—the two women exchanged greetings now and then, slight nods, even a faint smile—in a mansion almost as grand as theirs. Her uniformed chauffeur snapped to rigid attention at her appearance. A generous income allowed her the most stylish clothes from New York and Paris, cities she periodically visited with her mentor. Bejeweled at the theater, she sat in honored seats and greeted others who solicited her recognition. In restaurants she was a figure for display and admiration.

My sister Olga's wedding reception was held in the house of a relative in El Paso, a house like a relic, large enough, but lacking furniture, so that one room looked like another. It had two stories—as I had noted with delight on entering. To me that was a manifestation of elegance, no matter how drab both stories might be. Several dozen guests were gathering noisily, all as well dressed as was possible during extended tough times: the men in proper suits and ties, a few with hats exhumed for the occasion and properly removed before entering the house; the women in dresses retained for such an occasion, many also wearing hats. I detected the medicinal odor of mothballs when a breeze whispered into the house. There was all the usual brouhaha of Mexican weddings that occurred even in this higher, but poor, echelon of Mexican immigrant society.

Discarding my awkward jacket on a chair somewhere, I slunk around winding in and out of people grouping to discuss how beautiful the wedding had been, the women dabbing at tears of memory, the sad happiness of such an occasion. My sister and her husband had walked in through showers of rice and congratulations, rushing past greeters toward the largest room, where the cake that looked to me like a castle was waiting on a table. My mother stood nearby to greet my sister with a dozen little blessings, sighed aloud and echoed by celebratory outbursts that seemed to emanate from the center of the cake surrounded by circles of guests in this noisy tearful ritual. My sister Blanca, with her rigid German husband, Gus, beside her, stood with a polished knife for slicing into the mounds of sugar.

For me, it all passed in fast motion, the shrieks and applause when my sister daintily removed the strange sugar figures, like tiny featureless puppets, on the highest tier of the snowy cake; the actual cutting of the cake, my sister and . . . her husband? . . . together cutting into it for the first slice and intensified applause; the deliberately loud popping of corks as bottles of "champagne"—sparkling wine, the best affordable—were opened, poured into paper cups, and passed around. At least one gentleman, and surely one or two more, had managed to sneak a beer, instead, into his cup. Mounting toasts! Loud applause! Joyful tears at evoked memories!

I stood glaring at my unfaithful sister.

Very soon—too soon—it would be time for the couple to leave on a honeymoon, to Mesita, in New Mexico (where Billy the Kid was said to have lingered and Bonnie and Clyde might have made a visit in honor of his memory). The small town was just a few miles outside El Paso, but that economical honeymoon seemed to me then like a trip to Paris.

I ran about the rooms of the house, trying to find a hiding place where I might be discovered, with difficulty, when my sister would begin frantically looking for me, leaving me for the last in her abundant farewells amid drenching tears, jubilant and sad salutes, good wishes, and blessings. Then she would take me aside to deliver a special farewell, an acknowledgment of our enduring closeness, and a promise to clarify this baffling event, a promise that once this silly stuff was over, she would come back and be my cherished partner, without that odd man in a tuxedo. She would not say "good-bye"—we had figured out that that had unwanted finality to it—no, she would say:

"So long, little brother. I'll be back in a few days."

As I roamed the house that was becoming vaster and emptier for me—though people mingled about, trying to locate a place to sit, balancing paper cups of "champagne" with pieces of cake that crumbled on paper plates—I dodged into one room propitious for hiding. A doorless closet ahead would be perfect. Before I could head for it, I was almost knocked down by an older man and his wife looking startled out of their primness as they hurried away from that one room, although it was not occupied—

Except by one person.

Alone, slowly smoking a cigarette.

She sat on a drab couch out of which tufts of cotton had begun to protrude. It had to be her. No one else would look like that, not in El Paso, not in the world that I knew. There was no doubt that there sat the kept woman of Augusto de Leon.

Remaining now at the edge of the door, and hiding behind the frame, I stared at her in stunned awe. It was as if the room had been vacated for her, except for a scrappy framed drawing of a countryside, on a wall whose paint was peeling, and a lamp whose shade had been patched. Nothing more was needed, because the kept woman challenged the drabness of the room, splashed it with a grandeur it had never possessed, not even when new. The ragged couch she sat on was her throne.

She wore a gray dress that caressed her body. The few creases that dared to appear on it when she moved, breathing, were instantly transformed into silvery-gray streaks, the exact color of her shoes. In a hint of elegant decorum, her breasts did not peek out of the top of her dress; they were only outlined as if hands were molding them and then sliding down along the curves of her body. She wore the hat she had worn in church, wide-brimmed, a paler shade of gray, slanting to the right so that a portion of her face was shaded. Even under the breath of a veil sprinkled with velvet dots, her lips were a bold slash of crimson, stark on her creamy skin—no, her skin was the color of cream into which only a touch of chocolate had been blended. Her eyebrows arched—didn't hover—over her eyes, which were—

From where I stood, I could not tell what color; I hoped amber, a favorite shade, the color of fall leaves that I had once painted in watercolors. I didn't have to see them to know that she had long, curled eyelashes.

Not until she shifted on the couch—and they glistened—did I notice that she wore tiny earrings, specks of diamonds, I was sure. Her hair was dark brown, but strands that caught a gleam of light from the window against which she sat burnished it umber. Although later I would discover that she was not tall, as she sat on the converted throne her legs looked long, her stockings so sheer—no woman, not even a kept woman, would dare shock with bare legs in El Paso—that they disappeared.

There was about her an aura of sublime aloofness—or welcome isolation. I was sure then that never again would I glimpse a creation as spectacular as the one my eyes, dry from staring, remained fixed on.

I must have been holding my breath, because when I released it, it came out as a sigh louder than I had expected, which made me pull back against the door frame so that, if she located the origin of the awed sound, she would not retreat from my sight.

Whether because she had become aware of my presence or whether at some private thought evoked by the sounds of congratulation rising now distantly about the wedding couple in another room, her lips tilted, the inception of a vague smile.

As if deciding not to complete the smile, or because the memory aroused had turned bitter, her scarlet lips parted, instead, to receive the cigarette she brought—almost thoughtfully—to her lips. She held it there at the exact verge of brushing her lips before she allowed it to touch in a movement that occurred without transition, and she inhaled imperceptibly—no sound even of her breath, the barest rise and fall of her breasts the only indication. A slender streak of smoke arose, lingered about her before it evaporated. The cigarette remained touching her lips as if reluctant to separate. Then her free hand rose and rested lightly on the elbow of the arm whose fingers held the cigarette, and she completed an intricately graceful choreography of slight movements as she withdrew the cigarette from her lips but kept it close, as if considering whether to inhale from it again, a moment of suspense. The hand with the cigarette drifted away from her face, was lowered, and she touched the tip of the cigarette so lightly to an ashtray that the ashes merely vanished.

She rested the cigarette on the ashtray and allowed one of her sheer legs to slide over the other, simultaneously adjusting the hem of her dress, which had risen, barely, above one knee. Her hands soothed the silvery rivulets sent scurrying about the dress.

As she reached again for the cigarette on the ashtray, she looked up and smiled, definitely smiled, this time—

At me!

No, it wasn't at me that she was smiling.

She was smiling at—

In the moments that I allowed my eyes to stray from her to locate any other possible direction of her smile, I saw a girl my age stationed at another doorway watching the kept woman as raptly as I had been. In those brief moments, I saw the girl raise one hand tentatively, on its way to her lips with what was, surely, an invisible cigarette. Catching me watching her, she pulled back out of my sight.

Was it at her that the woman had smiled?—as if bequeathing to her a glorious blessing? Or at me, bequeathing—What? At both of us . . . ? Bequeathing . . .

A harsh-looking woman invaded the room; the kept woman rose from the drab couch, smoothing her dress to banish any wrinkle that might linger; the sounds of the wedding party rose, laughter and snatches of songs and congratulations mixing; the harsh woman spoke, "Who—?" and the kept woman removed the veil from her face, and said, "I—" the wedding party was moving outside; I had to hurry—I heard curt words in the tense room, I heard soft words, words I thought I understood, words I didn't understand, words carried away by the sounds of the wedding party in the adjoining room, all occurring in a confusion of impressions, words that seemed to pursue me.

4

Cheers! Bravos! Applause!

Oh, but not, as it seemed to me for a moment, for the grand woman—no, the cheers were following the wedding couple on their way to their honeymoon.

I had to leave this room. My sister would now be desperately looking for me, her incongruous veil tangling—and even ripping, I hoped—on a chair, making her search for me even more difficult. I tore myself away from the awesome presence of Marisa Guzman.

My sister! There she was, so pretty—yes, she was very pretty now—so young. As I withdrew to find another hiding place, a closet away from the spellbound room, I knew that my sister would be asking, "Where's Johnny? I want to say so long to him—not good-bye—assure him I'll be back tomorrow—"

I slid into the deep shadows of an empty closet. Let her work to find me! Let everyone start wondering where she had rushed off to, abandoning them all, abandoning her . . . husband . . . and—

No urgent footsteps neared my hiding place. No approaching anxious voice, no words of panic at my absence. I left my place and looked out the nearest window.

With her handsome husband, my playmate had already entered the car amid a rain of rice, and they were gone.

★   ★   ★

I finally faced the fact that my sister would never again be the tomboy who played with me when she and her husband returned from
their brief honeymoon and rented two rooms in a boardinghouse
nearby, and I went determinedly to visit her, to reclaim my special
place in her life. I knocked on the door. Sounds inside stopped. I
knocked insistently. Nothing. I jumped, high, trying to reach the
slightly open transom to see whether she was there, asleep in her
bedroom. I fell with a thud. Did I hear giggles? I waited long, longer
at the door. When the noises resumed, I left bitterly.

Señor died soon after the wedding.

His wife astonished us by appearing to convey the news
calmly. She wore a new hat with a flower and had put on a few
pounds. "Yes, he's gone. No more curses." She tilted her hat.
"May God and the Holy Mother be kind to his soul." She either
sneezed or tittered as she tugged at her hat to slant it at a flattering
angle.

Soon after, a rumor ran through the community of exiled
immigrants that a mysterious woman draped in black veiling had
been seen at Señor's last rites, which—I heard to my surprise—were
widely attended. Immediately after the funeral, the mysterious
woman had hurried into a limousine and left.

I never again saw the kept woman of Augusto de Leon.

Gossip about her—cruel, malicious—persisted as a favorite
topic, especially from my mother's two monstrous sisters, who
knew of and took every opportunity to bring up our connection
to Marisa Guzman by way of my sister's marriage to her brother.
Previously, when they had visited my mother—usually to carry
some talk that they felt somehow implicated her—I would avoid
them. They were, at best, very plain, and, I couldn't help notic-

ing, their eyelashes seemed about to slant downward. Everything about my mother irked them: mostly, I was sure, that she was the pretty one.

I had heard them make several pointed references to my Scottish father's "strange, foreign ways." "And how can you tolerate them, Lupe?" they would accuse without identifying his strange ways. Though I might have agreed with them had they identified my father's strange ways, there were times when I hoped my father would walk in on them because, no doubt, he would pursue them out of the house in a rage, even push them out; but they avoided him, always. I once saw them—they were always together—under the shade of a tree, fanning each other as if they were merely cooling off, waiting until my father walked past them, either not seeing them or ignoring them. Then they rushed to knock at our door with fresh judgments.

Now here they were in our house, having announced their presence as always with a shrill, *"Aqui estamos!"*—"Here we are!"—as if their presence were to be celebrated; I considered their cry an alert that allowed me to flee.

But not today. I situated myself in a neighboring room, the door open. I was certain that the subject of the kept woman would come up.

This is how it went on that hot Texas day when gray storm clouds threatened rain, saturating heat with sticky humidity and hurling bolts of lightning rumbling over the desert.

The homelier of the two sisters—although that designation shifted, depending on which of the two was saying what—addressed my mother sternly: *"Esa mujer que tu conoces bien—pues es parte de tu familia, esa mujer, no?*—"that woman whom you know—well, she's a part of your family, that woman, no?"—is being properly discarded by her keeper, that philanderer de Leon, now that she's thirty, old and homely. I read about it in the newspaper."

"I never thought she was beautiful, with that atrocious painted face, and I'm sure she's older," the second aunt said—and now she was the homelier of the two. "I'm sure she is older! When she dared to come back to affront Señor, didn't you see those dark circles under her eyes?"

"From her perdition," the now uglier of the sisters said. "However old she is, she's been moved into another house by that de Leon."

"A lesser house? No?" my mother protested.

"The newspaper said it was a larger one," the other aunt sulked, certainly the uglier of the two, "but no doubt only to mollify her, but it's farther away from the one he shared with his legitimate Catholic wife in the best neighborhood."

"That appeared in a newspaper—?" my mother began to ask.

"Yes, in *El Alacrán,*" one aunt said. *El Alacrán—The Scorpion*—was a notorious Mexican tabloid published in Juárez that carried only salacious stories, constantly disproved.

"—with their names? Really?" my mother persisted.

"Don Raynaldo doesn't use names," one aunt said in an indignant tone, as if the mere mention of the tabloid's columnist proved the story's authenticity, his morality, and his commitment to the Catholic church. "But he doesn't have to. Everyone knows who he's talking about, always."

"Who else could he mean, Guadalupe? He referred to a powerful man and his kept woman? Who else would be involved in such a sordid story but de Leon and that woman? Who else?" piped up the other aunt.

"Hundreds of rich *políticos,*" my mother offered with a chuckle. "Including our brothers."

From such occasional references—including my father's that he thrust out in judgment of my mother's family—I had pieced together that the two rich uncles in Juárez, one of whom we had visited the day of the women's duel, were involved in shady political trafficking—large sums of money and favors.

"Guadalupe!" the aunts gasped indignantly in unison.

"How can you speak that way about your own brothers?" The uglier one dabbed at invisible tears. With renewed venom she said: "That woman is a whore!"

"And why are you defending such a woman?" said the other.

"Yes, why?" the second sister demanded.

"Because she's courageous," my mother said.

Was it possible that my mother had once been involved in a romantic scandal? Is that what accounted for her ardent defense of the kept woman?

She had been a beautiful young woman, my mother. Long before the events surrounding my sister's wedding and during the years of the deepening Depression in the country, Tía Ana, my great-aunt, my mother's aunt, had enthralled me with a loving depiction of my mother as a young woman—green eyes ("like emeralds"), brownish hair ("lighter in the sun"), a flawless fair complexion ("like buttermilk"), and long eyelashes ("curled, of course, of course"). I had accepted as unassailable Tía Ana's account of my mother's having been so lovely that Pancho Villa, the marauder of the countryside during the Mexican revolution, had been swept away by her after a single glance and had sent one of his trusted lieutenants to kidnap her, forcing the family to flee to Juárez.

Although I would learn later that the same claim was made by other Mexican women of the time—and Villa had been a reprobate—I was sure that the true version was Tía Ana's, about my mother, a version that had subsequently incited the claims by others.

So it was that from my earliest years, I imbued my mother with an aura of sad romance, a woman whom my father, an old, angry, dejected man of fifty when I was born, did not deserve.

Out of that belief had sprung my longing for her to have a lover—although at the time I would not have known that word. The thought, perhaps undefined then, had occurred to me when I was about six.

At that time in El Paso, freight trains that rumbled only one block away from our house carried hidden, shabby men and women—not derelicts, no, but people displaced by the Depression, most often on their way to California.

In frequent raids, uniformed police would slide the train doors open—creating a loud, terrible, metallic bang. They flailed their batons at the bodies that spilled out in terror, men and women stumbling out to escape, some caught and handcuffed, others left to bleed from the blows, some escaping into nearby neighborhoods, hiding until they felt relatively safe. Several would turn up at houses nearby for sustenance.

Lean men and women, often handsome but dirtied, tattered wanderers, would appear at our back door. My mother always kept rice and beans to be served on tin plates, and steaming coffee in tin cups, for those who turned up. They would sit on the rickety steps. Often, when there were several, my mother would entrust me with bringing out the plates of food, the coffee.

There was a particular transient who came to our backyard. He had appeared alone, and he was handsome. I observed that because although like others he was sullied by days of hidden travel, he had stopped at the outside faucet in our backyard to wash his face and hands.

My mother brought him the usual plate of rice and beans and the cup of hot coffee. He smiled at her and she smiled back as he took the food. I saw this as I stood near the remains of a garage filled with debris.

When he was through, he stood and extended one hand toward my mother. He waited. Slowly she extended her hand to him. He brought it to his lips and kissed it.

The memory of that man kissing my mother's hand lingered with its hint of kind romance.

There had been another hinted possibility to explain my mother's defense of Marisa Guzman.

During those same years, a nun who might have been a spry eighty years old officiated over her own chapel, actually a small house she had converted into a chapel a block away from where we lived, another one in a row of desolate houses occupied by Mexicans.

Within that house, Mother Mercedes had erected an altar, decorated with broken pieces of bottles, a medley of shiny colors, an improvised altar that one of her neighbors had helped her with. He was the same man who planted her garden—a difficult feat, since what constituted the "lawns" in our neighborhood was only dirt, a grainy residue left by seasonal winds to be scorched by hot summer suns. Nothing grew there except scattered patches of ugly weeds.

The nun's "lawn" did grow—overnight. Her helper had imported rich soil from outlying farms; he had also brought clumps of grass and flowers, transplanted for her. Several people had gathered to watch Mother Mercedes bless the lawn, lush amid the depleted blocks.

Men and women in the neighborhood contributed to the chapel: too many crucifixes, which found their place in the small chapel, and pictures of the Holy Mother, most in her appearance as the Virgin of Guadalupe. A young woman drew stations of the cross on sturdy cardboard. Her husband mounted them and nailed them, tight against each other, on the close walls of the chapel.

In the daytime, Mother Mercedes took in the children of women who worked; they paid her a pittance, if at all, often in candles, which were always lit so that there was, in the small chapel, a rubyish glow that illuminated the altar where she had placed Christ in a robe, arms outstretched, a welcome sight to me since I always winced at the crucified figure.

On a spring day when even scraggly trees were blooming with bright-green buds auguring leaves, and the seasonal winds I despised had become a kind breeze that would soon be smothered by fierce summer heat scorching the leaves of trees prematurely, I was idling on my way home from school when I saw my mother sitting on the porch of the chapel—a single step before the front door—with Mother Mercedes. My father was away, as he often was now, on some temporary work he took under the Works Progress Administration, formed to alleviate the poverty and joblessness of the Depression.

My mother and the nun were so engrossed in some intimate conversation—which even from my distance seemed whispered— that I was able to watch them secretly for several moments. My mother bowed her head, and Mother Mercedes blessed her slowly, mouthing some words. Then my mother, smiling, her hand on the nun as if to share the view, looked up at the sky, which had been swept azure by the spring breeze.

When she noticed me, my mother stood up hurriedly, came to me, held my hand. We both waved back at the nun, who now stood up watching us as we headed back to our decrepit house along the blocks.

I was sure my mother had been confessing to Mother Mercedes. But confessing to what? Perhaps—I grasped for this— she had confessed a happy transgression, forbidden by the church but allowed and blessed by the nun. I longed to give to my mother even brief times of romantic happiness.

Whatever those moments might have actually been, they established a powerful bond between my mother and the nun. That was why, I was sure, she once defended Mother Mecedes with fierce courage.

"Guadalupe, Guadalupe!" One of our neighbors had come knocking at our door. "They're going to arrest Mother Mercedes!"

"What! Who?" my mother demanded.

The quivering messenger wrung her hands; tears streaked her face. "The bishop!"

"The bishop is going to arrest Mother Mercedes?" My mother's indignation turned her face livid. She was not often enraged, not even at my father after his violent rants. She had already grabbed her purse and was rushing out of the house. I ran along with her.

When we reached the nun's chapel, others had gathered. Perhaps seven women—the men would be away at whatever jobs were available—were kneeling on the imported grass, and they were taking turns kissing the hand of a heavy man in a cassock, his starched white collar so stark and ringed with gray perspiration that it seemed to be holding his head up. I doubted that he was the bishop; probably he was just a parish priest.

"Where is Mother Mercedes?" my mother asked, softly, in Spanish after she had barely but dutifully kissed the priest's hand. That's what we were taught to do, kiss the hands of priests. I hated that, especially when I saw bristly hairs on their fingers. I would pretend to kiss the outstretched hand. With a moistened finger, I would bend my head and touch the waiting hand, to create, I hoped, the feeling of a kiss. Once a priest had grabbed my own hand and kissed it, leaving saliva.

Now, in practiced Spanish, the Anglo priest said: "The woman you call Mother Mercedes is inside doing penance for her grave sins."

The women, still kneeling, began to pray, "Hail Mary, full of Grace . . ."

My mother faced the priest. "Forgive me, Father, but may I ask you: What grave sin could a holy woman like her, a nun, commit?"

My devout mother questioning a priest!

"She's not a nun!" the bishop said.

Gasps, including one from my mother, interrupted the prayers.

I saw Mother Mercedes, her face framed by her habit as she peered out the window.

"She claims to be a member of an order that doesn't exist," the priest sneered. "She commits a mortal sin each time she dares to hear confession and even—even—!" He could hardly finish: "—say Mass!"

My mother had recovered from whatever surprise the priest's accusation of the nun had created. I watched her intently, admiring the courage it took for a Catholic woman to continue to face a priest. I was sure now that a confession had occurred that other spring afternoon, a confession that had caused my mother to smile up at the sky.

"Father, please, I don't mean to be disrespectful of your sacred office, but doesn't God listen to a holy woman's prayers?"

"Señora! You must watch whom you defend!" Impossible as it had seemed, the priest's face had grown redder, the white, smeared collar seeming to choke him. "The sacraments are allowed only to an ordained priest, a legitimate priest, who has taken vows, not a ridiculous old woman who claims to be a nun."

More gasps at the priest's harsh denunciation. The women there, standing now, stared at my mother as if waiting for guidance as to whom to support—the priest, or the nun who had ministered to their children, provided comfort without reward, and said Mass at odd times when work kept them from going to a large church.

The cleric, breathing fiercely, also seemed to be waiting for what my mother might say next. In irritation, he pulled his hand away from an old man who had just hobbled up and was attempting to kiss it.

My mother said: "Forgive me for asking this, Reverend Father: How can the kindness of an old nun offend so?"

"She's pretending, a fraud!"

"Father, she's confided this to me. It's true her order no longer exists. That's because she's the last survivor of it. She *is* a nun."

The priest turned his back on the improvised chapel. With a harsh bellow of air, he said, "Enough of this! Know, all of you, that you are gaining no favor with God by supporting this sinful charade, nor are you fulfilling any of His sacraments! You are all, every one of you, in danger of excommunication."

His skirted cassock hissing, he stalked away. A driver awaited him by a black car.

Everyone became aware of a flutter at the door of the chapel.

"Mother Mercedes," my mother greeted the nun, holding her hand, helping her out.

Mother Mercedes stepped forward. She stood at the open door and raised her hand.

Everyone knelt as she completed her blessing and then invited everyone to participate in early Mass.

I had sought connections to explain the excitement I felt at my mother's defense of the kept woman, the possibility of a romantic scandal, the defiance. But was that all that explained my growing fascination with the kept woman, beyond the obvious allure she would hold for a boy attempting to seize whatever was exceptional out of the drab horizon of life in El Paso?

5

That's how I viewed my life then, a bleak landscape.

From the beginning of my memories, I felt myself an outsider formed by contradictions. I was poor but with inherited memories of gentility. Of "mixed blood"—Mexican and Scottish—I was considered a *guerro,* a Mexican who didn't look Mexican by entrenched standards. My complexion was fair; my hair was almost blond in summer; my eyes were blue like my father's, although I often insisted they were green, like my mother's. Though I was constantly told that I was very good-looking, it was difficult for me to make friends—I didn't want to make friends—among other Mexican children in our neighborhood, who, at times, stared at me. One boy, two years older than I, followed me around. I asked him: "Why are you always staring at me?"

I thought he would run away, perhaps having thought I had not noticed him, perhaps not wanting to answer. I waited; he waited. "You're like a ghost boy," he said. "You don't talk to anyone. You seem to be studying others around you, judging others. You act as if you're not where we are."

A ghost boy. I remembered those words when I saw a photograph of my father's children's troupe—sometimes he wrote brief skits that I performed in. In the picture I was wearing white pants, a white shirt. I looked as if I were part of another picture. Although for a brief time it pleased me to appear separated, I soon tried to abandon the aura of a ghost boy, especially because, looking at another photograph, of my father's dead son from a first marriage—the boy had died at the age of eight—a photograph taken during the boy's first communion, when he was dressed in angelic white, I saw how much we looked alike: twins, the dead boy and I.

As I grew up, I came more and more to view El Paso as a desolate desert city swept by relentless winds that lasted from early February, a violent beginning, and sometimes into May, even early June, winds that howled and thrust sheaths of dust against the city as if in vengeance, gathering tumbleweeds into tangled spiny giants clawing their way into the city, urgent winds thrusting needles of dirt at our faces as we made our way from school, pushing against the windy current.

As a child of five, I had seen hurtling toward me a tumbleweed growing larger, huge, as it raged along the blocks collecting splinters loosed from other dry weeds. I dodged, the tumbleweed dodged too, I dashed away from its path, it dashed toward me, I ran to one side and then another, it pursued me until it crashed against me. Trying to break away from it, I flailed at it, but it pushed against me, finally capturing me within its cage of dried twigs, shredding my skin bloody. Trapped inside the tangle of dead weeds, I pushed and pushed, until I had disemboweled it. In nests of seared weeds, it spun away, tumbling across the horizon, gathering its shed parts, racing across the city, and, finally, back into the hellish desert.

That feeling of being entrapped outlasted the nightmarish experience, trapped in the ubiquitous poverty of the Depression, trapped in an atmosphere of potential violence as my father's depressive moods festered dangerously.

In winter, the windstorms abated; icy nights replaced them. Our whole house—four rooms with scant furniture—was heated with a coal-burning stove, a big-bellied iron contraption that glowed with embers and dark crumbling cinders. The panes of several windows were broken, and eventually cracked and fell in shards to the bare floor. We patched them with cardboard from boxes gathered outside grocery stores. The cardboard, attached with tacks to the frames of the windows, had to be replaced often; especially, rain or snow made it soggy.

My two brothers slept in one bed. I slept on the floor, on a slender pile of blankets—only when my brothers left for the army would I inherit a bed of my own. My mother slept in what would have been a living room, with my two sisters—the older, Blanca, would marry young. My father slept alone in the front room, the door closed. Very early in my life I became afraid of his flaring temper. I slept uneasily, sitting up at any sound that might precede his footsteps.

I detested poverty. When the cardboard on the windows was new, I would paint pictures on it, birds, flowers. The rain would eventually streak them into colored tears. When my mother was away shopping for groceries, I would try to rearrange the house, covering a scraggly sofa with a towel, rolling up a blanket to place at the head of my mother's bed so that it might look like the satiny rolled pillows of movie stars' beds. I wanted to surprise her with something pretty.

I watched her outside in the barren yard washing our clothes in a tin container propped up on bricks, the water heated by burning wooden boards underneath the tub. Angry that that was required of her, I stood on a box and helped her hang the clothes to dry on a line, breathing in the scent of fresh clothes washed by her.

There was a fearful time when I was hardly a boy. My mother's mother, who lived in Juárez across the border, was dying. My mother rushed to her side and remained until she died soon after. It was only when she was not allowed to return to the United States that I learned—and not even then; I understood it later— that my mother had crossed the border illegally from Mexico into the United States years ago. Now she was being detained by the immigration authorities. When she didn't come home for what seemed to be weeks but was probably only a few days, I was despondent. Finally, my father, through his lingering contacts among the powerful, was able to arrange for her return to Texas, to El Paso, to me.

Cold, dark winter nights in El Paso required expensive electricity, no matter how early families might attempt to go to bed.

There was a device known as "El Diablo," the devil, a two-pronged wire that was attached to the light meter located inside our house and that short-circuited the meter, keeping it from recording the amount of electricity we were to be charged for.

Inspectors from the electric company roamed poor neighborhoods, paying surprise visits. When an unfamiliar car was spotted cruising the streets, out would go the lights, not only in our house, but along whole blocks of houses, presaging a rapid disconnection of El Diablo. Then the lights would come back, house by house.

As my father's ability to support our family continued to diminish, Robert, the older of my two brothers, dropped out of high school to work as a professional pool player to help out. The younger of the two brothers, Yvan, continued in school, as did I and my sister Olga, still children. My sister Blanca, at seventeen, married a solidly built German man named Gus, to escape, I sometimes thought, our dour household.

On a cold December day when I was ten, my mother wrapped me and Olga in every sweater she could find to take us to the movies, at the Colón theater, the only Mexican theater in El Paso. Along with the usual Mexican melodrama about a wayward son abandoning his mother—typically, to become a bullfighter, and living to regret his unnatural cruelty when his mother is at death's door and his sister begs him to return to ask forgiveness—a famous Mexican magician, Paco Miller, would be performing on stage.

As we watched the magic in fascination, Paco Miller pulled an enormous eagle from his cape and held it, flapping until—

An incongruous man in a suit rushed onto the stage and whispered something to him.

Part of the act, of course. No. Paco Miller, putting the eagle back into a cage, stepped forth to announce:

"An atrocity has occurred in the world outside. Japan has attacked Pearl Harbor."

There were gasps; many people left. I had little idea what that meant. I understood the impact soon after when both my brothers had to go away, the younger one to the infantry, the older to the air force. My father would shed his gloom to follow closely and proudly the advance of the Allies, victories he ascribed solely to my brothers.

During those sad war years, that, however, began to end the Depression, virtually every house in El Paso displayed a proud cross indicating that a family member was "serving America." Very often the cross was replaced with a gold one, marking yet another death. The accumulation of gold crosses signaled the passing of those turbulent years, the toll of death.

My sister Olga and I—and my gentle mother—became the objects of my father's wrath, fueled by his extending decline. My sister escaped by making friends with girls her age, staying over at their homes as often as possible, often coaxing me to come with her; but I wouldn't, feeling I had to protect my mother.

Toward me, my father became an enigma of contradictions. When he discovered that I had begun to write one-page stories (always titled "Long Ago" and illustrated with costumed characters, the sort I had seen in his theatrical productions), and despite his own artistic background, he disregarded them: "You're too moody, go out and make friends." And yet, my mother attested, to others he would brag about his "artistic son." "You're too pretty," he would castigate me—although he had always cast me as the lead in his children's skits, insisting that I look the best, to stand out. "Go out for sports like your brothers," he demanded. "I do," I rebutted. "I'm very good at gymnastics, and I run track fast." That was true. I preferred activities that allowed me to perform alone, compete with myself. At school, I could do sit-ups—and show off doing them—until my stomach wrenched. I could run in record time around the playground. "Those aren't sports," he dismissed them; "those are substitutes!"

Just as unpredictable as his unprovoked outbursts at his own declining status, there were moments of regret. He might appear with a bunch of fresh flowers for my mother after his outbursts; flowers that assumed a despairing beauty when they entered the sad house. My mother would hold them, smiling sweetly. I waited for the flowers to wither and die so that I could throw them out. After raging at me for whatever reason he concocted—I would cover my ears, not hear—he might return, in the evening, with a present he could not afford: once, a pair of shiny cowboy boots I had longed for, and, another time, a small movie projector.

On her saint's day—we did not celebrate my mother's actual birthday, only her saint's day, the day of the Holy Virgin of Guadalupe, after whom she had been named—he appeared outside her window at dawn with two or three scraggly musicians playing guitars to serenade her with the romantic "Las Mañanitas." My mother would linger by the window, greeting the serenaders with a smile. At those times, always, there was a loveliness about the morning, a loveliness that seeped into the day, hopeful interludes, very soon broken again by my father's blind rages.

Between me and him, periods of angry silence lengthened into days, shattered without warning by his escalating anger and threats aimed at me and my mother. He became for me a despised stranger, an old man, fifty years older than I.

There were times when pity for him swept away my anger. During a broadcast by the Metropolitan Opera of *Carmen,* his favorite opera, which he had staged throughout the years, productions that grew more and more bravely ragged, he commanded my sister Olga, my mother, and me to sit facing the radio. As glorious music soared into the house, he stood with his back to us, and with an imaginary baton, he made passionate motions as if he was directing the orchestra himself, as he had once done. His baton sliced up and down, around, his head keeping pace with the music and the flow of his tears.

The afternoon when newspaper boys ran about the city, screaming, "Extra, Extra, the war is over!" even my mother—my father was already outside—rushed out with us to add to the crowds at San Jacinto Plaza in the center of the city amid loud and prolonged jubilation, overflowing with soldiers from Fort Bliss, grabbing, kissing, and dancing with pretty Mexican girls.

Soon, my brothers would return home, safe but with memories of death and explosions.

It was on the eve of their returning home that the wedding of my sister Olga to Luis caused so much turbulence in the city, the time when I first saw the kept woman of Augusto de Leon.

In the seventh month of her pregnancy (so that it was possible to claim a premature birth, to my mother's sighed relief, despite the child's nine full pounds and the virulent aunts' persistent inquiries about the *exact* date of birth), my sister bore a boy, whom I gleefully proclaimed to be ugly, although my sister, my mother, and everyone else who saw it—him—thought otherwise.

Although other families in El Paso had struggled out of extreme poverty to moderate poverty during the war, ours seemed entrenched. Soon after his triumph over Señor's threats to stop my sister's wedding—and the added triumph of playing his music during the ceremony—my father's musical pupils abandoned him. He had to accept menial jobs, finally as a caretaker in a park.

Back home now from the army, my brother Robert quickly married but continued to help support the family. He got a job in a lens-grinding factory, soon becoming its foreman—and, for me, much more of a father than my real, aging father. Every payday, my brother bought pastries, which he spread out before me, still a boy.

Yvan returned to college under the GI Bill.

My brothers had always been popular athletes. Now they extended that popularity in school and city leagues, continuing to fulfill my father's expectations. On one of those strange El Paso nights when the horizon seemed on fire—the sun spreading an orange glow against the purplish horizon—and when the wind only threatened to rise, spurts that shoved everything into motion for seconds and then abandoned debris on the streets, only to stir it up again, my mother, my sisters Olga and Blanca (their husbands had night jobs), and I traipsed across the city to watch the final playoff of the City League basketball season.

My father, excited, was already at the site of the game. Often, when my brothers made what he considered an error, he would march onto the court ready to shout at them, only to be rebuffed by the referee, to whom he would then turn his wrath. When another player interfered with my brothers' moves, my father would shove ahead and threaten him, fists preparing to punch, while the players and the referee—and my brother Robert—kept him away and my face burned with embarrassment.

The game was over, a cliff-hanger. My brother Robert had, in a succession of moves, shot three baskets—one from a long distance away, winning the game by seconds. My mother wept, thanking the Holy Mother. I could see my father hopping onto the court, probably to lecture my brother on what he might have done even better. My brother, sweating, elated, kept looking up at us and waving, especially—I was sure—to me.

I jumped up and ran down to congratulate him. He and the other players, exhilarated, sweating, exchanging camaraderie, had already headed for the showers.

I walked down the corridor where they had disappeared, to the right. The door had been left open. I walked in. I reeled.

All around were naked men, some dripping with water; others were still in the showers, water running down their bodies. Some had begun to dress, slipping on their shorts; others were still in jockstraps. A few sat on benches conversing and drying themselves; some had their backs to me.

I stared at the naked flesh about me, the patches of hair between the legs matted with water or sweat.

My brother saw me. I had forgotten why I was there.

"Johnny!" my brother called. His middle was wrapped in a towel. "What are you doing here, little brother?"

"I—" I remembered. "I came to congratulate you, brother. You won the game."

He placed his hand on my shoulder, thanking me.

I turned away and ran out of the steamy room.

By then, my belief in God—and it had been ingrained in me that God was Catholic—was waning. Still, I went to church, usually with my mother and, when she decided at the last moment to join us, my sister Olga with her baby. During Mass I found my mind wandering over inconsistencies in what the priests demanded that we believe. Although I found the figure of Christ crucified gory and cruel, the almost naked body was beautiful, and sexual. Didn't all those folks, men and women, who knelt before him see that? That he had a body that made him look as if he worked out regularly, did dozens of crunches to get carved obliques? All the men depicted in the stations of the cross, especially the Roman soldiers, were muscular and good-looking. Yes, and the women were beautiful, but they were always covered, every inch of them. Only their hands, clasped in prayer or wrenched in pain—and their faces painted like those of movie stars, with rosy cheeks and curled eyelashes—revealed flesh. Under their cowls and dresses, what? I imagined it often. The legs would be curved just slightly, and right at the intersection, the V—what? It would be different from what I had seen that day in the showers after my brother's basketball victory. In my imagination, I had to stop at the point when my mind wandered during Mass and I imagined lifting the skirts of the glamorous saintly ladies.

I had entered the limbo of thirteen. I became gangly. Looking through one of my sister's movie magazines left behind—I think it was *Screen Romances*—I saw a photograph of Burt Lancaster without a shirt, muscular chest oiled. I rushed to the mirror and studied myself without a shirt. A wave of despair swept me away from the mirror. What had become of the boy who was constantly being complimented for his good looks?

Once I had accompanied my mother to church when she was performing a novena; nine consecutive days of reciting the rosary before the Holy Mother Mary. I had been able to endure only one day of what seemed endless torture. Today, after school, I knelt before the statue of the lofty lady in the Immaculate Conception Church. Her face was gorgeous, soulful and strong at the same time. Her eyes were brilliant, her features perfect, sublime, gleaming marbles of whatever color filtered through the stained-glass windows. Although her body was clothed in shimmering azure, she was surely well shaped; the folds of her dress indicated wonderful curves—I forced myself not to imagine lifting her skirt. Today she resembled . . . No, not the kept woman; she was not that sensational. No, she resembled Magda Holler—the actress who had played the Holy Mother, my mother, in *El Monje Blanco*.

For long afternoons, I knelt praying before the beautiful image. There were usually one or two *beatas* about, old shawled women who spent most of their time in church beating their breasts and confessing to nonexistent sins, fussily tending to the altar, kneeling dozens of times as they navigated back and forth, thrusting signs of the cross at the altar each time. An occasional nun, not sweet like Mother Mercedes, would float by soundlessly in her full winged habit, standing over me for whatever purpose and startling me because I hadn't heard her approach. Then she would drift away like a cumbersome specter.

I did not trust silent communication, even with the Mother of God. Making sure that no one was near me, I whispered aloud the words of my petition, the purpose of my devout novena, quietly but with grave devotion and resurrected belief:

"Please, Blessed Mother Mary, make me handsome again."

One day I was fourteen, then quickly fifteen and again handsome. I now had pubic hair like the men I had seen naked in the basketball players' showers long ago.

And I was now able to confront my father's rages by disconnecting myself entirely from him, even at the dinner table. Both of us were encased by silences that extended into days.

6

A pretty girl by the name of Isabel Franklin transferred out of Bowie High School; gossip immediately sprang up in my high school about why she had transferred—and how she had been able to enroll in the "rich school."

Bowie High was known as the "Mexican" school, where the poorest children from South El Paso went. The demarcation between the South Side and the North Side was emphasized starkly by railroad tracks that cut off one side of the city from the other. My family lived just one block into the North Side. By that slim coincidence I, and a few other Mexicans, were enrolled in the "American school," where the students were predominantly the children who lived "up the hill," in Kern Place, the rich people's neighborhood.

Isabel Franklin's complexion, although lighter than dark, might have exposed her to vague suspicions that she was a "light Mexican." But that deduction was clouded seriously by her last name and predominantly Anglo features.

She spoke to few of the other students—only cursorily when necessary. She walked haughtily by herself from room to room, although she often smiled, even when the smile was not being directed at anyone specifically, as if she was practicing a smile in order not to arouse malicious antagonism. She drew admiring looks from both

Mexican and Anglo boys—and snippy looks from most of the girls—
both of which reactions she rebuffed with an enigmatic smile.

Because I was developing my own defensive arrogance, I
would pass her as silently as she passed me. I assumed we shared the
arrogance of the outsider who is nonetheless admired physically, as
we both were.

My "Anglo" coloring contributed to allowing me to become
a "popular student" at El Paso High School, a position I sought
aggressively, becoming, eventually, president of several clubs, a student council representative, and, at the time of Isabel's arrival, editor of the school paper, *The Tattler*. Still, my ambiguous identity as
a *guerro* exiled me doubly. Other Mexican students were cool.
Among "rich Anglos" who did not know I was Mexican, I felt like
a trespasser. I had begun to gravitate toward those students exiled
as geeks, unattractive boys and girls, who were often the smartest.
Even among them, I was looked at with suspicion. Daily, I surrendered my compromised popularity when classes were over.

Two teachers I would cherish forever provided respite from
those conflicts. Maude Isaacks, a prim, smart lady, encouraged me,
proclaiming me "definitely a future writer of note." Fanny Foster,
a flamboyant onetime actress who demanded attention by aiming
her cane at any student who lapsed in concentration, introduced
me to Shakespeare while acting out scenes with dyed spools on a
huge dictionary atop her desk—Hamlet was a dark brown spool,
Ophelia was pink, Queen Gertrude was scarlet. Othello was very
black, and Desdemona was white. "And you, young man, will one
day stand out," she prophesied, searching through her colored spools
as if to find one for me.

In school, students who could not afford to eat the hot meals offered in the cafeteria might apply for a "free token," granted, after

a detailed interview about the extent of their poverty, by a staff counselor. All the students who applied were Mexicans. With the token, such students might choose only from the sandwich counter; they had to stand in a separate line from the Anglos. I chose not to apply for the free token. I ran home for lunch during the midday break. I returned breathlessly before the bell rang signaling the resumption of classes.

It was not only because of lunch that I ran home from school. I did so also when school was over for the day so that no one would know where I lived—our house remained dingy, although my mother relentlessly cleaned it, ordering everything in it, the few pieces of furniture we had.

On one rare occasion, I impulsively accepted an invitation to go to the movies with two popular Anglo boys from school. I gave a wrong address to be picked up at, one that corresponded to a pretty two-story house two blocks away from where I lived, three blocks from the telltale railroad tracks. When the time neared for the two to pick me up, I rushed to meet them at the fake address.

That had been so from my earliest years. When I was only six, I would get up early, to the consternation of my brothers and sisters. Those mornings at dawn, I would wander over to Montana Street, which, then, was lined with beautiful two-story houses— two stories would always remain, for me, "special." One house rested, by itself, alone, aloof, on one whole square block, green with perfect grass. There was no necessity for gates then. The lawn edged onto the public sidewalk. The house had four white columns and a tall entry door that led, I imagined, up twin flights of stairs under a huge chandelier.

Those twilit mornings, I would sit on steps that led from the street to the lawn of that grand house. I would pretend indifference, imagining that those driving by would look at me and sigh and think, "Look at that lucky boy, so rich, living in that beautiful house he takes for granted." (Many years later, as an adult, I would learn that my haughty grandmother, my father's mother, had once owned property on that very street, and had, "out of spite"—in my sister Blanca's indictment of the woman who had humiliated her because of her darker color—let the property go so that my father, and more importantly my mother, would not inherit it.)

I became sure—as I was sure she was sure—that we, Isabel Franklin and I, were aware of each other as vague conspirators in exile, looking as if we "belonged" but not belonging, or perhaps really even wanting to belong. That would surely enhance her interest in me.

It was a crucial time of adolescent confusion, and everything seemed to conspire to aggravate it. My journalism teacher, who supervised the school paper, often stayed in her classroom to plan the next week's edition with me.

I was reading a lot by then, whatever the librarian at the public library recommended—Hawthorne, Poe, Melville, Emily Brontë, all instant favorites—and I had begun to write. At this point in my "career," my stories were loose retellings—this allowed me to think of them as "original"—of movies I had seen (Marie Antoinette, in my version, was saved from the guillotine at the last moment by Tyrone Power)—and of operas my father had staged. In one of the latter—I want to believe I was no older than ten then— Madama Butterfly said to Pinkerton, "You know what, American sea captain? I am going to have your baby."

In high school, I had recently completed a much more ambitious story, a longer one titled "The Thing." It was profoundly influenced by Poe; it concerned a woman going insane, or not; sensing a presence, not knowing whether it was real. That story was obviously pilfered from some movie that I had seen and whose name I can't remember. I thought it was a masterpiece. I mentioned it to my journalism teacher.

"That sounds good, Johnny. I'd like to read it," said Miss Edwards. She was a nice woman, unremarkably pretty, an older woman, as I thought then: perhaps thirty. I had noticed her breasts, which were full, especially for such a slender woman, because at times, when we were alone, she would lean over me to check something or other while I sat at my desk. That embarrassed me because I was sure she was unaware of what she was doing, and sometimes it made me start perspiring, and I didn't want her to notice, or, worse, to smell me sweating.

Elated by her attention to my story, I told her I'd bring it to school next week to give to her, after we had completed the pending issue of the paper, which involved going downtown, with others on the staff, to the print shop where the columns of type were set on galleys.

"Why don't you bring it over Saturday?"

"No school on Saturday," I reminded her.

"Oh, that's right. But why don't you bring it over to the hotel where I live?"

It was not rare for people to live in hotels; small hotels seemed to be all over the city. They were more like apartment houses, except that there would be a desk for registering. Usually, there was some kind of dining room, often with a dimming chandelier. The inside of those buildings had a twilight mustiness that attested to age, to another time when Texas was more Southern than Western.

If Miss Edwards was eager to read my story, this certainly meant that my brief description of it had excited her. I saw that development as my first opening into the world of . . . literature! She told me where she was living. We arranged the time: midafternoon.

I went over to the hotel–apartment house, thrilled by the prospect of discussing my story in private with a teacher who had become, for me, the best authority in the world on literary quality, a quality that my story would clearly exhibit and so overwhelm her. I told the man at the desk that Miss Edwards was expecting me. I added proudly, "She's going to read my story titled 'The Thing'— I'm a writer." Not impressed, he nodded me toward a room along a corridor and gave me a number.

My anticipation growing, I knocked where he had designated. Miss Edwards opened the door, not fully, as if she was hiding from someone. I couldn't see her entirely yet.

"Hello, Johnny."

"Hi, Miss Edwards," I said.

She opened the door. I went in. She closed the door quickly behind me. "I brought my st—" I stopped. She was wearing a nightgown—or so I considered what must have been a negligee, with lace trimming at the top. It opened to exhibit the crescent of her breasts, now even more surprisingly large—or did they just loom that way for me now?

"Am I early?"

She laughed, touched my head lightly, rumpling my hair. "No, you're just in time." She took the story from me and laid it on a table in a small corridor at the entrance.

"Come on in and relax," she said, gliding through the corridor—she was barefoot!—into her bedroom.

I looked back forlornly at my story, and followed her. I wasn't sure what I felt: a sudden unfocused fear, yes; of course disappointment that she wasn't going to read my story right away, yes, that; but something else I had never felt before, fear definitely, but also anticipation, and, yes, yes, a strange excitement, not entirely welcome, that seemed to grip my throat, especially now that she was sitting on her bed in her negligee and I was standing directly before her.

If I had blacked out, I would have believed that this had occurred before I recovered; but I hadn't blacked out. I was there, and I saw it. I saw her hand reach out toward my pants, saw it open the buckle of my belt, saw it moving down, down, toward my—

Standing over her, I could see deep into the parting of her breasts, which were being shoved into increasing prominence by her motions—mounds of flesh pushing out, out, almost out. She leaned her head slightly down. Her breasts burst out.

I froze—no, I grew hot—at the sight of the startling twins of white flesh that had just popped out, a smirch of red on each one. More panic, more excitement, more apprehension, more fear, a confusion about running away or staying—all at war. This was definite: I couldn't breathe—was I gasping?—because she had opened my fly, and was pulling my shorts down. Did this happen? Yes, I saw it: She took out my cock, which sprang out hard, so hard that it seemed pasted against my groin, firmer and longer than I had ever imagined it could be. Hot, sweating, embarrassed, terrified, I wanted to demand that it return to its normal stage—no, that it spring out even more—no, that I could hide it, knowing she would be upset with me, scold me, yell at me, send me away, accuse me of—

What?

I couldn't move, I didn't know where to move—or how to move—whether to move, where to go, what to say, what—

"Relax, Johnny," she said softly. She shrugged off her nightgown. It fell like froth to her hips, the firm breasts even whiter; the reddish smears that had crowned them, darker circles—with nipples.

What was one of my hands doing cupping one of the extravagant breasts? I hadn't put it there. Had she? That hand felt as if it was being struck by hot lightning bolts, small ones. Now she was guiding my other hand, also burning, over her other breast, and I seized it, hard.

"Yes, Johnny!" she said.

No, no! I thought as I squeezed harder. I don't want to do this! But I did! No, I didn't! Yes, I did! Her hands were stroking my fiercely upright cock. Did she know what she was doing? Did she know what would happen if she continued? Did she know that I would burst open right in front of her and spatter—? Why did my hands refuse to remove themselves from her breasts? Why were they pinching her nipples?

When had she pulled my pants and shorts down? When had she opened my shirt? Stumbling on my pants gathered about my feet, I fell back on the bed, my legs straight out before me. She took off my shoes, my socks. I was naked!—and so was she, the nightgown clinging only in patches to her body, intensifying the whiteness of her flesh. Were my hands really roaming all over it, over that startling, astonishing, naked white flesh?

My cock was pulsing, moist.

"Not yet, Johnny!" she said.

She thrust herself back quickly on the bed.

"Quick! Get on top of me! Quick! Now! Now!" She parted her legs wide.

I saw a patch of hair—so that's what was there! It gleamed as if she had applied something to it—brilliantine?—a small patch of hair so abrupt that I stared startled and awed that a woman would have pubic hair, and into that moment, there entered the memory of the day I had gone to congratulate my brother in the showers and there had been slabs of naked flesh interrupted by patches of hair—

Somehow, somehow, I was straddling Miss Edwards and her naked body was under my naked body, and I was about to burst open somewhere, everywhere.

"Fuck me!" Miss Edwards cried.

My cock was in the furry nest! Inside her?—inside a moist velvet smoothness that nevertheless clung to my cock tightly and made me want to pull out and yet stay and stay as she trembled and made sounds like a kitten and my body convulsed as if I was about to die, once, twice, and then again, coming to life again, coming to—coming—

I lay exhausted on top of her. I didn't know what to do next. She decided that for me.

She jerked away from under me. I fell facedown on the bed—but I quickly turned over and sat up.

She straightened her nightgown and shouted at me:

"What did you do, you dirty little boy? Get out, get out! What did you do?"

I put on my clothes, dashed into the corridor, closed the door, remembered my abandoned story, pulled on the door expecting it to be locked—but it wasn't. There lay my story unread on the small table. I grabbed it.

Before I could run out, I heard Miss Edwards's sudden sobs.

In class, Miss Edwards acted as if nothing had happened, except that she no longer stayed to plan the school paper with me. I wondered whether she had forgotten what had happened; I longed for that to be so. The very day that I had fled from her apartment, I had felt a sense of something not completed, despite the orgasm, something not yet fully satisfied that made me sad.

7

At school today, as the new girl walked by as usual ignoring me pointedly, I stopped for a moment, disoriented, doubly disoriented. I had a vague feeling that I had seen her before. Where? Who? Yes!—Isabel Franklin was the girl who—what? Any association I had been about to make vanished.

Smoking was forbidden even within the environs of the high school, but groups of teenagers would congregate, a few in each bunch, under the steps of the school or at other places hidden from open view though known to the teachers, who probably resignedly preferred to ignore the activity.

As I was rushing home from school for lunch, I saw Isabel Franklin moving surreptitiously under some shaded steps outside the school, apart from where the others congregated during the noon break.

I halted before she could see me but close enough that I could see her.

She brought an unlit cigarette to her lips—no, not yet to her lips. She was holding the cigarette as if contemplating what to do with it. In an odd sort of exaggerated arc, she finally brought it to her mouth, but didn't light it—I did not see a match spark.

Of course. She was rehearsing smoking before she exposed herself to anyone else. That would be typical of the haughty girl, yes.

She saw me—and quickly looked away, then just as quickly down, searching around her with exaggerated earnestness as if she had lost something—the cigarette had disappeared from sight. Dropped? Discarded? As if she had found whatever she was looking for, she stood up and walked away, stopped, turned around, and—

She looked at me again as if challenging me, although I had no idea what the challenge was, but I did know this: Isabel Franklin was the girl I had seen staring at the kept woman of Augusto de Leon the day of my sister's wedding, the girl who had been as enthralled by the glamorous apparition as I had been.

After the long sullen period during which I nurtured my resentment about her marriage—I had made sure not to reconcile with her too quickly, to punish her for getting married—my sister Olga and I became close friends, even closer as adults. We were confidants. I visited her often. These visits were times of respite away from the clouds of my father's lengthening moods that hung over our house, especially now that my brothers and sisters were all married and I was the only son left to witness the decline of someone who had become for me an intimate stranger.

I had come to like my sister's husband, who worked as a car salesman. Their child, Louis—Louie—had become, I now admitted ungrudgingly, a cute playful kid; he was always happy to see me, though I forbade him ever to call me "uncle," a title that didn't fit my developing image of myself.

My sister was always full of news. She seemed to know everything about everyone, and she delivered the information with unabashed authority, often dramatizing her stories, even mimicking the voices of those involved. Her main sources of information about her husband's family were Tina, her sister-in-law; and, unlikely as it seemed, Señor's wife, who visited often and who had become quite heavy, to the point that I had not recognized her when I had seen her leaving my sister's house—fat and sassy, a sassiness emphasized by the fact that she never appeared without a proud plume on one of the jaunty hats she had begun to wear after Señor's death. I had also learned from my gleeful sister that Señor's wife doted on my nephew, Louie, as if to affront the memory of her dead husband. "To think," she had once said to my sister, "that that madman would have stopped this angel from being born!" (I had been astonished to discover that, in her wedding scrapbook, my sister had pasted on a special page, alone, Señor's newspaper notices threatening to stop her wedding.)

Now I did not want to think that my sister had become a gossip. My tomboy buddy grown into a gossip?—my buddy who had given me my greatest baseball triumph? Never! The gossipy aunts looked like gossips, unattractive, speaking in whispers that occasionally stumbled into a loud blurt, whereas my sister Olga had become so beautiful that I was sure she now could win the role I had submitted her for long ago, even over Yvonne de Carlo, whom she was coming to resemble.

Today, her husband was at work, Louie at preschool. I planned my visits around those absences so I could have my sister to myself and enjoy her stories. We had settled in her living room in the small rented house she now occupied—not yet entirely furnished. I had just mentioned to her the girl at school; I always attempted to make my sister jealous, as I had been about her husband. I had added that I was sure the new girl had been at the wedding, wondering whether Olga would remember her.

No sooner had I mentioned the name Isabel Franklin than my sister folded her hands over her chest, firmly, and sneered: "Isabel Franklin? Oh, really? That's Alicia Gonzales."

"Olga, I'm telling you, she's in school with me and her name is Isabel Franklin."

"She just calls herself Franklin," my sister said. "Franklin is the last name of Tina's second husband. Not even Tina uses his name since she divorced him; she calls herself Gonzales, Alicia's father's name."

"Isabel—

"*Alicia,*" my sister corrected.

"—is Tina's daughter?"

"Yes."

Then the girl who had been as enthralled by the glamorous apparition as I had been, the girl I had seen practicing secretly how to smoke at school, that girl was Alicia Gonzales, who was now Isabel Franklin, who was—

The kept woman's niece!

A sharp image pounced into my mind, the entrancing memory, sharp, intact, as if I were seeing her again, the kept woman of Augusto de Leon. It was an image that must have been implanted deep in my mind, ready to spring forth, exact:

As if deciding not to complete the smile, or because the memory aroused had turned bitter, her lips parted, instead, to receive the cigarette she brought slowly—almost thoughtfully—to her lips.

That assertive image had been evoked, yes, by the discovered association with Isabel, that day of my sister's wedding, but there was more that kept pushing the memory forward, now at this moment of my sister's disdain for Isabel. It was a memory of words overheard, spoken in the drab room that the kept woman had ruled proudly, words—

"—Isabel was always her middle name," my sister had gone on, and stopped. "Little brother?" she nudged my attention back.

"Olga?"

"Where were you? You weren't listening to me."

"I was." The memory of the kept woman dissolved.

"I wonder, though," my sister resumed, "why Alicia's at El Paso High now. The last time I heard from Tina, she was going to

Bowie. Maybe that's why she changed her name—Gonzales was too Mexican for her. Hmmm. The only way she could transfer to another school is if she lied about her address." She paused in a way I had come to recognize as preparation for the height of the drama she was recounting. "I always thought, you know, that Alicia is ashamed of being Mexican."

My voice edged toward anger. "I think the matter of Isabel is much more complicated than what you've assumed. You know, Olga, you don't know *everything*. Something else, too, Olga—I think you're becoming a gossip. No, I take it back, I don't think you're becoming a gossip. You *are* a gossip."

That was all I could say now to my sister—who smiled indulgently—in order to end the conversation about the new girl who had transferred to the Anglo school, had changed her name, and was suspected of being ashamed of being Mexican.

In El Paso at the time, shame at being Mexican was an easy, often unfounded, accusation to make; it was sometimes routinely made of *guerros*.

I had always been assumed by strangers to be Anglo. As a kid, before I learned English, I would necessarily respond in Spanish to whatever might be asked, in a store, at the barber college we went to for the cheapest cuts, at the library, on the bus. Then, someone would often protest, saying something like, "Oh, you must be Spanish, you're too fair to be a Mexican, don't say you're a Mexican."

I had witnessed many manifestations of discrimination in El Paso against Mexicans—there were very few "Negroes" then in the city. Anglo waitresses at the Newberry lunch counter pointedly hesitated to wait on Mexicans, so that, often, a family so disdained would walk away. Though I never denied being Mexican,

I saw little reason to court the kind of cruelty that often attended such identification, cruelty that I had experienced on my first day at school.

In the kindergarten classroom where about thirty children, all five- or six-years old, congregated, the prim teacher—a knotted bun planted atop her head with no relation to her hair—went about the room touching some of the children lightly on the shoulder and smiling, avoiding others and frowning. When she passed me, she brushed me on the shoulder and smiled. She instructed those she had touched to stand up. I stood up, to join the others so designated. The teacher then ushered us out of the classroom—"March, one, two, three"—toward the playground while the others remained in the room with her.

As we were filing out along the corridor, a girl in my group said something to me in English. I answered her in Spanish, shaking my head to indicate that I didn't understand her. Overhearing me, the teacher—a deadly frown crinkling her white-powdered forehead—yanked me back, mumbling something, while leading me back to rejoin those still in the classroom.

In the classroom, she snapped her fingers and flung her hands up, signaling us to rise. We—the fifteen of us, all Mexicans, who remained in the room—stood bewildered, and now somewhat afraid. Her hands now sheathed in transparent gloves, she went to each of us, one by one, parting our hair in several places, inspecting all of us for lice. Humiliated, I pulled away from her and ran home.

Every morning, the same teacher led us all in a stiff Pledge of Allegiance. Then she made us all—even those of us who didn't know the English words—sing "Home on the Range," with this change: She made us block out the word "seldom" from the line "Where seldom is heard a discouraging word and the skies are not cloudy all day," as printed in a mimeographed song sheet she passed out. We then had to substitute the word "never"—she spelled it out slowly—"because, after all, this is Texas, . . . where *never* is heard a discouraging word."

In another classroom, for half an hour, Mexican students were again separated from "Americans." We could hear the Anglo children through the windows laughing in the playground while the sturdy teacher attempted to teach us the profound mystery of the difference between "ch" and "sh." "Tcha, tcha, tcha, tcha, *tcha!*" she would fire at us, beating on her desk with a stick. We would respond, "Shuh, shuh, shuh, shuh, *shuh!*" Her face growing dangerously red, she would shift to this example: "Tchildren, Tchihuahua, tchildren, Tchihuahua!" and we would respond: "Shuldrin, Tchihuahua, Shuldrin, Tchihuahua."

My older sister, Blanca, had been the object of similar cruelty within our own family. Because her name meant "white" and her complexion was darker than my mother's—and certainly my father's—my determinedly "Spanish" grandmother on my father's side ridiculed her. She called Blanca *la India,* inflicting pain that would bruise my sister all her life, despite the fact that she became very beautiful, a queen at a yearly bullfight in Juárez, where she once was courted by a matador with the ear of a slain bull.

My two brothers were opposites in coloring. Yvan, athletic, good-looking, would have been an all-American type except that he was brown; Robert, the older, was fair, with blue eyes, and as handsome as Robert Taylor, whom he resembled. My sister Olga, eventually to blossom into a beauty, looked entirely Spanish.

My mother often said that if the haughty grandmother had been alive, I would have been her favorite because I looked "so entirely white" and had "such long, curled eyelashes."

Many years later, my beautiful sister Blanca would legally alter her name to Blanche, attempting to banish the pain the grandmother had caused her by mocking her about her darker color.

★   ★   ★

In the same kindergarten and grammar school where, daily, Mexicans were separated from Anglos to be checked for lice and to learn to pronounce "chuh," and around the same time, my name was changed. Knowing not a single word of English, I sat confused through a silly game that involved a colored ball of yarn to be pinned onto the back of one of the children. I knew only that before the count of ten, the child so pinned had to guess what the color of the yarn was.

"One—" the teacher began.

I got up.

"What?"

"Juan," I said, pointing to myself and smiling at having been called.

"No, no. Sit down."

She began again: "One—"

Exasperated myself but thinking she had decided to make amends for having called my name and then making me return to my desk, I went up to her, not smiling.

"One!" She understood. "Not Juan."

The Anglo children laughed raucously.

"I'm going to call you Johnny," she said. "You look much more like a Johnny than a Juan. Doesn't he, children?" she asked those who understood English.

"Yes, yes!"

I did feel more like Johnny than like Juan.

But I was sure of this, after I left my sister Olga's house and I replayed her accusations of Isabel Franklin—Alicia Gonzales—never had I been ashamed of being Mexican. Regretting poverty, yes. Ashamed of being poor, allowing people to think I lived elsewhere, yes . . . But ashamed of being Mexican?

No, no, never.

8

I got an after-school job in the call office of the Acme Laundry, picking up bundles of clothes from cars and bringing them to the checkout desk, then writing out a receipt. There were two other clerks, freshmen in college, both Anglos. I was paid fifteen dollars a week and allowed a 50 percent discount on laundry. My mother no longer had to do the washing. I gave my salary to her and kept two dollars for myself.

One early evening my rich uncle Carlos came across the border from Juárez into El Paso to visit us and show off his new Cadillac. In front of our house, the Cadillac was parked like the ship of an invader, an alien in our Texas neighborhood of run-down cars that had to be cranked up daily. The Cadillac gleamed, standing out rudely, disdainful. Kids roamed around it; one touched it and then fled as if it had singed him.

Since his wife, Carmen, slightly sober, was with my uncle, I assumed she had managed not to kill any of her cronies during her raucous poker games—or, at least, she had not been caught. She smelled faintly of perfume and strongly of whiskey. She was wearing spangled earrings and kept elbow-nudging me in the ribs to indicate how good-looking she thought I was, eh?

"Do you know how to drive?" my uncle startled me by asking when I admired the gleaming Cadillac.

"Yes!" I said quickly. My brother Robert had taught me in his own cantankerous Nash. I had even acquired a beginner's permit.

"Would you like to drive the Cadillac?"

My mother protested that I was too young, my father roused himself out of silence to warn that I would wreck the car and wasn't worthy of it, and Robert attested to my excellent skills: "My little brother," he said, "is the smartest of us all." I thanked him, and insisted he was—and he was at least as smart; he had given up an opportunity to prove that by choosing to go to work to help out, even after he was married, instead of continuing his education.

I did not pause to wonder at the astonishing offer my uncle had extended, this stroke of generosity. Nor would it have mattered that it might have something to do with his vaunted disdain of wealth, including his own—he was later identified by some government agency or other as a "rich communist." The Cadillac was last year's, because, in one of those strange regulations that only regulators can understand, foreigners were allowed to buy new American cars but only last year's models.

My uncle handed me the magical keys as if they were petty change.

"Remember everything I taught you," my brother said. "Let the clutch out . . . smoothly . . . if it has one."

"I will, brother." I held the keys in my hand, disoriented momentarily by what I was about to do. My first clear thought after that was this: I would call Isabel Franklin! Because of the lack of what was now possible—a good-looking car—I had never thought to date a girl until now. My brother's Nash constantly needed repairing. He spent more time under it, tinkering with the engine, than he and I did driving. When he lent it to me, I would not drive far, a few blocks, around, enjoying driving, just that. The girls whom I was attracted to in school, and who might be attracted to me, were all from the "rich" neighborhood, Kern Place. The thought of asking any of them out, and waiting for a bus—if they accepted—was dismaying.

But now! Now Isabel and I would go to the drive-in diner, where everyone from school who had a car, and money to go there, went on weekends. Everyone would see us there, together.

I began to run out of the house raising my hand to grasp my mother's benediction when I realized I didn't have Isabel's telephone number.

I retreated into the house—"I forgot something"—and sauntered back to a small entryway where our telephone was. Only recently acquired, it was a party line, and the first time it rang, my mother clasped her hands with joy at the marvelous acquisition. I looked up Isabel's mother's name, praying it would be listed, as almost all numbers were then. Ernestina Gonzales—there it was: Main-8282-J. I ran out before anyone could ask me what I had forgotten.

I glided along the street in the beautiful spaceship—it had fins, of course—until I located a public telephone. I inserted the requisite nickel, picked up the telephone.

"Operator."

I was speechless and quickly hung up.

Would Isabel—I must remember to call her that and not the name she had rejected, Alicia—recognize my name, or even me when I turned up, if she agreed to go out with me? Had I been misleading myself into thinking her avoidance of me at school was a deliberate avoidance, as pointed as mine? Worse still, if she recognized me, might she turn down my invitation? Even if she did say yes, might her decision be based on my mentioning the grand Cadillac—should I mention it at all?—and offering to take her where everyone would see her in it? Well, there was this: She had smiled at me that one day.

Had she? Or had she just looked back?

There was something else that was entering into my decision, not yet made: that she was related to the kept woman of Augusto de Leon, that we had shared the image of her years ago.

"Who?"

The telephone had been answered by a woman—Isabel's mother, Tina?—and I had asked for Isabel Franklin.

"Who?" the voice asked again; I detected an edge of annoyance. At me? At anyone who called her daughter? Then I remembered: "May I speak to Alicia?"

"Oh, yes, she's here, yes, I'll call her."

As I froze in terror at what was already happening, the woman called out, "Is-sa-bel!" Did I detect a trace of pointed sarcasm in the way she phrased the name, stretching each syllable?

I might still hang up; she would never know who was calling; I would . . . If Isabel didn't recognize my name, that would mean she hadn't inquired about me, as I had about her, and then—

"Hello?"

I stopped myself just in time from calling her Alicia: "Isabel?"

"Yes."

Emboldened by the courage I was dredging up, I identified myself—"Johnny." Johnny? The name I didn't use for myself had come forth without my intention, and I quickly identified myself again: "It's John." No reaction from her, more panic for me. "John Rechy. From school." Into the deadly silence that extended, I shoved added words that I believed formed an invitation to her to go with me to the Oasis Drive-In. Before the vile silence could extend again, I added, "In my uncle's new Cadillac. Will you?"

"Yes," she said, "that would be nice."

Had the Cadillac cinched it? What if the address she would have to give me—my relief leaped to anxiety—was the one she had made up to transfer to El Paso High and was not really where she lived, if my gossipy sister was right? And what if when I reached it, she would not be there?

Doubts and questions intruded on my happiness. Had Isabel been out on dates?—and so would be much more sophisticated than I? I felt reasonably sure she hadn't, the way she acted, so aloof, the way others came eventually to react to her, matching her indifference.

She had given me an actual address, of a small neat house in one of the poorer, though not the poorest, sections of the city, I noticed as I drove up. There was no way she could have given this address and been allowed to transfer across the tracks. Did she know that I, too, lived in a poor section—but not across the tracks—and had she therefore told me where she really lived? Or was she just as eager to go out with me as I was to go out with her and that was it, just that?

I walked to the door, knocked, greeted her mother, Tina, the kept woman's sister!—that thought took my breath away. She was pretty but not beautiful. I bowed slightly before her, to impress her with my good manners, which my mother had drilled into us. (Even when we were poorest, she insisted that we cross our forks over our knives on the plates, to signal that we didn't care for "seconds," although at that time we hardly could afford "firsts." Among some of the formerly privileged immigrants, poverty was not talked about, as if the subject would be rude.)

When she saw me, Isabel did not react in surprise. That assured me that she had known all along who I was when I called. She looked prettier than ever, much prettier, so pretty. Was it possible that eventually she might come to look like the kept woman, her aunt?

In a blue dress fitted to her body, she seemed to me to have more curves than any of the other girls at school. Was that only because the dress was meant to show her off?—unlike the loose sweaters and blouses the others wore. And—was she wearing stockings? Older women wore them all the time, younger ones on special occasions, but most of the time younger girls wore white socks, bobby socks. Yet there it was, yes, she was wearing sheer stockings and high-heeled shoes. Perhaps I was only now allowing myself to look at her fully, without pretending that I didn't notice her. Was it possible that, this very evening, I would be able to erase the feeling I still nurtured of something very wrong in the encounter with Miss Edwards? I was so enthralled by Isabel's presence that I hadn't answered her hello until now:

"Hello, Isabel." More doubts instantly: In the course of the evening, would I have to explain my pretended cool demeanor of previous times, thus revealing my infatuation? Would she leave me isolated with a one-sided declaration?

She did not seem awkward at all as we walked toward the finned spaceship that managed to gleam especially brilliantly even though the sun was just about to sink into deep dusk. Nor did she seem particularly impressed, as if she would expect nothing less. Her poise annoyed me because I was sure that, despite my rigid intent, I seemed anxious and awkward. I was holding my hands firm to keep them from shaking.

She was waiting for me to open the door for her.

"Thank you."

"You're welcome, Isabel." I took that opportunity to practice the name she went by.

"Oh, yes," she said easily, "you may be wondering about this. I don't really live here, you know. I just come here to visit now and then, a poor friend—and I happened to be there when you called."

At the telephone listed as her mother's? No question now; she had given a false address at school.

She stepped into the car gracefully, tucking her dress neatly under her lap, and then, discreetly, smoothing her stockings to obliterate any possible wrinkle. She placed her small purse carefully beside her. Then she did this: She held her hands in her lap—properly, I assumed; yet it seemed a strange dissonant detail, as if she was hiding something.

Now what? While I was wondering how to fill the looming silence in the car, I noticed that her eyes were . . . appeared to be

. . . amber, even in measured light, amber, not brown—although perhaps I only hoped so. And her eyelashes—would there be a time when I would not be compelled to notice this?—were not only curled but very curled and long.

I flooded the silence with music from the radio. It issued a loud blast of Mexican music, country Mexican music, *charro* music my uncle's wife had probably been listening to.

"You like Mexican music?" she asked me.

I didn't. It seemed old-fashioned to me. In the poorer sections of the city, the air would be suffused with a cacophony of sung laments, loud, pulsing into the air, Mexican male and female singers, and strumming guitars; romantic songs in which women sorrowed over lost opportunities at love and in which men yearned for what was lost, for what was never found, deeply lamented, longing for what was still sought, what was never recovered, almost crying voices. Younger Mexicans listened to American songs, Harry James, Frank Sinatra, jitterbugging music. On the radio I had acquired years ago, by collecting stamps from the comic strip page of the newspaper, I listened to dramatic shows—*Lux Radio Theater* was my favorite—and mysteries: I loved the dramatizations of Poe, creepy voices, screams, secrets. And I listened to classical music, sitting outside on the steps we called a porch. Those times, I would notice my father lurking about, as if to share the sounds of the music he, too, loved but not daring to commit himself to the sharing.

Alicia—*I must remember to call her Isabel!*—was waiting for my answer. Now it became even stranger to me that she continued to hold her hands on her lap, rigidly, guarding whatever she was guarding—or hiding? "Oh, sometimes, I do like Mexican music," I felt it safe to answer—I did like, very much, "Las Mañanitas," the Mexican serenade my father still sang to my mother on her day, now accompanied by two or three old musicians. "Do *you* like Mexican songs?"

"No," she said.

I turned the radio off, not knowing how to shift the stations. There were so many panels on the dashboard, so many knobs.

"It's not too hot today, is it . . . Isabel?" *I must implant that name in my mind.*

"Not too, no." She turned to smile at me. It was a dazzling smile. It was so: If she wasn't beautiful yet, she would be soon.

"Do you like school?" she asked.

I wasn't sure; sometimes I did, sometimes not. Some classes I did like especially: English and mathematics, although my arithmetic teacher would throw me into confusion when he sent me to the board to solve a problem and at the same time stroked my neck. I didn't like gym unless I could be alone on the bars. Then, I liked the sense of my body challenging motion, and, too, I noticed what calisthenics did for my body, forming muscles.

"Yes," I said, "I like school. Do you?"

"No. I can hardly wait to get out and leave."

Leave? It seemed like a curious betrayal, now that we were getting together. "Where do you want to go . . . Isabel?"

She looked out the window, away, her silhouette against the declining light that was etching desert mountains against the darkly brilliant sky. There seemed to be for her a lingering moment of longing when the hands on her lap seemed to release whatever she held. "To Mexico City," she answered.

"Oh," was the only response I could think of.

At the Oasis Drive-In, there they were, the students from school, munching on hamburgers dripping with yellow cheese, slurping malted milks, sipping Cokes, gobbling fries in their cars; "rich" Anglos, the popular ones. I recognized a cheerleader, giggling as she did constantly at school; she stopped giggling and gaped when she saw us in the Cadillac. My spirits soared; no one was driving a more spectacular car. I waved at those staring. Isabel barely smiled in their direction.

When I parked outside the glass enclosure that was the drive-in, an octagonal shape, a round counter inside, to await the waitress who would attach a tray to my side of the car and take our order, I applied the hand brake with an assured pull.

Why did the hood of the car spring up?

Perspiration broke out on my forehead—and probably all over my body—as if a bucket of scalding water had drenched me. I had pulled a lever that opened the hood, which remained there, slanted, defiant, merciless.

"The hood's up," Isabel said, as if I hadn't noticed.

"I know. It—" After, in a haze, I found the actual brake, got out, and slammed the hood down—I had not dared to look around to note whether anyone was snickering—we ordered from an older waitress in a low skirt, white and orange.

"Some car you got there, boy," she said.

"It's pretty, yes," Isabel acknowledged.

But now another horror loomed, that I would not have enough money if Alicia—*Isabel!*—ordered more than I could pay for, with my two-dollar share of what I made at the laundry.

"A lime Coke, please," she said.

Ten cents! Now I could afford the vanilla malt I asked for, for fifteen cents.

"Do you smoke?"

Was she suggesting that I smoke to calm my nerves? Was it so obvious that I was nervous—and excited to be with her? Was I still sweating? "Yes, of course," I answered her, and added, "I smoke a lot." I had never smoked.

She released her hands.

So that's what she had been holding, a pack of cigarettes. She tapped the box on one palm so that a cigarette popped out for me to take. I did, not knowing what I would do with it, just holding it for now. She took one herself after another tap on her palm.

Hesitating so that I would not pull another unexpected lever, I tested the cigarette lighter. It glowed.

In a wide, showy arc, Isabel brought her cigarette close to her lips, and held it there, barely touching, as if deciding whether to allow it yet to touch. When she did finally bring it to her lips, lightly, I extended the lighter out to her, retaining my own inert cigarette in my free hand. I missed the tip of her cigarette with the lighter—because her hand holding the cigarette between her fingers was . . .

Trembling!

She was nervous!—like me.

Poking my cigarette between my lips, I held her hand to still the trembling while I tried again to light the cigarette for her. "I'm nervous, too," I said.

She stiffened, clearly rejecting my assumption that she was nervous, an acknowledgment of awkwardness.

"Really, it's all right, Alicia—" Too late to withdraw the forbidden name or the offending suggestion.

She jerked her hand away from me with a whimper so slight that I barely heard it as she opened the door and ran out, dropping the unlit cigarette on the floor of the car.

9

A man and a woman came often—very often, sometimes with only a small bundle—into the call office of the laundry where I worked. They never honked for service. Whenever either of the other students who worked at the counter with me attempted to wait on them—even when customers were protesting about the slowness of the service—they lingered until I was free. Once I saw them waiting at the curb in their car until two other customers had left.

He was a heavyset man, about fifty, who breathed audibly, every now and then inhaling to catch his breath. Perhaps because of his girth, he seemed to waddle. His wife—he had introduced himself and her to me formally as "Mr. and Mrs. David Kippan"—was his opposite, reed-thin, with deep-set anxious eyes. She seemed to float in, noiselessly, beside him. They had in common slight frequent smiles contradicted by deep frowns.

The first time I had waited on them—a slow day—they had asked me about school, my ambitions, alternating questions between them. I told them I was going to be a writer. They seemed thrilled. I suspected that one or the other or both might be writers themselves and that that accounted for their sustained interest in me, and so I responded warmly.

When they invited me to dinner at their home, I was flattered by the invitation from sophisticated adults, surely writers. Too,

I had continued to discourage friendships outside school. The encounter with Isabel Franklin had left me feeling sad. On the night of our shared catastrophe, I had considered driving after her, but I was sure—afraid—that she would reject my offer.

Mr. and Mrs. Kippan offered to pick me up, but I didn't want to give them my address—so I borrowed my brother's car and drove to their house. It was an attractive house in a "good" neighborhood, a very good neighborhood—I never failed to notice such details.

"What a pleasure that you're joining us for dinner, John Rechy!" Mr. Kippan greeted me in his booming voice. He was wearing a jacket and a tie. I had not even considered dressing; I wore jeans and a sweater. I had only one suit, which my brother had given me, not yet worn out.

Mr. Kippan ushered me into a house that seemed an extension of each of them, in equal parts. There were several delicate porcelain figurines on shelves of dark solid wood. The books on the shelves looked musty and old. Over a dormant fireplace hung a picture, in a lacy frame, of a fierce horse about to pounce.

"John Rechy is here," Mr. Kippan called into the house.

Emerging briefly from the kitchen, Mrs. Kippan greeted me: "John Rechy, welcome to our home!" She confided, "I don't often cook. David and I eat out most of the time. But, tonight, I've made a special meal for you, Johnny." I simply accepted being called "Johnny" as a form of affection.

We sat at the dining table, set with white plates and shiny cutlery. They faced each other on opposite sides of the table. I was seated in the middle. Uncomfortable at first, I rehearsed what to say to retain their impression of me as sophisticated enough to invite for dinner.

Mrs. Kippan had cooked a "home meal"—a roast, potatoes, corn on the cob, along with a crisp salad. She served iced tea in a sweaty pitcher, a Texas staple. At home, even in winter, we drank iced tea.

Eventually, the conversation became easy. I answered their questions—some already answered at the laundry—about school; I told them I edited the high school newspaper.

"So ambitious!" Mrs. Kippan complimented me, her hands constantly touching her hair as if to make sure it was not messy.

"And accomplished," Mr. Kippan barked in his authoritative voice.

"Thank you."

"And you're only—?" Mrs. Kippan abandoned the question as she disappeared into the kitchen with dishes, returning with ice cream for desert.

"Seventeen," I answered when she was back.

"Imagine that!" Mr. Kippan said. He paused to regain his breath, which resumed in loud heaves.

"And already so smart—and attractive, forgive me for observing," Mrs. Kippan said.

"Thank you." I certainly didn't mind the observations.

"I'm sure girls pursue you all the time," Mrs. Kippan said.

"Not only girls, I wager," Mr. Kippan said with a raspy chuckle.

What had he meant?

Both were staring at me.

"You're right, David," Mrs. Kippan broke the uncomfortable silence, "I'm sure it's not only girls who are attracted to him. There are, you know, some pretty teachers."

"Precisely," Mr. Kippan said.

I was as relieved by what seemed to be a clarification of Mr. Kippan's remark as I was unsettled by the new reference to teachers. How could Mrs. Kippan know about Miss Edwards? I forced myself to relax, but that was becoming increasingly difficult.

"Do you have a special girl?" Mrs. Kippan asked with what seemed to be grave interest—she leaned toward me for my answer.

"Yes," I said. Who?

"So you are a writer!" Mr. Kippan finally changed the subject.

"I'm going to be, yes," I said.

"I, myself, you know, am working on a radical essay about films and the importance of subtle shadings." Mr. David Kippan leaned back importantly to underscore the profundity of his radical essay.

I didn't know what to say. I wasn't sure what *he* had said.

"Why, you and David have so much in common—both writers." Mrs. Kippan moved her hands nervously, lightly, about her face, as if to detect her expression.

I didn't welcome having much in common with Mr. Kippan. The silence deepened.

"You must read a lot, for a young man your age," Mr. Kippan said after he had waited too long for me to remark on our similarities.

I welcomed an introduction to discuss writers I was now reading. I had just discovered Dos Passos and Farrell. Shamefully, I didn't mention that I was reading Kathleen Winsor's sensational *Forever Amber,* which all the congregants at Mass in the Immaculate Conception Church had been sworn never to read.

"Have you read Henry Miller's *Tropic of Cancer?*" Mr. Kippan dismissed my proud listing of readings. "Would you like to?"

Henry Miller? Forbidden. Banned. Censored. "Sure, I—How? He's not allowed in the country, is he?"

Mrs. Kippan leaned over me to whisper, "We have a copy David smuggled past customs!"

"I'd like to borrow it," I said, curious about the notorious book by the notorious writer, but, also, to return the subject to books I had read.

"We don't let it out of our sight," Mr. Kippan said.

I felt trapped without knowing what the trap might be.

Mrs. Kippan went to one of the musty bookshelves and pulled out—very carefully, edging it out—a worn book without a jacket. She held it out toward me. "Henry Miller's *Tropic of Cancer!*"

When I reached for it, she pulled it away. Mr. Kippan took the book.

Mrs. Kippan uttered a sigh. She pressed her hands against her temples. "Migraine," she said. Then to me: "I'm sorry, Johnny. I have to lie down in the dark until it passes."

I stood up, concerned, ready and eager to leave. "I'm sorry. Thank you very much for the delicious—"

"No!" Mr. Kippan said, restraining me with a firm hand.

"You must stay," Mrs. Kippan encouraged. "David will be happy to read to you from Mr. Miller." She left the room quickly.

Mr. Kippan linked one heavy arm through one of mine, leading me to the living room. "You sit here," he instructed, indicating a chair with a large footstool.

"I really have to go—"

"You don't want to hear the banned words of this great writer, this towering intellectual? You—a writer yourself? *Every* writer owes it to himself to read the man's work! Why, it's fraught with subtle shadings; I intend to discuss that in my radical essay. Now sit *down* and take advantage of this rare opportunity."

Sit down? He was ordering me! I didn't move.

"Please, sit down," he said smiling and frowning.

I sat down slowly, to indicate I was only deciding.

Quickly, David Kippan sat on the footstool in front of me, hardly fitting on it, so that I had to lean back, into the chair.

He opened the book to a marked passage. In a declamatory voice he read to me—not about "subtle shadings"—but about thighs and cunts and cocks and lice and smells and buttocks and lice and odors and cocks and cunts and lice . . .

"Exciting, isn't it?" he asked. He had had to interrupt his reading now and then to catch his breath, at times a wheeze.

I shook my head. No. The characters were dirty, disgusting.

"Listen to this—" He went on reading, rushing now breathless. More lice and odors and—"Aroused?" he gasped at me.

"What?"

"Are you aroused!"

"No!" I stood up so abruptly he almost fell off the stool. "I have to go. I told my brother I'd have his car back early."

"You *have* to leave?" Mr. Kippan asked, his voice softening as if he was suddenly very sad.

"Yes. Please tell Mrs. Kippan that I enjoyed the dinner very much, and I hope she gets well soon, and thank you, Mr. Kippan, for reading to me. I enjoyed the 'subtle shadings.'"

In my brother's car, I felt angry at them, but, more, at myself. How had I invited this strange evening?

During the following days when I had my brother's car, I drove around Isabel Franklin's house—the house where I had picked her up—considering stopping by, even thinking that I might ask her to accompany me to the approaching senior prom. But I didn't. I couldn't picture her coming out to greet me in the unimpressive Nash, let alone getting into it. Too, she'd be angry that I hadn't believed her story about a friend living there.

At school now, she and I would pause to greet each other, just that. Eventually we merely nodded. Finally we ignored each other.

Then she stopped turning up in classes. She was considered only absent at first.

Each time I saw my sister Olga, I realized how far we had come from our childhood roles. I would look at her and try to grasp the evolution that had transformed the girl who had been my buddy, a plain tomboy, into the woman I saw now. I felt that the added closeness between us—or rather, the extension of our closeness—

had come about in significant part from my having told her what I had withheld for years, how unhappy I had been when she had left on her honeymoon without saying "so long" to me, how I had hidden, certain she would seek me out.

"Oh, how sad!" she agreed. Instantly she was crying.

I assured her that I had long since recovered. That seemed to annoy her.

Although she was still beautiful—her skin, like my mother's, unblemished—she was increasingly prone now to gain a few pounds, lose them, regain them. More often than not, she was—I chose the best term to award her—"lush."

She had accepted her role as the family gossip, or, more kindly, as the family chronicler, constantly increasing her dramatic powers of presentation. By tacit understanding, we did not speak about my father, who now, in my life at home, I thought of as lurking like an avenger of something I couldn't grasp; and when my rage at him allowed momentary surcease—pity—I would wonder whether I would ever understand, if I continued to try, the violent anger he aimed at me.

As kids, my sister and I had haunted the Texas Grand Theater during Revival Week, after I had confided to her that I used to sneak in, alone, by a side entrance, an entrance we then used together. When, once, my mother joined us, we told her we had special "student tickets" for ourselves and would meet her inside. That time, we sat, my mother in the middle, all three of us holding hands and crying as we watched Mata Hari led to the firing squad.

Often now, I would detect in my sister's stories something borrowed—no, integrated—from those grand old films. When she was annoyingly judgmental about someone, usually about Isabel— "Her name is Alicia, Alicia, *Alicia!*" she would insist—I reminded her that she herself had been the object of gossip before she married, and about Señor's threats, especially among the vicious aunts.

"*Those* stories," she said, "were just rumors."

"Then you weren't pregnant when you married?" I had never considered that she had not been.

She burst into laughter: "You think it's possible to give birth to a nine-pound boy at seven months? Our mother still does, God bless her. Besides, the rumors never bothered me. I was in love, little brother, and of course I was pregnant, and so we married."

Knowing that she remained close to Señor's wife—who was now nothing less than fat—and to her sister-in-law Tina, I turned to her for information about Isabel Franklin.

We had lunch frequently, my sister Olga and I—always awkward sandwiches; she was not a good cook—in her new two-room apartment while her husband was working and the growing boy had been sent to play in another room.

We had just finished that day's awful sandwiches when she settled her slightly expanded form—plump today—on her favorite soft chair.

When, oddly, she hadn't brought up the subject, I asked her about Isabel Franklin.

"I knew you were waiting to ask, weren't you, little brother?" Having, I suppose, determined my enduring interest, and having decided to add suspense by withholding her information for me to draw out, she said, "Of course you mean Alicia Gonzales. She's gone."

"She ran away?"

"Tina was too embarrassed to tell anyone about it till now. Alicia left a note that said only, 'Good-bye, don't look for me, I'm OK.' Imagine!"

"Where did she go?" I had convinced myself that she would still be in El Paso. I felt rejected.

"Tina has no idea, and she's despondent, sobbing on the telephone; she's called her ex-husbands, both of them, to see if Alicia went to see them. No word. Imagine Tina's sorrow over that nasty brat! She probably went to Hollywood to be a movie star, with all those airs she has. I never thought she was all that pretty, did you?"

"Yes," I said, "she was and she is."

My sister shrugged.

"I'm sure Isabel will come back for graduation." I was hoping that she would.

"I'm not so sure Alicia Gonzales will ever be back, little brother," my sage sister prophesied.

Had Isabel gone to Mexico, as she had said that disastrous evening?

"Little brother, do you still have a crush on Alicia?"

Still? I had never told her I did. I wanted to deflect her question: "Why don't you like Isabel?"

My sister started pretending to count on her fingers Isabel's many faults, exhausting one hand, going on to the other.

"Stop it, Olga. Why? Are you jealous of her because you think I like her?"

"Oh, hush . . . How can anyone like someone who leaves her mother without telling her where she's going, or why? And how can you like someone who's such a fake?"

"A fake?" I stood up, ending our lunch.

As the ritual of the high school senior prom approached, I felt I had to go, to assert my place as a "popular" if still remote student. I wished that Isabel were back. Perhaps because she wasn't, I was certain I would have recovered enough arrogance to ask her out.

10

On the day we were to be measured for the caps and gowns we would wear during graduation, I ran into a pretty girl I had often said hello to in the hallways; a few times, I'd stopped to talk to her, briefly, a fact she seemed to welcome. She even seemed to seek the accidental contact by slowing down when she saw me approaching, as she did today. She was a sophomore. Her name was Virginia Taylor. Like the movie star her name evoked, she had black hair and a very fair complexion, and she had violet eyes, yes, violet, and she was Anglo.

"Will you? To the prom?"

"Oh, yes," she said.

We lingered for a few minutes. When recess between classes ended, she gave me her telephone number.

I had asked an Anglo girl to go out with me! That wouldn't have happened if Isabel had been around, I told myself, blaming her for my feeling uncertain about what I had done when I learned that all the other Mexican students in the school were going to the prom—if they were going—with Mexican girls.

My brother Robert was delighted that—after wavering—I had decided to go to the prom. He helped me polish the old car. Did I have enough money for the essential corsage? I didn't. He gave me two dollars to add to mine.

With my sister Olga's help, I ordered the corsage by phone on the afternoon of the prom. "It has to be delivered," my sister had instructed, "so she'll be wearing it when you pick her up. Carnations, that's always the best for a girl." She was enjoying the activity, although I could tell she was piqued. "Is she pretty?"

"Very."

"Prettier than me, little brother?"

"Much prettier," I said jokingly, causing her to elbow my ribs.

"The address to deliver it?" the voice on the telephone asked, after I had agreed to go by and pay for it.

Oh, God, I had the telephone number but not the address. I kept scrutinizing the paper Virginia had written on as if the address would magically appear.

I called the telephone number to get the address from her.

A woman answered. Immediately I was tense.

"Is Virginia there?"

"Who wants to know?"

"Me. I'm John Rechy. I have a date with her, we're going to the senior prom. I want to send her a corsage."

"Oh?"

The woman's voice was odd. She was extending the silence that followed as I waited for her to call the girl.

"I'll be picking her up later."

"You will?"

Now the voice was sarcastic, taunting.

"Yes."

"Virginia told me you asked her out."

"I did." I wanted to hang up the telephone before something horrible could happen, what I knew was about to happen.

Her voice harsh, the woman rushed words, stuffing them into the telephone before I would be able to stop them:

"I know who you are, boy. Over my dead body will my daughter go out with a Mexican," she spat into the telephone and into my ear, and the telephone clicked off.

After I had paid for it, I gave the corsage to my mother, who accepted it with her usual gracious smile, the way she had once accepted a kiss from a handsome transient, long ago. She did not question what had occurred concerning the corsage.

I did not go to the prom.

Much later, after anger replaced pain, I wondered:

How the hell did that bitch know that I'm Mexican?

At school, I saw Virginia Taylor. I forced myself to walk over to her, certain that she would apologize for her mother. She pointedly turned away.

I was glad to be about to graduate from high school, to leave behind its cruelties, not only Virginia's harsh rejection of me but what had began to seem to me the determined viciousness of "popular" students against those not in their circle, the desire to thrust them far away to preclude any attempt at entry. From my undefined vantage, I saw it all.

There was a pretty girl named Wilma whose body had matured beyond her age, sixteen. Her voluptuous breasts, which she was clearly proud of—wearing blouses that exhibited them as much as possible—had made her popular among male students, all Anglos, including several athletes. But she was popular only after school, when she was picked up by one or another of the boys, who later claimed that she was an "easy fuck." When, during lunch break, she tried to insinuate herself into the company of the boys who bragged about having sex with her, they would turn away as if they did not know her. They would sidle over to their safe girlfriends of supposed good reputation, girls among whom a football queen and princesses would soon be announced.

I was in a math class with Wilma, my last year at school, when a student monitor, one of the popular girls who disdained her most, arrived breathlessly with a message for Wilma that was important enough—from the principal's office—that the teacher allowed her to receive it. The messenger said in a loud whisper: "Congratulations, Wilma!" Wilma tore the envelope open, read the message, stood up and shouted ecstatically: "I've been elected football queen; the principal wants to see me now."

Without waiting for the teacher's permission, she ran out of the classroom. Trembling, she returned a few minutes later, her makeup stained with tears. The note had been a prank initiated by the boys who "dated" her after school, and by the girls. For days Wilma did not attend school.

I felt for her, for her crushed feelings; but also because I saw a similarity in her situation—perhaps that's why we had never talked. My own popularity was compromised, too, ending when I rushed home to a secret address. That had not protected me from Virginia and her mother's rejection of me. If I went to college—a consideration clouded by the fact of our limited means—I would not care whether or not I was popular.

Although I had still hoped that, at the last moment, she would come back, Isabel Franklin did not turn up for the graduation ceremony.

If it had not been required because I was one of the top ten students, I would not have attended either. I was assigned to read a rosy patriotic speech by someone named Benjamin de Casseres. It was about the bright future that awaited us all; it ended—and although I could not see her, I knew that in the audience my sister Olga would be giggling:

"I am democracy in action, I am the United States."

It garnered loud applause, most spiritedly from my mother, wearing a new hat and dress my brother Robert had saved up to buy for her. My father was there, sitting beside her and my sister and her husband, along with my sister Blanca. My father's presence surprised me.

I had never mentioned around him that I was writing stories. But soon after the graduation ceremony, there appeared, on the table that I had converted into a desk, a secondhand portable Royal typewriter.

My father had placed it there.

I turned toward the open door, where he stood watching me.

"Thank you." I broke the silence of long days.

He nodded and turned away.

But his outbursts of anger continued as ferociously as before. He lived now in an angry trance of remembered crushed dreams of musical glory.

Wherever she was, wherever she had gone, wherever she had fled to, Isabel Franklin—I thought of her only by the name she had chose, over the name she had abandoned—had left El Paso, as I longed to do. In my young life I had been away only as far as Chihuahua, on a brief early visit with my parents and Olga. The fact that Isabel had fled intensified my own feeling of wanting to flee this city, despite the crystalline skies and blue mountains that I loved.

There was an immediate situation that I wanted to flee, get out of. My rich uncle's wife, Carmen, the boozy lady who held court with a gun over her poker sessions, was preparing a *quinceañera* for her pretty daughter. That meant a celebration of her fifteenth birthday, a coming out. In the upper echelons of that society, there would have been an orchestra, a gleaming hall, gentlemen in tuxedos, ladies in long dresses, the honored girl in a dress that resembled a wedding gown, her escort in a fitted tuxedo. A few rungs down, the whole became an attempt to imitate and at times gaudily surpass its precursor: The orchestra became a popular band, the setting a vast rented patio, gentlemen wore their slick dark suits, several of the ladies displayed flashy dresses, the *quinceáñera* often wore an exaggerated version of the usual gown, and her escort—

That was me, in a suit borrowed from my brother and temporarily fitted to my body by my mother.

Why I was chosen for the affair, which would take place in Juárez, was a puzzle to me. I had seen the girl only once; we had said hello. That was it.

"I don't understand why they want me to be the escort," I told my mother as she was altering the suit.

As if it were merely to be taken for granted—nothing exceptional—my mother said, "Because you look like an American."

In attendance after the church ceremonies were my proud mother and my uncle and his wife, whose cronies, draped in loud jewelry, were already tipsy. I wondered whether any of them had a secret gun, to deal with whatever affront might occur.

I went through the determinedly elegant affair, stiffly, danced the first dance with the slender girl—in a surprisingly subdued and pretty gown—who looked like a white tulip. Then I led her to her actual boyfriend, a dark young man, and I left.

11

I was seventeen.

One of the two local newspapers, the *El Paso Times,* gave me a scholarship, fifty dollars for tuition to attend the small college that adjoined the vast desert surrounding the city. It was called Texas College of Mines and Metallurgy. Although it had a few liberal arts departments, it specialized in courses for engineers. Its rugged campus—we had to climb stony hills to get to the classrooms— appeared at times to be taken over by lanky cowboys from the interior of Texas, and by their blonde girlfriends, who, it seemed to me, had come only to join one of the several sororities there.

Still, there were some good professors, most of whom had chosen the warm climate because of lingering illnesses; a few came here to die.

Dr. Sonnichsen, the head of the English department, was a graduate of Harvard. I never found out what had brought him here to this cowboyish college; perhaps it was his lusty Mexican wife. In his strict classes, I was introduced to a gallery of classical writers who would influence me in various ways: Milton, Pope, Dryden, Donne, Swift, and, eventually, James Joyce. Those led me by circuitous routes to others: Rimbaud, Verlaine, Djuna Barnes, Robinson Jeffers, Gertrude Stein. Concurrently I punctuated my literary explorations by reading, and enormously enjoying, famous best sellers: *Kings Row, Gone with the Wind, The Strange Woman, Leave Her to Heaven, The Foxes of Harrow*—those books, with their splashes of Technicolor prose, also influenced me.

For Dr. Sonnichsen, I wrote a paper upholding that Milton was on the side of the rebellious angels. I received, reputedly, the only A he had ever awarded. Eventually he would encourage me to take, long before it was ordinarily expected, just before the granting of a degree, the comprehensive English literature examination he had established as a requirement. I passed it easily when I was a sophomore.

I did not, however, fare as well with Dr. Ponsford, a woman with a face like a mask framed in dyed black hair; she was unbelievably white, and her one expression, etched disdain, seemed never to change. She forbade me to write a term paper about Marie Antoinette—"too vast a topic." In an earlier lecture she had informed us that we could narrow a subject by introducing it with "On." I wrote the paper about Marie Antoinette and titled it: "On Marie Antoinette." With her usual sneer, Dr. Ponsford surprised me by granting me an A.

As part of my journalism scholarship, I would be employed at the city newspaper as copyboy after school, sometimes on the late shift, until midnight, alternating with another college student. That allowed me to leave the laundry call office and avoid Mr. and Mrs. David Kippan, who had continued to lurk around me.

My father hardly ever worked now, having secured some kind of meager "pension." He continued to drum his fingers on his desk to unheard music, still venting his anger in curses, muttered and shouted, against me and my mother.

Neither the scholarship nor what I would earn at the newspaper, fifteen dollars a week, was enough to pay for all the college requirements, or even for the used textbooks I intended to buy. Although by now he had a wife and son to support, my brother Robert was determined that I, as "the smart one," must attend college; he would pay whatever I could not afford.

Even with what I earned and what my brother Robert continued to contribute, we could not afford the monthly rent for the run-down house just barely on the "good" side of El Paso. There was nothing to do but apply for a unit in the government projects on the South Side of the city. Because in El Paso many Mexican families were just making do, all the units were occupied. It was through my popular brother's contacts that we were able to move in.

Now I lived in the Second Ward, the section of the city identified as the "poor Mexican section."

The units were identical, boxlike, glued to each other. In front of each there was a concrete block, a mockery of a tiny porch. Grass had died from a lack of expensive water; weeds patched the dirt. Even in summer, trees there bore few leaves; their trunks and branches were grayish-brown. Garbage spilled out of inadequate cans that were quickly filled, secured with chains to a wire enclosure.

The few pieces of furniture we owned were lugged in by me and my brothers. My father's large, once grand desk did not fit in our unit. My brother took it with him to "store" . . . somewhere.

When we were moved into a "family unit" of two floors, I stood in the room upstairs that would be mine and I looked outside through the window, studying the desolation of the doggedly identical units. Instead of coming closer to the house on Montana Street that I had sat in front of, pretending to be rich, we had moved downward. The next step would have been the tenements just blocks away, flimsy, sweaty structures propped on stilts, tired walls pasted over with tattered posters of movies that played at the Teatro Colón, the only Mexican movie house.

With intact dignity, my mother settled into the projects. She continued to dress impeccably, altering her clothes as they became old, adding something here, taking something off there as she pumped at the pedal of her ancient sewing machine. Even just to go to the corner store that specialized in Mexican goods, she wore a hat and gloves, which she kept immaculate, drying them flat on a shelf. She became a beloved figure among the neighbors, all Mexicans, like a benevolent queen, always smiling. The neighbors never addressed her in the familiar form, *tu;* it was always *usted*—and it was always as Señora Rechy, never by a first name, as they addressed each other.

Knowing how deeply the move into the government projects, a defeat, had affected me, my mother tried to cheer me up. She pointed out that the government units were equipped with a washing machine, hot water, and other improvements we could otherwise not afford. She decorated the rooms as best she could—with curtains she made, a tablecloth she had embroidered—making them a grand setting for a poor queen. Young "gangy" Mexicans—whose older forebears had been called pachucos—looked at me skeptically, as if wondering what I was doing in their territory. They, as well as the other residents of the projects, assumed that I was Anglo, like my father, and that he and I were the only "Americans" in the whole neighborhood.

Especially now, I told no one from my "other life"—at work, at school—where I lived. I now gave as my own the address of my older sister, Blanca, who lived with her husband in an attractive white house near Grandview Park. A pretty vine flowered over the front porch, which was edged by grass, trimmed.

I didn't want to take the bus to college; that seemed like a further decline. Whether my brother Robert understood this or not, he offered me his car. He would come by early in the morning and I would drive him to work at the lens-grinding factory and then drive on to college. Sometimes I would pick him up later; most of the time he drove home with a coworker. When he couldn't come by for me, I would run across town, across the railroad tracks that separated the city, into the section we had moved from. Halfway up the hill that I had walked to go to high school, I would hitchhike to the college, getting a ride easily from other students.

At night I lay in bed, hot from the intense heat of the airless day, and I knew I had to move my mother out of the projects. I would buy her a house of her own, out of the neighborhood that branded us as poor Mexicans.

Today my brother needed his car.

After classes, I hitchhiked from the college to the center of the city, running across the tracks, to the projects. It was not a particularly hot day, but when I reached our unit—always an assault, the brick cracker box we now lived in, in line with all the others, blocks and blocks of them—I was perspiring and hot, my shirt open and moist.

I walked in. There they were, the malicious aunts. I considered walking out. But my mother had already greeted me and the aunts were leaning expectantly toward me, smiles slashed across their haggard faces. No doubt about it, one was just as ugly as the other. How the same parents who had produced them had produced my lovely mother was a mystery to me.

"*Hijo!* Son!" they addressed me. I winced; it annoyed me that they were related to me even as aunts.

"Hi." I started to walk up to the second level, to take a bath—there were no showers, just a clean bathtub.

"We were just remarking to Lupe," one of them said in a tone steeped in artificial caring, "how wonderful it is of El Paso to provide such nice shelter for the poor."

I inhaled, all that I was capable of doing at that moment.

"Yes," said the other aunt, "and Lupe, you've done so much to make it pretty—different from all the other units that look exactly the same from the outside, and, we suppose, inside."

"Thank you," my mother said, her eyes steady on me. I had not moved. Perspiration was turning cold on my body.

"What do the neighbors think about your American husband?" one asked my mother, but her smile was aimed, knifing, at me.

"I suppose—*no es así?*—that he's the only . . . *americano* . . . in the projects."

"We wonder how *he* feels about that?" the other one fired, and drew her smile away from my mother and on to me in judgment.

I wanted to rebut, to answer her hateful questions with something cruel. For once, I wished that my father would appear, that he would shout them away for judging him when he had already been judged so harshly by circumstances.

Sweating even more from the rage I felt, my breathing harsh, I was finally able to say to them: "You've always been jealous of my mother because you're so damned ugly and she's beautiful." Not enough yet, not enough. "*Y no se aperescan aquí jamás.* Don't ever come back again!" Not yet enough. "*Cabronas!*" I hurled the harshest word I could think of in Spanish, a word blunt beyond its actual meaning—something like bastards, damned bitches, but much, much more.

"Guadalupe!" one screamed over at my mother. She dabbed at tears, which were not flowing.

"Did you hear what your son called us?" the other asked. They were both sobbing extravagantly now.

"He called you *cabronas*," my mother said softly, "and that's what you are. Know this: We Rechys carry our pride with us wherever we live." She turned her head and looked at me. "Don't we, *m'ijo?*" she said.

When at the checkout desk of the college library, I asked for a play by García Lorca, whom Dr. Sonnichsen had mentioned, the librarian, Baxter Polk, introduced himself to me, offering to order whatever was not then available. He was a tall, slender man with mesmerizing eyes.

One afternoon, he told me that he wanted to show me a collection of foreign plays he had just acquired for the library, some books that might interest me. We stepped down laddered steps to the bowels of the building.

From a sparsely filled shelf, he pulled out a book and held it out to me. I took it. I saw a photograph of two excessively handsome men, both blond, about to kiss each other, their hands touching. Twins. No, not twins, or even two men. The photograph was of one man facing a mirror, as if about to kiss himself.

I looked away from the photograph. Mr. Polk's eyes were so intent on me that I pulled back.

"He's very beautiful, isn't he, John?" he asked me. His gaze held, unblinking.

I had never before heard a man referred to as "beautiful." "He's handsome, yes," I said. "But I don't see—" I wasn't sure what I had been about to say.

"His name is Jean Marais," Mr. Polk said. "I thought you would be interested."

"I've never heard of him, and I'm not interested in him," I said. I thrust the book back at him, thrust away the image of the blond man.

Mr. Polk took the book and held it close to himself, as if to warm his heart with it. "Oh, I didn't mean that, oh, no, no, not that at all, I meant you might be interested in the *play,* the writer of it," he said with a sly look at me, his gaze probing. "It's Cocteau's *Orphée.* Marais is the star of the film. I've noticed the books you've been checking out—"

"Mostly Lorca," I said.

"—and I thought you might want to broaden your . . . literary . . . horizons."

"I'd like to read the play," I said.

Mr. Polk held the book out to me again, like a precious gift not to be rejected; but instead of surrendering it to me, he put his hand on my shoulder. I pretended to reach out for another book on a nearby shelf so I could move away.

"I must introduce you to a girl you *must* meet," Mr. Polk said.

I met Barbara in Mr. Polk's office a few days later, a very pretty girl, about my age, perhaps slightly older, eighteen.

"Barbara, this is Johnny. Johnny, this is Barbara." Mr. Polk bowed individually before each of us.

I assumed that his referring to me as "Johnny" was meant to indicate fondness, although, increasingly, I disliked the boyish name.

"Hello, Johnny," Barbara said.

She said the name so immediately fondly that I didn't mind it from her. Mr. Polk stood back, as if reeling from the spectacle of both of us. "My God!" He touched his cheek in posed amazement. "You two aren't only enamored of the same writer—"

"Lorca?" Barbara asked me.

With an especially intricate configuration of gestures that seemed to be outlining our forms and bringing them together, Mr. Polk finished his propped exclamation, "You even look alike."

I recognized the girl then. She had aroused talk around the campus by having resigned from one of the college's most popular sororities, whose members were attractive and well-off girls.

Barbara and I now met often on campus, by conscious coincidence. We would go to the student union building at a certain time between classes. We would sit at one of the many plastic tables, a checkerboard of shiny colors, and drink coffee and talk exuberantly about Lorca. We agreed that we would translate Lorca's *Bodas de Sangre* (*Blood Wedding*) from its original Spanish into English, finding all other translations—we had each read one—"inadequate."

To seal the agreement, we shook hands, and then I elaborately kissed one of her hands, feeling immediately silly—but welcoming the memory of the transient who had long ago kissed my mother's hand.

"Wait now," Barbara said. "Do you know Spanish?"

"My mother is Mexican," I said.

As we began our translation in the college library before I would go off to my job at the newspaper, I soon noticed this about her: One moment she was exuberant, joyful; and then without warning, a look of sadness shaded her face. Her words trailing off, she seemed to withdraw into a private place of her own. When that happened, I would simply wait for the excited pretty girl to come back, as she always did within moments of the fleeting mood.

At times, when I was with her, the memory of Isabel Franklin would return. Why? There was no point of reconciliation between her and Barbara that I could find. In disappearing from El Paso, why had Isabel Franklin not diminished in importance in my life?

Because of my scholarship, I was eventually appointed by the journalism faculty to the staff of the college magazine, which was called, appropriately, *El Burro, The Donkey.* It was a paying job—twenty-five dollars a month. That and my job as copyboy augmented the money I contributed at home.

The editor of the college publication was a young man whose face was a field of pimples and who seemed always to be laughing hysterically at some new joke or cartoon he was clipping out to borrow from another college publication. Borrowed jokes filled the several pages of the glossy magazine. "Listen to this one! It's the best," he praised each joke.

Besides me and him, there were five others on the staff: a girl who seemed to have a permanent cold and, as far as I could see, did nothing; a "writer," a sullen young man who wrote funny captions; a photographer, who took photographs only of sports events and fraternity and sorority parties; and two "reporters," both male, who wrote flat captions to accompany the photographs.

At the end of the semester, the clowning editor left the college. I was appointed by the faculty board—Mr. Polk was a member—as editor. That position would pay more, thirty dollars a month. Despite my job at the newspaper—and the ongoing translation of Lorca with Barbara—I accepted this new job gladly. I was determined to convert the magazine into something much better when I published my first edition, the previous editor having completed an issue yet to appear featuring "Best Jokes and Cartoons from *El Burro.*"

My announced position as editor immediately gave me a certain prominence on the campus. It must have contributed to my becoming friends with two very popular young men at the college.

I was working out on the parallel bars in the gym, thinking I was alone because it was early in the morning, when I noticed another young man entering. He worked out briefly with a couple of dumbbells. When I was leaving, he introduced himself.

"Scott."

"I'm John."

He was blond, with a gymnast's body, and he was good-looking. We left the gym to go to the student union building "for coffee." Nervously, not knowing why, I hoped Barbara wouldn't be there. Scott introduced me to his best friend, who was waiting there for him. "Ross, this is John. John—Ross."

Ross was a school wrestler, compactly built, a fact he emphasized by twisting his head as if to unwind from some intense activity, rubbing his muscles as if to obviate any new soreness. When he walked, he kept his arms a few inches from his torso, to emphasize his wide lats. Both he and Scott were in what was considered the "best" fraternity on the campus—and the most exclusive.

As the three of us were sitting in the student union building, Barbara walked in. She saw me and I saw her. Pretending—I was sure of this—that she had just remembered something, she walked out.

"What were you doing with those guys?" she asked me bluntly as we sat in the library during our next meeting to discuss whether we would emphasize life or death in our definitive translation of *Blood Wedding*—and pondering what to do with the "moon" imagery.

"They're my friends," I said, ready to be defensive but realizing how unlikely the friendship might seem.

"Have they asked you to join their fraternity?"

We had never discussed her dropping out of her sorority; the cause was still a subject of speculation. The suspected reasons I had heard ranged from her being crazy to her being pregnant. I saw no evidence of either.

"No," I said, "they haven't." It was a ridiculous thought; I could certainly not afford what participating in a fraternity, especially that fraternity, would entail; joining didn't interest me at all.

"I wonder why they might want you," Barbara asked.

"What the hell does that mean?" I stood up.

"That you're too smart for that kind of bullshit," she said. I couldn't think of anything to rebut; I was searching for something that had to do with her having been in a sorority, but I could find nothing because she had, notoriously, left it.

"Do they know you're Mexican?" she asked.

Struggling to contain my anger at her, I sat down again and returned my attention to Lorca and the moon imagery.

Since they had seen me and Barbara in the student union building, Scott and Ross suggested we all go out together on a date on Saturday.

"No doubt about it, man, she's beautiful, a little strange," Scott said about Barbara.

"Yes," I agreed, "she's beautiful, and very smart."

"Smart don't matter," Ross laughed. "Dumb and pretty, that's my choice."

With trepidation I asked Barbara to go out with me and my two new friends and their girlfriends, certain she would say no; that way I could back out of the plan. She surprised me by saying yes. I felt trapped into going.

My new friends agreed to pick me up in Scott's father's car, a roomy Lincoln. I gave them my sister Blanca's address as my own. I took the bus there earlier. My sister was surprised by my unexpected visit, but she welcomed it. I told her some friends were picking me up there because they lived nearby; did she mind? I know she suspected nothing else—unlike my sister Olga, who would have immediately been on to what I was doing. I sat on the flowery-vined front porch and waited.

Scott and Ross had already picked up their girlfriends; just as I had expected, both of the girls were cheery and giggly and pretty. Whether they were smart or not, the vapid conversation would not reveal. We drove to pick up Barbara. I was in a good mood at the prospect of extending my relationship with her in this way; we would be allies, even saboteurs of the girls' inanity, almost predetermined.

Barbara's mother was watering the lawn of a two-story, recently painted house. She was a drawn, thin, woman, unsmiling when she saw me get out of the car. I thought of Virginia Taylor's mother, and my aborted date with her daughter; I considered pulling back.

"Is Barbara home, ma'am?"—of course she would be; I just wanted to acknowledge the presence of the harsh woman, and for her to acknowledge mine.

Not possible! The water spouting from her hose was nearing where I was standing. There was no way that she would be directing the water at me. A spray wet my shoes. I dodged back uncertainly, not wanting her to think I suspected she might be attempting to wet me. But she was—there was no question of her intent as the water came closer. I pulled back far beyond the water's reach. The arcing water swirled before me.

I shouted into the house, "Barbara! I'm here!"

The woman jerked the water hose away, turning her back on me. Barbara ran out. She did not look at her mother. Wordlessly, she got into the car. Scott and his girlfriend were in front; Barbara, Ross and his girlfriend, and I attempted to squeeze into the back, Ross emphasizing his impressive size by turning sideways, front again, sideways—"I'm just too big," he kept saying—until his girlfriend volunteered to sit in front.

After I had introduced Barbara—"Hello," "Hi," "How're ya, Barbara?"—Ross's girlfriend said to Barbara, "Aren't you—?"

"Yes," Barbara said, smiling, very pleasantly "I am."

"Oh."

I wanted to laugh. Whatever the girl had been about to ask her, Barbara had defused the question, obviating any unpleasant possibility.

But not entirely. Scott's girl seemed to clarify: "*We're* Chi Omega." she said—that was the other highly desirable sorority on campus.

"Oh," Barbara said.

It was a relief to be in the movie theater, where we didn't have to say anything; we saw a musical with Betty Grable and John Payne. Later, at a popular coffee shop, the two sorority girls talked between themselves about nothing. I tried to make conversation with Barbara—I don't even remember about what. She was withdrawing from all of us, so that I wondered, Why the hell did she agree to come? Ross and Scott were talking about weight lifting—"How much do you press now?"—and suggesting that I take it up soon with them.

The disastrous evening ended when we drove Barbara home. I got out with her. Her mother stood like a guard at the door. Barbara and I said good night. I considered kissing her, but she had already walked into the house, past her mother, as silently as she had left.

Had she agreed to go out with all of us only to get away from her mother?—and to persuade me to split away from Ross and Scott and their cheerful banalities?

When I returned to the car, Ross and Scott were kissing their girlfriends hotly. I considered walking back to my sister's house where they had picked me up.

12

Barbara and I continued our translation of Lorca's play. But our initial closeness, if it had not been severed, had not progressed. That had to do, I was sure, with my growing friendship with Scott and Ross, both of whom I had come to like, and enjoy being with, even if our conversations were never as lively as I might have wanted. They continued to talk about their fraternity, hinting that I would make a good "brother." Impossible, and even if possible, unwanted. But I was flattered by the implied association with the good-looking group of men on campus, since the matter would proceed no further than that.

They invited me to go with them to visit Ross's "widowed aunt" at her ranch, in Balmorhea, in Texas, for a weekend. Surprising myself, I agreed. I would be away only two days. When I voiced my constant apprehension at leaving my mother alone to face my father's moods, my brother Robert assured me he would take care of her.

I needed to get away.

When I told Barbara that I was going on that brief trip, to explain a break in our translation of *Blood Wedding*—which was proceeding well, to the point where we fantasized that she would play the woman and I would play the lover in what we determined would be our own production—she went silent and ended our collaboration for that day.

They picked me up again at my sister Blanca's house, the address I continued to give them.

In Ross's slick new car, a Buick, the three of us seated in front, we drove across miles of Texas desert and abrupt greenery—it burst out of the earth, a shock of immediate contrast with long arid stretches of dusty-yellow desert, distant mountains. In the deep blue sky of Texas, the bluest cumulus clouds melded and burst, now and then snuffing out the sunlight so that a gray glow veiled the landscape. When the sun escaped, the grayness would turn into a silvery brightness that lit the desert.

Ross's aunt wasn't home when we arrived at the vast ranch, acres of land about a sprawling house like a luxurious hacienda, with terra-cotta walls, a large courtyard, and a cultivated cactus garden, the cactus in bloom, large blossoms exploding with color out of tall needled green trunks. The widowed aunt had left word with a maid, a Mexican maid, that she would be back tomorrow and we should make ourselves at home.

It was late, almost midnight. The maid led us to a large guest room. Although she might have been waiting to show us another room, Ross and Scott, sighing wearily from the heat and the drive, put down their overnight bags. I followed their lead with my own.

The room was furnished in the style of the house: expensive wooden furniture, "Texas decor." There was one large four-poster bed, the posts carved elaborately.

"Too fucking hot! Let's go swimming!" Ross suggested.

"This late?" I didn't know how to swim and I preferred that they would not know.

"Yeah," Scott agreed. "Balmorhea has the largest outdoor swimming pool in the country," he explained to me, apparently having been here before.

The sky was a spangled field of stars, so many that the darkness seemed crowded—a Texas summer sky, stilled by rainless heat.

The pool was surrounded by a tall wired fence; the gateways were chained and locked, closed for the night.

Scott climbed and then jumped over the fence. Ross followed. I made my way over easily.

Scott and Ross started stripping off their clothes, T-shirts first, then shoes, socks, pants, shorts. Naked, they plunged into the water that mirrored the sky's dark brilliance.

"Come on!"

"Come on, John!"

They spattered about the pool, then swam a length, competing, their bodies bobbing up and down, bare flesh illuminated in streaks by the hot moonlight.

"Come on, John!"

"Come on in!"

I wasn't sure what was making me more anxious, the fact that I couldn't swim or the fact that I was being coaxed to take off my clothes and join their nudity.

Ross swam to the edge of the pool, where I was standing. "Take off your clothes, come on, jump in!"

Scott flapped his hands in the water and spattered my shoes. I pulled farther back.

"I'm embarrassed—" I started.

"Embarrassed? With us guys?" shouted Scott, his body shimmering toward the edge of the pool.

"—embarrassed that I don't know how to swim." It was easier to admit that.

"No shit? We'll teach you."

"Come on!"

At the edge of the pool, still in the water, they flanked me, reaching out for my feet, threatening to pull me in.

"Take your clothes off or we'll yank you in with 'em," Ross laughed, grabbing one of my legs.

Scott slapped forcefully at the water so that it sprayed on my clothes. "You want to get your clothes wet?" He had reached the very edge of the pool and was grasping for my other leg.

Wresting myself away, I took off my shirt, my shoes, my socks, my pants. I kept my shorts on.

Their bodies pushed out of the water, emerging out of the pool, water dripping in sprinkles off their bare flesh. They bounded toward me; puddles of water spattered on the pavement.

"Take your shorts off, man!"

"Or we'll pull 'em off for ya."

I took off my shorts, drawing away from the wet bodies romping toward me to pull me into the water. I backed away, farther, away from the pool.

They approached me there, movements exaggerated in preparation of grabbing me. I did not move.

Ross started laughing, doubling over, and then Scott laughed. Ross splashed water on me. I was laughing, too.

They shook off the water, drying themselves with their hands, letting the dark heat dry their naked bodies.

Dressed now, scurrying out of the fenced enclosure, we drove back to the ranch, laughing, laughing, laughing.

In the bedroom we would sleep in, the heat was stifling. The day had turned into one of those Texas nights drenched in moisture, as if the night itself was sweating. Despite the open windows, the air refused to yield even a breeze. Air-conditioning was not yet ubiquitous; some houses, even those of rich people like Ross's aunt, had it only in individual rooms, not the whole house. Even then, only refrigerated air worked to cool; conventional air-conditioning only added moisture.

It was past two o'clock. In the hot darkness streaked with distant flashes of sudden lightning that illuminated the tall cactus just outside, long shadows were thrust on the ground and quickly gone. Ross and Scott stripped to their shorts, sighing loudly to emphasize the relief of less heat. This time unself-consciously, I did the same, welcoming momentary respite from the encroaching heat.

"I'm not sleeping in the middle, I'm too big!" Ross said, and flung himself at the very edge of the large bed. He asserted his requirement for extra space by sprawling on the bed, pushing one leg diagonally across the mattress.

"I'm bigger than you." Scott began to struggle with him to pull him off the bed.

"The fuck you are." Ross resisted.

Scott grabbed Ross's legs; I grabbed his shoulders. Ross pushed away, powerfully. Pulling and tumbling, we all fell back onto the floor, sweat soaking through our shorts, outlining our groins, gluing limbs to limbs in shifting positions, two bodies on top, one on the bottom, two on the bottom, one on top, rolling sideways, sliding against hot moist flesh, hands grabbing, pushing away, bodies intertwined in sweaty friction, as we gasped breathless with increasing heat—our bodies', the room's, the overwhelming night's—laughing, falling back on the floor, exhausted.

The next day, Saturday, we drove around the small hick town of Balmorhea. Most of the men, the Anglo men—ranchers, I assumed—wore cowboys hats, expensive boots. Women in light print dresses that seemed new but from another time darted into and out of a Newberry store, the only somewhat large store in the flat landscape.

Mexican laborers idled in small clusters seeking the shade of scattered trees under the punishing sun, their wives or girlfriends fanning themselves nearby, children with them dashing about, indifferent to the heat, moist heat increased by a the brief shower that had followed the rumbling of thunder last night.

The single theater in the dusty town proclaimed that it was "Air-Conditioned by Refrigeration." That may have accounted for the number of people buying tickets. An old musical I had seen in El Paso with my sister Olga was playing: *Coney Island,* with Betty Grable and Cesar Romero—probably just reaching the town, which seemed to be isolated in the middle of the desert. Going into the theater was a cooling way to pass the couple of hours before Ross's aunt was due back at the ranch.

We bought our tickets—fifty cents—from a dopey man, cowboy hat sliding over his face, who woke up only when anyone rapped on the glass window he sat behind. When Ross took his ticket, the man chuckled something to him. Scott and I approached together for our tickets. The old man said, with a raspy chuckle: "Now you city boys be sure to sit on the left side, ya heah? Right side's for spics, Saturday afternoon's spic day." He snickered, or coughed, a combination of both that made a dirty sound.

Jolted, I asked the man, "What did you say?" while Scott and Ross waited for me at the entrance to the theater.

"Saturday's spic day," the man said, as if he were being asked to embellish an appreciated joke. "They get to sit on the right side, just one day a week, mind ya—they come in from the fields then."

"Come on," Ross goaded me.

Scott had already walked in.

I stood at the entrance. The movie house, square, without a trace of decor, looking as if it might double as a hall for town meetings or religious revivals, was lit in dirty orange light. The hall was divided by an aisle in the center, flanked by rows of seats. There was a scattering of people on the left side, all white. The right side was almost filled, with men, women, children talking expectantly in Spanish, waiting for the movie to begin, candy wrappers, popcorn bags rattling as they brought out prepared food.

I felt the gasps of refrigerated air on my body, cold on sudden cold.

Either Ross or Scott called to me, "Come on!"

I waited. Which side? I looked at the Anglo people. A few had children; they held them close as if to prevent them from bucking over to the other side.

I still waited. Which side?

A little girl, about seven, broke away from her mother on the Anglo side and ran into the aisle, where a Mexican boy was playing idly on the floor next to his seated parents. The white girl looked at the brown boy her age as if studying something foreign. Rushing into the aisle, her mother yanked her away.

On the left side, Ross and Scott, already seated, devouring popcorn, looked back at me, motioning impatiently.

Several of the Mexicans on the right side stared at me, curious now as to why I was standing there, calling attention to myself.

I took a step in, moving toward the right side. I waited, now the object of stares from both sides of the aisle. I took another step, another, faster, to the right of the hall, where the Mexican kid had been yanked in by his own parents.

"Hey!" the old man who had sold us the tickets stood glowering at me. "What the hell ya think you're doin', boy? I told ya—"

I joined Ross and Scott on the left side, only to avoid a scene that would involve my friends, just that. To have done otherwise would have created turmoil in the hall. The old man who had shouted had been prepared for that. I sat through the Technicolor movie only intermittently aware of it, surprised, and relieved, when it ended.

When we filed out, the Mexicans waited dutifully for the Americans to leave, and then they followed. The little Mexican boy who had sat in the aisle before the movie sprinted ahead of everyone. "Hello," he said to us.

All three of us answered back, "Hello, kid," "Hi," "Howre ya?" Scott patted the little boy on the shoulder, a gesture that clearly pleased his father, a dark-brown man, who said, "Thank you, sir." The few white people who had been in the theater turned back, waited, stared at us.

At the end of the block where Ross had parked, I noticed only now a greasy diner and the sign on its window:

"We do not serve niggers, spics, or dogs."

Ross's aunt was back at the ranch.

She was a woman of about fifty, a widow left with a ranch and lots of money. A stolid woman, friendly, with a wide welcoming smile, "Miz Crawford" greeted us with ample open arms. "My, my, my! Jest look at ya now, will ya?—better-lookin' all the time!" she greeted Scott familiarly, planting two loud kisses on his lips while she captured his face with her hands to ensure that he would receive the two full manifestations of her affection. She spoke with a deep Texas accent that seemed to have been deliberately deepened throughout her years. Her effusive words came easily—in puffs, I thought, as in cartoons.

Before Ross, she leaned slightly back as if the spectacle of her nephew required distance to be grasped entirely. "Why, Ross, I swear ya get bigger an' bigger by the day. Come here and let me feel your muscles, boy." She didn't give him a chance to come to her. Before he could flex—he started to eagerly—she was consuming him with enormous hugs and kisses.

She turned to me. "Hiyah, there, handsome!—where'd y'all get him?"—the latter to Ross and Scott. "Glad to have ya with us, hon," she said to me, and hugged me tightly.

"Glad to be here, Miz Crawford."

Already, she was offering us lush red fruit. "You'd think I picked it myself," she chuckled. "Well, I did, from the outdoor market!" When she laughed, her body shook, continuing to shake after her laughter had abated. She would be the kind of woman who could not do enough for you, who would follow you out the door lavishing candy, cookies—whatever was available.

"Lemonade? Cookies? Maybe something a little . . . tastier?" she winked. "How about some frosty beers?" Then: "My, my, my, how *good* it is to have y'all here."

Despite her excessiveness, I liked her. I complimented her on her dress. "Ready to give it away," she said, but it was obviously new.

"You gonna be a fraternity boy, I hear," she said to me, patting Ross conspiratorially on the shoulder, spreading the conspiracy with a smile at Scott, and then smiling her widest at me.

"Yeah, we intend to rush him for our fraternity," Ross said proudly to her but addressing me.

Scott put his arm around my shoulders.

"Well, I think y'all will be making a damned good choice," Miz Crawford winked at me, their confederate in announcing the news.

I smiled, curiously relieved that the futile invitation had been finally spoken—"Oh, wow, thanks"—and then I was instantly anxious. Since they had told her before we arrived, they must have been sure that I would accept their invitation—did anyone turn them down? How much further—no, closer—could I let this proceed before I stopped it, or before it was stopped, now that I had allowed another impossible step?

"Hope you boys are hungry, 'cause I've had Esperanza whip us up a big scrumptious meal, yum; just for y'all. She's the best damn cook this side of the border."

Miz Crawford ushered us into the dining room: a large, grand room that extended the appearance of a Texas hacienda. It had solid wooden chairs, a long dining table, colorful sweeping draperies on the floor-length windows that opened, like the windows in the bedroom, onto the cactus garden, where the bright moon was creating a configuration of elaborate shadows on the ground.

The table was carefully set, all correct, all belying the woman's folksy presentation. Perhaps the abundant suggestions of elegance had belonged to her husband.

The maid—a slim Mexican woman of about forty—served us quietly.

"Mesquite soup," Miz Crawford announced.

The Mexican woman smiled in appreciation—"Yes, miz"—and lingered as if for our approbation.

I picked up my soup spoon, at the same time that Scott and Ross did.

"Whoa!" Miz Crawford halted us, in her same friendly voice. "Not yet, boys."

She was going to say a blessing, I was sure.

"Now you run on along and tend to your business till I call you, girl," Miz Crawford instructed the woman. She lowered her voice as the woman hurried out, "She's new, ya know, helps Esperanza when we have guests. Esperanza's daughter went and got herself pregnant—again!" she explained in her regular tone now, still merrily: "I can't eat—I have to confess it, it's the God's truth, Lord forgive me—I jest cain't eat when one of them is new to me and around me before I get to know them . . . Now you boys eat up the mesquite soup!"

"When who's around?" I lowered my spoon over the chilled soup. The subsequent cling! sounded harsh, like a bell.

"Why, Messican field workers, honey," Miz Crawford answered. "I can abide Esperanza—just love her like family, ya know, she's been with me for a coon's age. But this girl—forget her name—she's been here only a week. I think she was a picker before she came here." She sampled the soup and proclaimed it delicious with a smack of her lips. "I love their food, but I can't eat when they're in the room with me, and that's the Lord's truth," she seemed to want to emphasize for me. "Now y'all go ahead and eat up, eat up."

"Then I shouldn't be here." I said that quietly and wished I had said it much louder.

Ross and Scott looked at me, just looked.

"Ya think I'm an old bigot, don't you, handsome? Well, I'm not," Miz Crawford addressed me. "I treat my girls, all of 'em, real good, give 'em clothes, furniture. It's jest that ya gotta assert some standards of de-corum, and if—"

I stood up. "If you can't eat when Mexicans are in the room with you, ma'am, then I don't want to be here to ruin your dinner."

Ross and Scott had stopped eating. Miz Crawford seemed unflapped. In the same, unbudgingly friendly voice that she had been speaking in, she said, "What ya mean by that, handsome?"

"That my mother is Mexican, Miz Crawford." I didn't look at Ross or Scott—I didn't want to—I looked only at the woman.

Not even then did the smile relax, as if she could not comprehend anything that could possibly indict her, wrest her away from her cheerfulness. No, wait, the face allowed a slight frown, a tilt of the lips downward, briefly, and then it smiled and smiled and smiled.

"Well, now, that's OK by me. Ain't it, boys?" she asked without addressing them. "Just sit down and enjoy your meal, handsome. Let's forget all this nonsense. Eat up!"

Now I did look at Scott and Ross. I couldn't read their expressions, because they were staring down at their plates. In that room, I felt alone, isolated, separated, saddened.

I walked out of the room into the garden. The cactus, in sultry bloom, gleamed silvery under the incandescent moon. There seemed to be more stars than I had seen last night, probably because the ranch was away from even the small city's intrusive lights and the brief shower last night had wiped the sky clean.

I would forever remember that sky, yes, because of that night, and because of its beauty, yes, and its clarity. I would always remember, too, the pursuing image of the kept woman of Augusto de Leon that wafted into my mind:

She inhaled imperceptibly—no sound even of her breath, the barest rise and fall of her breasts, the only indication. A slender streak of smoke arose, lingered about her before it evaporated.

Why now that irrelevant memory that aroused in me a feeling— already fleeting—of peace?

My grandfather, a famous and prestigious doctor (to President Profirio Díaz of Mexico), Mexico City

My grandmother (from my father's side), Maria, with my father's child from his first marriage

My father, a child prodigy, with his piano in Mexico

My father (left) with one of his bands in El Paso

My privileged father in Mexico with his prized dogs

My sister Olga walking into her wedding reception with her husband, Luis, in El Paso

My father's theatrical group; this one a children's group. The "ghost boy" in the first row, center, in white is me; I'm almost invisible. Third to the right from me is my sister Olga (with longish hair). Second row, extreme left, is my sister Blanca looking like Hedy Lamarr.

My sister Olga as a bridesmaid, El Paso

Olga at her first communion (belated!), El Paso

Olga, a bridesmaid, again

Olga, football princess, El Paso

My sister Blanca
with her husband, Gus

My sister Olga with her husband,
Luis, wearing Luis's football-captain
sweaters just before or after they
were married.

A street-photographer photo of me and my sister Olga, El Paso. I believe I'd be maybe ten. She was right on the brink of losing her tomgirl aspects and becoming beautiful.

A favorite photograph: Olga in Los Angeles at the time she was mistaken for Ava Gardner, with her husband, Luis, and their second child, Rebecca.

The Rechy family about 1950: standing, from left, sister Olga, me, my brother Yvan, my brother Robert, my sister Blanca; seated mother Guadalupe and father Roberto

Another street-photographer photo: My mother, my brother Yvan, and me, now leaving my "gangly" period, El Paso

13

After a while, Scott came out looking for me. He put his arm around me. Then he coaxed me back in. I followed him, but not into the dining room. I went into the bedroom and lay in bed. Later, Scott and Ross came in silently, as if not to wake me—or not to talk about what had happened. Scott slept in the bed and Ross slept on the floor—I heard him whisper to Scott: "I'm too big to sleep on the bed with you-all." I slept only sporadically, eager for the night to end.

It finally did.

In the morning, we prepared to leave. Miz Crawford had fixed—or had her cook fix—box lunches of sandwiches and fruit and pie, everything she could think of. She hugged and kissed Scott and Ross. She approached me, smiling. She held out her arms to me. I resisted pulling back because the smile on her face seemed to me now—in retrospect—to be the only truly friendly one she had awarded me since dinner, friendly and, I thought, or wanted to think, a touch regretful.

"Now, handsome, I mean it, you come back and visit any time, and you'll be welcomed with open arms." She opened her arms, and I allowed her hug without returning it.

★　★　★

On the way home and over the music from the radio—I chose to sit in back—we talked in friendly tones. Nothing was mentioned about my walking out, or the reason for it. Ross kept the radio on, even when the music faded and there were only the clamoring voices of evangelicals that populated the deepest parts of Texas, jabbering on about sin and evil and Jee-zuss Christ. We laughed uproariously at their rantings.

We arrived in El Paso late at night, Scott now at the wheel while Ross dozed between us. They dropped me off at my sister Blanca's house.

As they drove away, I stared at the fraudulent house. I started to walk the long, long way to the projects. Soon I was running. The steamy night, as if it had followed me from the ranch, clung to my body, drops of perspiration clouding my eyes. When I had reached the house where I lived in the projects, I waited for minutes, welcoming the sweat as if it might wipe away the days past, the accusing regrets.

I found this out from Barbara, who tried to underplay its significance, kindly, "Oh, did you know—?" I accepted it unassailably the moment she had spoken it. The reason that I had been considered for the famous fraternity was that it had been put on probation by the college. A certain grade average was required for the fraternity to be allowed on campus. My high grades would have given the fraternity a passing nudge. The fact that I was good-looking had further paved the way for the unexplored invitation. It had not been known—because of my careful subterfuges—that I lived in the government projects and, the conclusion was easy, that I was Mexican.

★   ★   ★

Since that night in Balmorhea, I was haunted anew by the memory of the kept woman of Augusto de Leon. The reason why that memory had so powerfully asserted itself, after I had walked out on Miz Crawford and stood alone in the cactus garden at her ranch, baffled and eluded me. Before that, the memory had recurred, yes, goaded by the fact that Marisa Guzman was an enduring subject of speculation in the city. But I had not remembered her with the insistence of that recent night, and without an apparent impetus to spring the memory. When I deliberately evoked that night, the details of the recollection, the memory trailed off, once finding a new focus on Isabel Franklin, as if she existed in the penumbra of Marisa—in the shadows, as I had seen her under the steps at our high school. Then those associations were carried away again by the memory of the kept woman as she sat in the drab room smoking, her motions precise, elegant, a choreography of movements. I would rehearse those in my mind, as if within them lay an elusive connection. Then the spell of the memory was shattered, just as the spell of the kept woman had been by the intrusion of the harsh woman who had invaded the room and the cacophony of the wedding celebration's sounds.

The kept woman's superb poise—was that it?

I remained friends with Scott, but the matter of rushing me died down. Our friendship became hurried greetings, exchanges of information about classes, little else. I began to separate myself more and more from other students. I returned to my original intention, abandoned so disastrously, not to court popularity.

With a new staff—still five—I dedicated myself wholeheartedly to the first issue I would put out of *El Burro,* a name I would change after my first issue, to ease the transition. I solicited stories through the college newspaper. I chose the best two—there were not that many more good ones. One was by a girl delineating her surprise upon arriving in the desert from Boston, a wistful story. The other was by a young man I had seen on campus, usually alone. The story was about a friendship between an athlete and a "smart kid," who is caught giving answers to his friend during a test.

I could not totally at first abandon the cartoons and jokes the students had learned to expect. But I chose the ones I thought had not been overused. I chose them from schools I considered sophisticated. For the cover, I asked Barbara—using that as an excuse to call her after we hadn't met for a few days—to pose in the school auditorium, in her ballet leotards and shoes. I directed the shooting, made sure that the theater's curtain draped exactly, its folds highlighted. She and the photograph were beautiful, the photographer agreed, shifting his allegiance to me in small increments of approbation.

I wrote an essay for my first issue. It was titled: "Modern Art: A Shattered Mirror." It was pretentious, but I did not see that then. The article was illustrated by a young art student, a girl who had just arrived from the East. The illustrations were of various figures, men and women, in colorful distortions.

I went down daily to the printing office to make sure that the magazine was exactly as I and the new staff—I had managed to convert them, too, conditionally—had planned.

I would still have to wait for weeks before my first issue as editor of the magazine was printed and run and appeared on campus.

For a week, Barbara did not appear at the library, or at the classes I knew she was taking and that I would find a reason to pass by. Pretending not to be bothered, but becoming angrier and angrier at her unaccountable absence, I continued our translation, which was going nowhere.

There was another girl I met at the same time in college, a pretty girl who had recently transferred from somewhere in the East. We had a class together, a class in philosophy taught by a rabbi so boring that students would walk out unnoticed as he rambled on.

When the girl, who had exchanged smiles with me, walked out of the class one day, I followed her out, mainly because I hoped that Barbara, back from wherever she was, would see me with her and become jealous. As we walked out, a boy in the front row looked at me, and then at the girl; he made a spinning sign with a finger pointed at the side of his head. What? Obviously jealous, and that made me feel good.

The new girl looked like a gypsy to me. She even dressed somewhat like a gypsy, spangly earrings, flairy skirts, blouses that more than hinted of abundant young breasts; yes, like a reckless gypsy, but not, oh God, not like the grimy gypsy girl who had once terrified me by trying—I realized this only eventually—to kiss me that distant day when I had thought she was going to breathe a vaporous potion into my soul. This girl had long, abundant dark-reddish hair, which she emphasized by periodically pushing it away from her face with a dramatic twist.

That day, early afternoon, the wind was howling, tossing tumbleweeds against buildings and then exploding into myriad splinters. Fighting the wind, still looking around for Barbara, marking time for her to appear and see us, I introduced myself to the girl:

"John. I'm a writer."

"Anne. *I'm* going to be an opera star!" she shouted over the howling wind, which, however, abated as if to catch its breath, allowing her shouted words full force. Several students—Barbara was nowhere in sight—turned, startled, to look at her.

I asked her to have coffee with me at the student union building; I was working the night shift at the newspaper and had time. At around the same time, I usually met Barbara there before we went to the library to continue our translation.

"Why don't we go to my house for coffee, writer ?" she asked me, overly flirtatious. "I live nearby. We can talk more comfortably. Oh, don't you love the wind, so free!"

I hated the wind. "I don't have a car," I said, always embarrassed to admit it; I didn't have my brother's car that day. Too, I didn't really want to go anywhere else with her, I was comparing her with Barbara and finding her lacking; she was extravagantly ebullient, her head pushed back as if to devour the hateful wind.

"I have a car." She grasped me by my waist. "Come on, writer!"

With the wind tossing her hair about, she looked even prettier— and older than I had thought, about twenty. I felt somewhat trapped, now that the whole intent of this encounter had failed.

"Come on, get in, it's wind-eeee!" she trilled joyously.

She had led me insistently to what looked to me like a new car, hers—a surprise; I had expected something less of the reckless gypsy.

She opened the door for me. Either she or a gust of wind— probably both—shoved me in. "Let's go-oooo."

She turned the radio on, a classical station, and hummed along with the music. "Don't you love music? It's the language of the soul." She drove a distance away from the college, an elaborate trip for coffee, but now I was letting myself enjoy the "gypsy" girl's teasing company, feeling that I was spiting Barbara whether she saw me or not.

What the hell! We had entered Fort Bliss, the military base in El Paso.

"You live here?"

"Yes."

The daughter of an enlisted man, maybe a sergeant allowed to have his family with him in one of the Quonset huts converted into residences.

She drove on along the tree-lined street, the wind battering the car, dust scratching against the windows. We entered a section of large two-story houses with lawns and spacious Southern-style screened porches. In front of each house was a placard that designated the name of the main occupant, and his rank. Captain Evers . . . Captain Logan . . . another captain. I read the names as the sheets of dust abated.

As we moved farther along the street, which became wider, the houses were even more attractive; larger lawns separated one from the other, a greater distance apart; name placards were more prominent. Lieutenant Colonel Johnson . . . Colonel La Fountaine . . .

We parked in the driveway of the largest house.

General Welton, commanding general.

Anne sprang out and opened the door for me. "Here we are, writer!" she said gaily, offering her hair up for the wind to grasp.

I stopped before the placard on the lawn and looked at Anne.

"Who?" I shouted.

"My father," she shouted back, "but no one's home except the maid."

The free-living gypsy was a general's daughter? A commanding general's daughter!

Inside the large, well-furnished house, she led me into a spacious room. A record player, many albums in shelves or strewn about the floor; recordings of operas, open librettos; a couch.

The unexpected details of her life—and the powerful position of her father, who would be affronted by my background—gave me a peculiar pleasure to be here and with her.

"I am going to be renowned as the ultimate star who sang the greatest of all roles most memorably!" She planted her hands on her swaying hips and stood before me, as if before an adoring audience. "Carmen!"

I couldn't help myself; I laughed at the firmness of her grandiloquent intent and at her theatrical pose.

She slapped at my hand with splayed fingers, like an open fan. Apparently having forgotten her invitation to have coffee, she was humming strains from *Carmen* that I recognized from my father's productions. I quickly pulled away from that sad association as Anne swayed sensuously, like the gypsy woman in the opera, now singing phrases from Carmen's seduction song.

I had remained standing, watching her, taken aback by all this, trying to grasp where it was going.

She danced toward me, in practiced steps, one foot over the other slightly, then the other swinging over the first, advancing, dancing closer, now gyrating inches away from me.

Was this really happening? In her house? In the general's house! A commanding general's house, yes!—and she was his daughter, and all that was pleasing the hell out of me now. I did what she was inviting me to do with her extended arms and dancing fingers. I extended my own arms out and held her swaying body—still hesitantly, not knowing how low she might want my hands to grasp what.

Her movements slowed, tantalizing, before me. Did she really want me to do what I suddenly wanted to do—thought I wanted to do—wanted to do? Would she let me—if I tried—or tease me away? Challenged, I pressed against the quivering body of the commanding general's daughter and, in his own house, drew her to me.

She broke away from me, singing, "No, no, no, no-ooo!"—eyes seductively narrowed. Feeling suddenly silly, but more than silly, feeling a gathering of unwanted excitement—and suddenly aroused before I even realized I was, or wanted to be, I knew I had to act—she stood there wiggling and daring me, almost, almost pressed against my body. Do something, do what? Damn Miss Edwards—she had confused me, she had—damn Barbara!

I was able to add this in my mind: Not only was I with the daughter of the commanding general of Fort Bliss in his home, but if he knew that, and knew who I was—! I pulled away from her quivering body—still dancing?—trembling?—slightly, apprehensive at the last thought I had evoked to arouse me. It had aroused me but had also made me nervous. What if the general did walk in?

Before me, Anne tossed her head back with insouciant disdain—and mouthing something that sounded like, "Poor soul"—she shifted away from me, all of which annoyed me to the point that I surprised myself by grabbing her angrily—was she challenging me, sure she could control me, taking me for granted?—pulling her against my body, responding to a new urgency.

Her lips parted, her head tilted back, inviting. I felt her breath on my face as she gasped a few more strains, puffy phrases, from *Carmen*.

I leaned my head toward her lips, my heart throbbing, or was it my—?

She dodged my attempt. As if beating a fan against her thighs, she warbled, "No, no, no, no-oooo!" But she didn't move away.

I yanked her back—yes, awkwardly—or she flung herself at me; I wasn't entirely sure. But I was sure that I was pressing my body against hers, now wildly excited and wildly afraid. The general's daughter! She's the general's daughter!

My hands kept sliding away from whatever part of her I attempted to touch, or that she led me to—her movements making contact difficult, easy, difficult . . .

Determined not to let her take over—we seemed now to be fighting—I sat back on a couch and drew her firmly toward me, between my legs, not pausing now to disbelieve that this was happening.

"Yes, yes, yes!" she sang. "Yesssss."

I leaned back on the couch, coaxing her down in this unique battle. Still undulating to her own music, she lay on the couch and over me. I rolled over with her—she almost fell from the narrow couch—and now I was on top.

"Yes, yes, yessss!" Her fingers snapped behind her as if cracking castanets. We both pulled on her skirt—no panties! We both opened my fly. The general's daughter in his home, in Fort Bliss . . . breasts, whose?—Miss Edwards's, yes, no, legs in sheer stockings, whose?—sweaty male bodies in the showers, wet naked bodies, Miss Edwards, Henry Miller, hot bodies wrestling . . .

I barely touched her between her legs.

"Ouch!" she said.

I pulled my body back, but then quickly forward.

My bewildered cock, acting now on its own, independent of me, shoved against her exposed opening, a moisture—whose? Mine? Hers! She was humming—no, growling—the "Habañera" from *Carmen*! My father—no! The general's daughter! In his house! The general!

There was the sound of a door opening, distant but definitely within the house.

"Quick!" she said, "Quick!"

She spread her legs. I pushed between them, my cock—where was it? She closed her legs, tightly, very tightly, together—accepting my cock; no, pushing it out; coming, coming, coming!

She stood up, arranging her clothes. She whispered, "You didn't get in. I'm still a virgin and so are you! Now hurry, my father's here!"

I adjusted my clothes, trying to rub off the gummy moisture.

The general came in, all colorful ribbons, metals, and stars.

"Daddy, I want you to meet—"

She had forgotten my name.

"John," I said.

"John what?" the general demanded. "You have a last name, don't you?"

I needed to camouflage my name, quickly find another one, in case her father would vengefully track me down. His face was reddening. Quick! A name! "John Franklin, sir," I introduced myself, extending my hand. The general didn't take it; he merely glanced at his daughter, and then at me.

"I was just leaving," I said.

"Yes, you are," said the general, as his daughter began humming again.

"Good-bye," I said to her.

She waved an airy hand at me.

"Glad to meet you, sir."

The general didn't answer.

I stepped out, realizing I would have to walk blocks and blocks along Fort Bliss before I could reach the bus stop.

John Franklin?

What had really happened? Why did I feel so angry?

The next day, in philosophy class, I took my usual seat. The professor was not there yet.

In came Anne. In the aisle of the row where I sat, she paused. She smiled at me, a smile that turned sneery, a slash of bloody red. She took a step as if to occupy the seat next to me. Instead, she thrust her head back in emphatic disdain and, hips swaying, walked up the three ascending levels of the classroom, thrusting her hips about, to sit next to another student, another good-looking one. After class, I didn't wait to see whether she would leave with him.

As I walked out, the boy who had made an ambiguous sign when I had left with Anne that first day leaned over the aisle and said, "I told you, man." He repeated the sign, spinning his finger next to his ear. "She's crazy—I told you, man."

That same day, I saw Barbara talking to a man I didn't like, a hulking guy, older than the other students, probably thirty years old; I knew he was in the engineering department. He seemed quite arrogant, with a ruddy skin and a swagger to his walk. He might even have a tattoo on his upper arm; inky scrawls crept out under a short sleeve. Barbara was smiling at him.

I turned away from her, hoping she hadn't seen me. If *she* had been contriving to have me see her with that guy, just as I had done unsuccessfully with Anne, I didn't want to allow her the pleasure.

Why did it upset me doubly that the man she was talking to, so friendly, was older? Did she see me only as a smart kid—she was, after all, a year older than I—a smart kid who might have a crush on her? What did I really feel for her, this mysterious girl who, in the middle of laughter, might stop abruptly as if throttled, and who seemed to move away into a private terrible place of her own?

14

As the time approached for the appearance of my first issue of the college magazine, I became increasingly nervous, needing to leave the campus as soon as my classes were over, even going to work early at the city newspaper during the day shift. Then, at night, I would take refuge from the campus world in the public library.

A handsome white building with thick columns, it looked like a Southern plantation. I spent as many hours as I was able to there, impatient to finish one book so that I could start another. I read eclectically—Nietzsche, Marx—and I would place the impressive volumes, faceup, on a shelf visible to all the reporters of the newspaper I worked for. I would check several books out at the same time, shifting from one to the other, discovering Dostoyevsky, Flaubert, swept into their worlds, and, gratefully at times of most tension at home, away from mine.

On another floor of the library, I would regularly consult magazines and books about theatrical productions, all in preparation for the time when Barbara and I would put out into the world our thrilling translation of *Blood Wedding*.

Tonight, I had noticed a man enter and pause as if to see what I was reading, or as if to talk to me. He was tall, somewhat awkward, a slender man of about twenty-three; he wore bookish glasses, and looked, to me, like a young professor. I realized that

I had seen him before, here in the library. But where else—and just as recently?

He walked on to another table and sat facing me, looking up, smiling. I looked away, again enforcing my recurring desire for separation. When I was at the library desk returning the magazines and books I had been consulting, the man lingered by the desk and then disappeared into another part of the library.

Outside, as I walked along the tree-lined paths that led from the library to the street, heading home across the tracks to the projects, I heard footsteps quickening to catch up with me. I turned to see the man from the library. I hastily shifted my direction, to avoid signaling that I was going across the tracks to the projects, an unyielding source of battered pride. I stopped in a small plaza across from the courthouse, where a bus that traveled up the hill to the rich houses of Kern Place stopped. I pretended to be waiting for that bus.

"Are you a frustrated actor or a frustrated writer?"

I quickly recovered from the question. "Neither. I'm too young to be frustrated; I'm only eighteen."

"Some young people I know are the most frustrated," he said smiling, a smile that was entirely warm. "And the most talented." He added the last in a wry tone, as if bemused by the fact, and without any malice. "I thought you might be one or the other because I've noticed the books and magazines you've been reading."

I relaxed. "I've been reading up on theater because I'm translating Lorca's *Blood Wedding*."

"Wow! That's pretty ambitious." He shook his head, as if greatly impressed.

"Do you know the play?" From his presence in the library, I had inferred that he was at least educated, if not as familiar with Lorca as Barbara and I were.

"I think, yes, I've read it. Are you enrolled at the local college?" he asked. His questions didn't seem so much probing as friendly.

"Yes."

"I'm in the army, at Fort Bliss. But I come into the city; I rent an apartment, to get away from the army. I was drafted," he explained quickly as if otherwise I might infer that he was a career soldier. "You must know Spanish very well to translate Lorca."

"I do, yes," was all I said. "I'm doing the translation with my friend. She's going to play the lead when we stage it," I improvised. "As a dance-drama." My words, spoken aloud for the first time to someone other than Barbara, made the endeavor even more impressive to me now. "She's very talented; she dances and acts and—"

"—translates Lorca," he finished. "Is she your sweetheart, or just your collaborator?"

"Both," I said; was she? Our relationship remained waiting for definition.

"Are you going to play . . . ?"

The lover. "Maybe. We've talked about it. But I'm not really an actor, or a dancer."

"Oh, what are you?" he asked, the warm smile lingering.

"I'm a writer," I said, "like William Faulkner—"

"Oh."

"—and in addition to translating Lorca, I'm writing about a woman I saw, once, very briefly. She was the kept woman of—" What the hell was I saying? That wasn't true, but the image of the mysterious beautiful woman, smiling, had again swept into my mind unexpectedly.

A bus was pulling up. Its designation indicated the rich neighborhood up the hill. I was stuck having to board it.

Seeing me prepare to board the bus—and I would have to take the same bus back and then run home across the tracks to the projects—he asked quickly, "What is your name?"

"John Rechy."

"I'll see you tomorrow, in the library?" There was a note of wistfulness in his voice, a questioning of the possibility.

I didn't want to commit myself to seeing him tomorrow. Instead, as the bus opened its doors to let me in, and wanting to be polite, I asked quickly, "What is your name?"

"Wilford Leach," he said.

Wilford Leach, Wilford Leach . . .

Wilford Leach!

In the bus, I recognized his name—and him. I had seen a photograph of him, perhaps several, in an issue, or more, of *Theater Arts* magazine that I had been consulting in the library. He had directed a famous production of Brecht's *Mother Courage*. One of the pictures I had seen was of him receiving an award—I couldn't remember which, and didn't want to remember. Everything I had said to him, about translating Lorca, about staging it, about being a writer like William Faulkner, made not only my face but my whole body turn hot with mortification.

Wilford Leach, not then as famous as he would become later as one of Broadway's most admired and prizewinning directors, became one of my closest friends, one of my very few friends.

I continued to meet him in the library on the nights when I was not working at the newspaper or at the print shop for my debut issue of *El Burro*. Each time, he was clearly pleased to see me. "I'm glad you came, Johnny."

I liked him, especially because he made no reference to our first awkward encounter. He was witty; he was smart. I longed for that. He was also, at times, when he became excited about artistic subjects, overly emphatic, dramatic, with a repertoire of breezy gestures—theatrical influences, nothing more.

When the library closed, we would sit on one of the benches that lined the trellised walks outside. When it was time to separate—he going back to the base at Fort Bliss—we walked to the bus stop where I had met him. I was still stuck with the false direction away from the projects. Nightly, I took the bus to Kern Place, and then got off as soon as I thought he would have caught his own bus back to Fort Bliss. I would then head for the projects.

Although I had made up a story about how I was writing about the kept woman—with no intention of doing so—I had already begun a novel, almost finished, called *Pablo!* It was set in modern Mexico. Perusing books on theater production, I had come on one, misplaced on the shelf, about Mayan legends. Fascinated, I began writing the novel during idle time at the city newspaper. I had never been to Mexico, but I imagined it, the Yucatán, the Mayan Indians.

I was especially entranced by a Mayan story about the sun and the moon, before the creation of the world. The moon had fallen in love with the sun as they waited for their place in the constellation. Blinded by its own brightness, the sun did not see the moon. When the world was created, the moon, in anticipation, decked herself in bridal veils, gauzy clouds. The sun remained removed. Like a specter in the sky, the moon was allowed only longing moments to see the sun. Only during the short times of extended dawn did she glimpse the indifferent dazzling sun.

I was using the mythical frame to tell the story about a Mayan woman, her husband, their beautiful daughter, and a narcissistic boy. Fleeing from the plantation of a much older man who has attempted to take over his life, keeping him in isolation, and keeping him from becoming the great dancer he longs to be, the boy wanders into the jungle, lost. A beautiful Mayan girl falls in love with him, but he does not reciprocate an impossible love. In the background there are witches demanding violence, forlorn animals possessed of human souls, the infamous Llorona of lore screaming into the night—all Mexican legends. I was reading Paul Bowles at the time.

I told Wilford about my novel, avoiding the tone I had adopted in telling him about Barbara's and my translation of *Blood Wedding*.

"May I read it?"

I was flattered, especially now that I knew who he was. "Yes," I said. "I'll bring it next time I see you."

That night Wilford invited me to his apartment, a long large room facing the library through a tall window. He had decorated the room sparsely, with two couches—one of which he used as his bed—many books and records, a canvas chair, and a table littered with papers, stage designs, and letters he was writing.

I was sitting on the canvas chair, he on one of the couches. He had just finished playing a recording of Bartók's *Music for Strings, Percussion, and Celesta,* the first of many times when he would introduce me to "modern" music that my father would probably have disdained.

"Do you live with your family?"

The pointed question surprised me. At my age it would be likely that I would live with my family while going to the local college. I had spoken about my love for my mother, suggesting the prominence she had in my life, and had said hardly anything about my angry father except that he had once been prominent in music. Why, then, that question now. "Yes. Why?"

"You're a fascinating boy—"

I bristled.

"Young man," he corrected. "I wonder about everything that concerns you, like your family."

Was he indicating that he wanted to meet my family?—suggesting it subtly, cautiously. That was not possible. I would have to expose my charade of living not up the hill but in the projects. But there was more than that. I was considering the impression he would make, not on my mother, no, but on my father, even my brothers if they happened to come by—and not my sisters Olga and Blanca, but, yes, on the neighbors, the tough types who hovered about the blocks. What would they think, seeing this tall, lanky man who walked with a swinging gait, whose hands often windmilled? I pretended to be concentrating on the haunted music.

Silence.

"I'd like to meet your sweetheart," Wilford said.

In substitution? He meant Barbara, the only girl I had mentioned to him. Had he sensed my unease at the hinted invitation to my home?

"I'd like you to meet her." I was glad to be able to answer without intrusive considerations. Barbara would respond to him. They would charm each other.

One reason for asking to meet her was this, which he told me only later. He was conferring with the head of the liberal arts departments at the college about directing a series of plays there. His already substantial reputation in theater would guarantee the releasing of funds now available, as the college grew, for visiting artists. He had been highly encouraged by the head of the English department, Dr. Sonnichsen, who was formidable at the college.

"You'd be perfect as the bewitched boy," he added.

"What?"

"The Witch Boy John in *Dark of the Moon*. I directed a production of it in Urbana at the University of Illinois. Maybe your sweetheart would be right to play Barbara Allen."

I knew about the play; I had seen an article about a production of it featured in *Theater Arts* magazine. I looked it up later to see whether it was Wilford's. The title and the brief description of the story had intrigued me. A small photograph accompanying the article had shown a lean young man, barefoot, without a shirt, crouching and facing a young woman in a girlish dress. The setting was of shadowy trees, limbs as if struggling to capture the boy and the girl, grayish clouds smearing a dark sky. What surprised me now with Wilford was that I had then imagined myself in the role, a witch boy attempting to discover whether, finally, he will remain a witch or become human. An exorcism may free him to be with the girl he loves, Barbara Allen, or it will destroy him.

"I'm not an actor," I said. I did not tell him about my role as the boy Jesus; I didn't want to fall into the trap I had plunged into when I had first tried to impress him.

"Oh, I think you are," he smiled. "I think you are a very good actor."

"Guadalupe, Guadalupe, we've come back! We know neither you nor Johnny meant what you said that terrible day."

They had come back, the monstrous aunts.

I doubt that they would have had the nerve to enter our house if I had been there, especially considering the reason they had barged in again. But I wasn't there; my mother gave me an account of their odious visit, and I pictured it in detail.

"Lupe, it's better you hear this from us rather than as ugly rumors from others."

"So we're here to tell you—"

My mother thought they were going to provide new gossip about Marisa Guzman, whom, when they could dredge up something mean, they continued to associate intimately with our family because of my sister's marriage to her brother.

"—about your son," the second aunt finished for the first.

"About Johnny," the other emphasized.

My mother was tempted to ask them to leave, but if they had information that concerned me, she would certainly want to know what it was.

The uglier of the two aunts lowered her head, to indicate the weight of the information she was about to convey, and the difficulty in doing so. "My son, Beto"—that was her fat son, as ugly as she—"has seen Johnny—"

"—several times—" the other aunt said.

"—with a strange man—"

"—sitting in a park outside the library, late at night!"

"The man is—"

"—effeminate!" cried the other aunt.

My mother stood up. "If you didn't understand me before, that earlier day, understand me now. Leave, and don't ever come back or I'll shut the door in your faces."

My mother left the story there. I imagined the reaction of the aunts, the nasty creatures waddling out weeping, lamenting that they had intended only to help—only that! Was there no gratitude left in the world?

When she had finished her account of the poisonous visit, I looked at my mother, without saying a word. She looked at me, smiled, waited. She had told the story in an amused tone, as if dismissing it all, making the aunts seem as ridiculous as they were. So I did not feel that I had to defend Wilford against the insinuations of the goddamned aunts.

When I did not react to the story at all, did I see the slightest frown on my mother's forehead? Did I imagine it?

Always attempting to add a few dollars to what I contributed at home, I worked a few hours a week—the work also earning me units as a course in journalism—in the shop of one of the famous book designers in the country, Carl Hertzog, who ran the college printing press. He printed routine pamphlets and publications for the college. In exchange, he was allowed an office, the use of the press, and funds to publish beautiful limited editions for individuals and companies. My job was to read all the material for typographical errors, correcting spelling and punctuation.

He asked me to read a slim, elegantly rendered volume he had been commissioned to do for a large, lavish new store in Dallas. One section contained advice to heads of departments, including this: "If a white person rushes in barefoot and dirty, don't kick them out until you find out if they just struck oil."

Mr. Hertzog's pending project was a personal "history book" for a billionaire ranch owner. Among the many corrections I made, including dozens of misspellings, was changing his various references to "negroes" to "Negroes." The corrected galleys were returned to him for approval.

Mr. Hertzog was out of the office, and I answered the telephone.

"Who the hey-ell is this?" a harsh voice drawled.

I informed the caller that Mr. Hertzog was out.

"I said, who the hell are ya?" the voice commanded.

"John Rechy," I said, ready to hang up if the harsh voice continued.

"You the wise guy changed my spelling of—?"

I wasn't sure whether he had pronounced "Negroes" in a deep Southern-Texas accent or whether he had said "niggers."

I answered, "Yes, I capitalized the word."

"Boy," said the voice, "You know who this is? If ya don't ya better find out. Now I don't want no one givin'"—again the slurred word—"nigguhs any capital letter in my book, ya heah me, boy?"

I said I did.

"Good. Now ya leave my spellin' the way I wrote it, heah?" Click.

"He's wrong," I told Mr. Hertzog.

"Keep it the way he wants," Mr. Hertzog said.

"It's incorrect."

A look of impatience. "He owns half of Texas."

I saw Barbara only infrequently now; I had seen her a few times—and ignored her—while she sat at the student union building with the shaggy "older" man I had seen her with earlier.

I spent with Wilford whatever spare time I had from my jobs. I had brought him a carbon copy of *Pablo!*—just finished. He had told me he was eager to read it—"straight through without interruption," he pleased me by saying.

My visits always included listening to music I was unfamiliar with, Stravinsky, Prokofiev—and Harry Partch, a bizarre composer he championed, who played eerie gongy sounds with large crystal jars, a composer my father, having found his voice in the sad romantics, would have derided with angry passion.

Wilford had written to Partch about me, a fact I discovered when he told me that the esoteric composer had said he would welcome hearing from me, about myself. Complimented, and wanting to please Wilford, I did write to him, telling him what courses I was taking at school, where I worked. I sent the letter with Wilford's return address.

When I saw Wilford next in his apartment—unexpectedly, since I had thought I was working that day but was off—he was reading a letter that had just arrived. Glancing at the envelope on the table, I saw that it was from Partch. Wilford put the letter back in the envelope.

"Did he say he received my letter?" I asked him.

"Uh, yes." Wilford was seldom hesitant.

"Something you prefer not to tell me. Why didn't he answer me?"

Wilford was too honest to disguise further. "He just said he'd prefer not to write."

"Why the hell not?" I was determined to have him tell me or to show me the letter.

He pulled it out of the envelope and handed it to me, pointing to a paragraph:

"Please tell that guy that I don't want to hear from him again. I have no interest in anyone who gives so little of himself and seems to know even less about himself."

Wilford touched my hand lightly. "He's just being Harry Partch. That's all."

"To hell with the goddamned asshole," I said.

As if in compensation—he not yet reacted to *Pablo!,* a fact that annoyed me—he told me that the college seemed very willing to have him direct there. "Would you like that, Witch Boy?"

When I saw my sister Olga next—"You must be very busy, little brother, I haven't seen you in ages"—I was tempted to tell her about the prospect of the play at the college, about my friend Wilford, and about what the vile aunts had told my mother. But, just as I had withheld telling her about the debacle in Balmorhea, at the last moment I decided to retain the information, assuring myself that if I did decide at any time to tell her about those matters, she would "understand," being my steadfast ally. Even if I had decided otherwise, she would not have given me a chance to do so today. She announced excitedly:

"Alicia Gonzales is in New Orleans! She's claiming she was born in Spain."

"Olga, you're making that up. How the hell could you know that? What movie are you borrowing from?"

"I know it from Tina, that's how. Alicia's father hired a de-tective to locate her," she poured out more words eagerly. "She works in a fancy place that serves only tea. She claims she was born in Madrid, that her parents were connected to a long line of ar-ees-to-crats." The last word, spoken with sly contempt, wasn't a word my sister had ever used before, although like me she had been born among people who sometimes loftily claimed such an asso-ciation, which had never impressed her. "She's changed her name legally. So now she's really Isabel Franklin."

I tried to place Isabel Franklin where my sister had identified her. Why in New Orleans? The girl I remembered, and the girl who was emerging in my sister's account, would have a distinct purpose. If what my sister was telling me was true, not only had Isabel erased parts of her identity, but she was trying to re-create her background. To invent what new identity?

"Maybe they'll send her to the plague island," I heard my sis-ter say.

"What!"

"Wasn't it New Orleans from where they sent Bette Davis in *Jezebel* to the plague colony? Maybe that's where they'll send that creature, too, and it would suit her right."

When I arrived that evening at Wilford's apartment, he took a let-ter he had been writing and he placed it on a table before the couch where I usually sat; he cleared everything else away. Then he ex-cused himself. No question that he wanted me to read the letter. More about Partch? His defense of me to the weird musician? Still, I wasn't sure I wanted to read it, although I couldn't locate a rea-son for apprehension, for a sense of something disturbing being imminent. I glanced down. I saw my name. OK, good, he was putting that Partch guy in his place. I read: ". . . is John Rechy . . . magical combination . . ." Without hesitation, I read now: "His name is John Rechy. He is a magical combination of masculinity— and aching sensitivity. He is talented in a way that . . ."

I stopped reading, not knowing what I would do when Wilford returned to the room. It was obvious that he had intended to make his description of me flattering. But I wasn't all certain that I was flattered. What had he meant by "aching sensitivity"?

When he returned, he stood looking at me. I looked away, not wanting to convey that I had read any part of his letter, although he would know I had from its altered position on the table.

"I just dropped in to tell you I can't stay today; I have a test tomorrow."

"He wants to meet you," I told Barbara, using the occasion to break my determination to avoid her. She had been on her way to the student union building. "Why have you kept away from me?" she asked me, and she looked prettier than ever. I shrugged. "Just busy."

We agreed to meet and go to Wilford's apartment. Just as I had expected, and hoped for, they immediately took to each other. She and I sat on one couch; he sat on a canvas chair. He told her about the probability of a production at the college.

"You'd make a wonderful Barbara Allen to John's Witch Boy," he told her. That seemed to please her. He had obtained copies of the play. He wanted to rehearse us in a scene, the scene where the Witch Boy first sees Barbara Allen and falls in love.

Facing her, as she assumed the character of the sensual young woman—standing seductively, hands on her hips—I was dumbfounded as to what to do, suddenly too embarrassed to perform before Wilford with Barbara. I opened my mouth to speak the first line; instead, I gasped. The moment was so awful that Barbara broke up laughing.

"If you hadn't been wiggling so funny," I accused her, restraining myself from a substitute defense of informing her that I had starred in a famous Spanish drama; what had she ever starred in?

"I'm sorry," she apologized very seriously.

"Don't worry," Wilford told me later when we were alone. "I'll rehearse you, and you'll become the enchanted boy—and you'll look terrific, barefoot, torn pants, no shirt." He had a way of arching his eyebrows and smiling that signaled that he was appealing to my vanity. "Everybody will love you," he said, "just like they love the dancer in your novel *Pablo!*"

"You read it," I said excitedly.

"You're very talented, Johnny; it's exceptional. I'd like to send it to my agent in New York."

"Thank you." I kept myself from becoming effusive.

Wilford had easily become the first friend I thought I could trust, someone I laughed with, even when he gently satirized my vanity. I told him stories about my family—about my wonderful Tía Ana, who practiced white magic; about my mother's stalwart nobility in keeping the family going through the worst times, her never wanting to speak English, her defense of the nun over the priest—and even about my father, deliberately sympathetic stories about his roaming around the courthouse to be appointed for jury duty, to enjoy the air-conditioning on hot days.

Out of those stories—about Tía Ana, my dauntless mother, and my father—Wilford, years later, would write and direct a play in New York, a unique musical comedy, touched with wistfulness, called *Trapdoors of the Moon*.

But no production of *Dark of the Moon* occurred in El Paso. Unexpectedly, Wilford received transfer orders. He would be leaving Fort Bliss, to be stationed in Virginia.

In the intervening days before he would transfer, I knew how enormous my loss would be, how very much I would miss him, how much he meant to me.

In my brother's car, I picked him up at his apartment the night before he was to leave. We drove around town, talking; he had sent my novel to his agent and would let me know the agent's reaction as soon as he received it. As I drove through Memorial Park, he suggested we park and talk.

He said, "I'll miss you a lot, Johnny. Eventually, I'm sure you'll leave El Paso. I'll be out of the army soon, and eventually in New York. I hope that you'll come."

"Oh, sure," I said. At the time, I did not try to imagine my future; most often I seemed to be anchored in El Paso.

Wilford touched my shoulder. His hand remained there.

I forced myself not to pull away from the unexpected gesture. I sat tensely, feeling the weight of his hand increasing, the weight of his touch, knowing that the gesture was about to become an embrace.

"John, I want to say that I—"

I pulled away, stopping words I inferred, words I had naively dismissed from any place in our friendship. Now, even though not spoken, they had resonated in my mind as if, all along, they had been shouted but left unheard.

"I'll miss you a lot, too, Wilford," was all I could say. I started the car. I drove back to the bus stop where I had met him—he wanted to be dropped off there—and where he would leave for Fort Bliss, his last time in El Paso.

He wrote to me almost every day, letters full of memories of our brief encounters. Without his friendship, El Paso had become for me more of a desert than ever before.

Another letter arrived. He had received a quick answer about *Pablo!* from his agent. He quoted the agent: "Of course, this novel has in it everything but the kitchen sink. That said, it is clearly the work of a very talented writer. I predict his talent may outshine a top half dozen of our highly praised writers. To submit this manuscript now would do him a disfavor. He is still very young, his talent growing."

I was exhilarated by the praise, but dejected just as quickly by the implicit decision—and then I was confused: Why hadn't Wilford sent me a copy of the agent's letter? Why had he only quoted from it? Had he invented those remarks, trying to smooth something harsh from the agent?

One day Barbara and I ran into each other at the library. She appeared as if dazed. Although the day was hot, she wore a long-sleeved sweater over her blouse. She could hardly speak. When I asked her what was wrong, she ran out. I followed her outside. Under a sweaty Texas sun, she removed the sweater as if momentarily to cool off. She replaced it quickly when she saw me approaching. In those brief moments I had seen that both her wrists were bandaged.

"Barbara!"

"Johnny, please—"

There had been such an urgent plea—she had turned away quickly—to be left alone that I did not follow her.

I didn't see her around for days. Baxter Polk, the librarian, took me into his office and told me that she had tried to kill herself. "That mother of hers," was all he could offer. I remembered the gaunt woman who had refused to call Barbara the day I had gone to pick her up with Ross and Scott; remembered how when she returned, the woman had stood at the door like a guard. I remembered Barbara's moody withdrawals, her choked laughter.

"Where is she now, Baxter?"

Baxter paused as if to prepare what he was about to say. "She's married, Johnny, and she's left El Paso."

"What!"

"She married—"

He mentioned the man I had seen her with on campus.

Isabel Franklin had fled El Paso; Barbara was gone; Wilford was gone. I was still here.

The first issue of the college magazine with me as editor appeared. It created a furor I had not anticipated. Telephone calls were made and letters carried by a group of students to the head of the journalism department, protesting: What the hell was happening to *El Burro*? Why so few jokes, hardly any cartoons? Who the hell was interested in photographs of a girl in ballet poses? And the weirdo stories? And those ugly drawings—what were they? And worst of all, that whatever-it-was on "modern art"? What the hell was that all about?

I was summoned before the publications board and fired.

"What were you thinking?" Scott asked me, ushering me gently out of the student union building, where students with copies of my issue of *The Donkey* were glaring at the magazine, and then at me. "Look, John, guys are talking about you . . . being . . ."

"What, Scott?"

"Strange."

I thanked him and didn't ask him what exactly they were saying. I didn't have to.

As I was walking alone out of the building, a tall, hulking guy intercepted me. "What the fuck is this, man?" He thrust the magazine at me, opened to the story about the smart kid and the athlete cheating on a test. "What's with these two guys? Are they fuckin' queers?"

"No," I said, "they're not."

As I moved away, the rage I had withheld ricocheted on me, intensified incongruously by an image which I did not expect but which I now accepted.

. . . her free hand rose and rested lightly on the elbow of the arm whose fingers held the cigarette, completing an intricately graceful choreography of movements that extended as she withdrew the cigarette from her lips but kept it close, as if deciding whether to inhale from it again, extending a moment of suspense.

15

One more issue was pending before I would officially leave as editor. I rushed it into production. I wrote a prose poem titled "Babbitt Went to College." It was a broad parody of school activities that attempted to echo Eliot's *The Waste Land*. I illustrated it with recognizable cartoons of the students who had most loudly protested my version of *The Donkey*. Most prominent was the hulk who had accosted me. I drew other deliberately obscure cartoons. One was a box full of dots. The caption: "I'm one of the crowd." Another was a cartoon version of the *Mona Lisa*. The caption: "I prefer the Mona Lisa."

My swan song for *The Donkey*.

After that, *El Burro* returned to being what it had been before, with this exception: The next issue carried two pages of letters excoriating my ventures. The letters included one from the young man who had written the story about the close friendship between the athlete and the smart kid. He wanted to separate himself, he wrote, from having anything to do with those "sick issues of *El Burro*."

Often now, in the middle of the hot summer, I hiked out of the city, walking all the way from the projects, miles, into the desert, to the edge of the Franklin Mountains, up to Mount Cristo Rey. At the top, there was a crude stone statue of Christ, fifty feet tall, looming over the city. On holy days, gaudy processions, mostly Mexican men and women, some children, marched up to it, led by a trio of priests, praying, along the circuitous path that had been cleared for religious rituals up the mountain. Led by the priests, the congregants knelt before each of the crude representations of stations of the cross embedded in tall stones along the path to the very top.

On the days when I was sure no one else would be around, I climbed up by myself. I did not take the circuitous prepared path. I climbed up the steep slopes. I grasped the edges of rocks, dug my feet into crevices to keep loose rocks from crashing down. The resultant fissure often pulverized after I stepped higher. I'd reach the top, exhausted, drenched in sweat.

No religious inclination goaded me there. I had shed every vestige of my childhood Catholicism. What coaxed me to climb was the spectacle of the crude giant statue—arms outspread—overlooking the desert, El Paso, and Juárez, taken up stone by stone laboriously, the nearly impossible but triumphant labor of a Mr. Soler, who had envisioned it.

On a fiercely hot afternoon, after having rested briefly at the top of the mountain, I was climbing back down, shirtless, sweating, sunburned, thirsty—I never thought to bring water—I heard the distant clopping of horses' hooves. I quickened my step, moving across the tracks that cut across the desert at the base of the mountain, where, a short distance away, a small village called Anapra huddled, all flimsy clay-patched hovels where only Mexicans lived.

From that far vantage, I saw two men on mounted horses— the border patrol—racing toward the river, which was full today, a rare occasion, a foot or more deep with dirty water. Moving

ahead, I saw a group of people—a family?—in the river, attempting to cross the border. I could now make out a man, a woman,
three children, plodding across the water, their pace slowed by
the sluggish mud at the bottom. As the mounted men approached,
the man and the woman tried to scatter, clutching their children's
hands. They all fell, splashing in mud, the man and woman pushing the children up. The patrolmen halted, as if to prolong their
observation of the spectacle of the family, falling, rising, falling,
thrashing in the mud. I heard the screams of children mired in
the sandy river.

The hooves of their horses digging into the sand, halting,
the patrolmen corralled the group, pulling them out with heaved
ropes, bunching them together. Roped, the family members
were marched, the horses seeming to prod them on, to a station
wagon that had been waiting on the nearest road. Pushed into
the wagon, all five disappeared as the vehicle sped away, arousing angry dust.

Now at the river's edge, holding my shoes and shirt above
the water, I moved along carefully, the water deep enough to pull
me down. When I reached the farther edge of the river, I looked
up to see the same two border patrolmen waiting for me.

"Whoa, there, *amigo!*" one of them shouted at me.

"What's the matter?" I said.

"He speaks English good!" said one. "Where'd ya learn—?"

When he saw me close up—the horses snorting in protest
against the abrupt order—one of the patrolmen, a heavy middle-
aged man with a florid face, laughed. "Thought you was a wet-
back, sonny."

"I'm American," I said.

The other one joined him. "Shouldn't go around wadin' 'cross
the river without a shirt, buddy, all sunburned and everything."

"What were ya doin'? Fishin' in the pond?" Now they were
all humor and nasty camaraderie.

"I climbed up Mount Cristo Rey," I said.

"Well, you better say your prayers tonight that we recognized you as white, cause we coulda shot you if you'da run," one tossed back as they both moved away on their horses.

I felt indignant and ashamed.

The Korean War, which had come into my awareness as bloody events in newspaper headlines and droning voices on the radio and television about devastating bombings and mounting casualties, became close when I graduated—with a BA degree in English literature—from what was now called Texas Western College. I faced the certain prospect of being drafted. I might have asked for a deferment to acquire a further degree, but I opted not to.

To get the intensifying menace of conscription over with, I volunteered to be drafted. That would allow me to be in the army only two years, as opposed to the three if I volunteered in the regular manner. By then, my father seemed to have exhausted his rage—his curses were only muttered to himself. I would be leaving without betraying my mother.

I told no one other than her, my brother and my sisters that I was going into the army. Only one day before I left to be sworn in, I visited my sister Olga: "I'll miss you so much, little brother," she sighed. Overwhelmed by a possible wave of sad emotion, I asked her quickly for the latest news—and the last I would hear before leaving—about Isabel Franklin. The prospect of new gossip—information—livened her, a I had intended.

"She's left New Orleans, that's all I know. Whatever she was doing there, she did it. Let's see where she turns up next—and under what new name. What is she up to?"

It was particularly poignant for me to get this not entirely enticing news from my sister now that I was leaving. Olga's adamant belief that whatever she chose to believe was unassailable had further endeared me to her. I had long accepted, and now smiled at the fact, that she rejected any duty to cite any source other than the original conveyer of information—but only if she liked the source, usually her sister-in-law Tina.

"Good-bye, beautiful sister," I said.

"Shush! We don't say good-bye, remember? We say so long."

"So long, beautiful sister."

"So long, little brother."

Leaving my mother—especially leaving her still in the projects—was one of the most mournful moments of my life.

"*Que Dios te bendiga, m'ijo,*" she blessed me through her tears, matching mine.

Behind her, my father stood mutely, an ambiguous silhouette about to disappear. He extended his hand to me with something in it, which I took. A ring, a ring he had cherished, a ruby, he had said once, that was owned as a tie pin by his grandfather, converted into its present form by his father, given to him, and, now, to me.

Would that sad moment eventually be able to wipe away all the horrors he had inflicted on us, horrors that, only later, I would allow myself even to recall?

I was processed at Fort Sam Houston in San Antonio, from where I would be assigned to a regular unit elsewhere for basic training. Because of its proximity to Louisiana, many Negro—that was the word then—inductees and "Creoles" were being herded there daily with the rest of us.

The tension between Negroes and "Americans" simmered, threatening to erupt. Fists would clench ready to strike at a perceived insult; accusations piled on accusations, threats on threats, for any tiny slight. The heat, the sense of dislocation, of being pushed crowded into flimsy wooden barracks in a distant place not our own, dirt ground into prickly dust by thousands of marching feet, dust mixing with the stench of sweat—all of that stirred tension in the crowded barracks.

"Motherfucker, whatcha lookin' at?"

It was the first time I had heard that startling word, aimed by one recruit at another. I thought I had misheard it, but there it was again:

"What d'ya mean, motherfucker?"

The second time, hearing it exactly, I was shocked even more.

"Motherfucker, if I ever catch—"

From Fort Sam Houston, I was sent to Camp Breckenridge, Kentucky, for basic training, assigned to the 101st Airborne Infantry Division, to a compound of red dust, more heat, and pale-yellow barracks. We wouldn't jump from parachutes; we were only nominal members of that division, allowed to wear the famous insignia of the screaming eagle.

I was now able to send my mother more money. I arranged an allotment for her, and to augment that amount added my father as a dependent. A portion of my army pay would be deducted; a similar portion would be added by the army. That would nudge us farther out of the damned poverty, with my brother Robert continuing to contribute to our income although he was now in his second marriage.

At Camp Breckenridge, we were roused before dawn by a hillbilly sergeant shouting into the barracks:

"Drop your cocks, and grab your socks!"

That caused him, each time, to roar with laughter, a sound more grating than his shouted words.

We stood outside for endless roll calls, an endless chain of names that we must answer with "Here, sir!" Then we would be ordered to run—"Faster, faster!"—until the sweat had soaked through our uniforms and dripped to the ground.

I hated the subservience demanded of us, ordered by squads of sneering "regular army" sergeants who delighted in taunting and torturing servicemen in their ranks.

When the sixteen weeks of infantry basic training were completed, every member of our company, about one hundred of us—and hundreds more of the several other companies throughout the camp—would be getting orders. Those orders might send us to Korea, where the war was bloodier each day; or, if we were lucky, to Germany, which was still scarred by the occupation. We woke to the awareness of the probability that before long we would be facing death in a deadly foreign conflict.

Basic training ground on, week after week, then months.

As intense as the heat, the cold of winter chilled the ground into ice. Every morning before dawn, we would rise for roll call, then run around the camp, our heated bodies warring with the cold. On the icy ground, we practiced bayonet training, ordered to shout, "Kill, kill!" as we lunged against a sand-filled dummy, the pretended enemy. The exacerbated shouts—"*Kill, kill, kill, kill!*"—resounded as a contagious frenzy contaminating the ranks. I resisted joining the angry cries, jabbing at the imaginary enemy only enough so that I would not be detected by one of the sergeants in charge and ordered to perform the ritual over and over.

When one of the soldiers in our training group went absent without leave, causing the whole company to be denied a contingent two-day pass, a mangy sergeant addressed the barracks: "If he comes back an' y'all wanna 'thank him' for ruining your pass, you can be sure no one's gonna question you about it."

The man returned. That night, I was awakened by cries and stomping. Several of the men had ganged up on him, and thrown him down the steps of the second level of the barracks, kicking him as he fell bloody and unconscious. True to the sergeant's word, no action was taken against them.

On the firing fields, where we had to qualify as, at least, "marksmen," the lowest allowed rung, I deliberately did not aim at the center of the target; I aimed only at its periphery, shot after shot, increasingly resisting the indoctrination to killing. Lying on the dirt on the firing range with my rifle blasting, I felt kicks at my boots. A lieutenant loomed over me. I could not hear, deafened by the shots from my own rifle and others firing nearby. I shook my head and pointed to my ears to indicate I was deafened. The lieutenant squatted down and shouted into my ears:

"What the fuck are you doin', soldier; you're not even attempting to score." I heard him then, but I continued to pretend not to, a growing defiance.

Despite the dismal grading that should have guaranteed failure, I was awarded a "marksman" designation—a plus for the company at headquarters—indicating that I was ready for battle in the real war in Korea.

There were hated maneuvers in preparation for war; sleeping in army bags on the chilled ground, eating vile canned meals. I avoided the communal toilets—rows of men squatting—as long as anyone else was there. I discovered that the recreation room—closed till early evening—needed cleaning every morning. I volunteered for the task to guarantee the privacy of the toilet there.

In the barracks, I tried to shower at the end of rows of sprouting water. The sight of naked men pushed me back uncomfortably to that time when I had invaded the showers after my brother's basketball game, the bare flesh.

Like all the others, I waited eagerly for mail daily, loving letters from my mother, from my sister Olga—"no really interesting news, little brother"—my sister Blanca and my brothers; and, almost daily, from Wilford, long letters of encouragement for my future life.

So it went.

The whole company had to go on bivouac just before Christmas. That meant living in muddy foxholes. At the same time, there was a competition for the best-decorated barracks in the camp. I bought poster paints of my own and drew, late at night when no one else seemed to be around, a screaming eagle on the window of the company oYce. Though feeling foolish, I painted a ridiculous Santa Claus hat cocked atop the eagle. Under it I drew a colorful Christmas wreath.

The captain in charge of the company did exactly as I had intended. He assigned me to decorate the whole company area. Since the deadline of the contest was nearing, I was allowed to stay in the camp during the days of bivouac, painting screaming eagles with Santa Claus hats on every front window of our barracks.

When the rest of the company returned, grim, from bivouac, I felt guilty; because of this, too: My two brothers had fought in the big war, one during the invasion, the other in the South Pacific. That had been another war, another time, a time of some clarity in goals. The war in Korea was a confusion of maiming and killing. I did know, of course, that by avoiding all the preparations for the battles in those jungles, I would not survive if I was sent to the front lines.

My company won the Christmas decorations contest.

★　★　★

Winter melted. As fiercely as heat had been replaced by icy cold, cold was replaced by heat, mounting daily. Seared yellow dust infiltrated our lives.

In that dry heat, there would occur a campwide test of endurance. Those who excelled in various physical exercises would be pitted against those from other companies in the camp, yet another of the army's tactics for creating ferocious competition that could turn into rage during war.

A crucial part of the test involved sit-ups, overseen by three sergeants and a lieutenant roaming the ranks, goading.

When a sergeant barked the signal—"Hit the dirt!"— everyone in our platoon threw himself on the ground. On more growled orders, we all began doing—or, for some, only attempting to do—full sit-ups, hands interlocked behind the head, knees propped, upper body crunched and raised so that elbows touched steadied knees, over and over and over.

Heavier men, many huffing, dropped out after one or two strained attempts. They were loudly derided by the sergeants:

"Fatso, what did your mama feed ya?"

"That's all you can do, pussy?"

"Your fat ass pull ya down, Miss?"

"That ain't sweat, boy, that's fat."

As more recruits dropped out, the monitoring sergeants began counting aloud, moving from one to the other of those still performing, calling out the number of sit-ups being performed.

At the count of "Twenty!" less than half the company was still competing. "Twenty-five!"—more fell out.

I knew I could go on much longer; especially in high school, I had sustained a rigid regimen of sit-ups to keep my waist tight. The weeks of anger against regimentation aroused in me the need to win, as if in doing so I would again best the army, denying it any prepared ridicule.

"Thirty!"

"Forty!"

Only a few of us—ten—remained. Those who had dropped out and regained their breathing gathered about us; the sergeants continued their taunting, a lieutenant laughed at each dropout.

"Fifty!"

"Only fifty-one? Droppin' out already, GI?"

Three more inductees dropped out, falling back, gasping, wiping away sweat with their hands, one or two dramatically emphasizing exhaustion.

Seven of us remained. I could feel the terrific strain of the exercise on my abdominals. I shut my eyes. I demanded that my body resist fatigue. The sandy dirt underneath me was soaked with my sweat.

"Sixty!" "Sixty-one!" "Sixty-two! . . ."

"Eighty!"

There were three of us left. One of the two soldiers flanking me would soon drop out—I could hear his breath choking. Another one, a lean good-looking young man—and that pushed me even harder—seemed to have gained new forceful impetus. I had to match him, overcome him.

"Eighty-five!"

"Eighty-six!"

The gasping recruit dropped out. The other quickened his pace. One sergeant was counting his sit-ups; another was counting mine. I was two behind, but moving more slowly would allow me to endure longer.

"Ninety!" That was me.

"Ninety-one!" That was the other soldier.

"Ninety-one!" That was me.

The soldier next to me twisted his torso, forcing it up, up, to touch his elbows to his knees. He fell back, groaning.

I had outlasted them all. That wasn't enough, I had to continue, go on, continue . . .

"One hundred!"

I pushed myself harshly, squeezing out three more sit-ups to ensure my victory, now over myself. My body contracted, my stomach wrenched, sweat evaporating under the searing sun. I exhaled, and let myself fall back on my own moisture.

"One hundred and three!"

I stood up, dripping wet, nauseated from the exertion, ignoring cheers that seemed to be muted because my body was pulsing, my ears thumping.

"Private Rechy!" A sergeant from the orderly room was calling out my name. "You have a telegram."

My father had died.

16

With limited funds provided by the Red Cross, I traveled by Greyhound bus back to El Paso. Along miles of shifting scenery, I tried to grasp what I felt toward my father—what I had felt, what I felt now. I tried to imagine what I might feel for him later, what I would want to feel, hope to feel.

Death had halted new memories; whatever was to be remembered had occurred, all evidence was in for a verdict on the intimate stranger who was my father. I grasped for a benign summary of his life.

With pride, my mother had often recalled his days of outrage at injustice, the time he refused to play with his orchestra in a hall in New Mexico that barred Mexicans; the escape he provided for the poorest Mexicans with his magical productions, converting field pickers into grand ladies and courtiers; the flowers for my mother during the most dire poverty; the serenades at her window on her saint's day, even, eventually, with musicians as tattered as he. Was it possible he really loved her? Oh, God, had she loved him?

The Greyhound bus ground on out of Kentucky, leaving behind the stench of dust at Camp Breckenridge, and it moved, still miles ahead, night and day, to El Paso.

My father. There were those times when he had presented my sister and me with many toys at Christmas when we were children, despite my mother's insistence that whatever meager money there was should be spent on clothes. He surprised me with the boots I wanted and the movie projector I longed for—it came with several colored cartoons for screening, giving me hours of joy.

The cherished moment when he had given me the Royal typewriter—I lingered over that memory, and how he had placed the typewriter on my "desk" for me to find after the graduation ceremony he had quietly attended.

He was a kind man violated by stark changes in his life, yes, a pitiable man worn down by the weight of crushed hope. During deepest poverty—I didn't want to remember this and then welcomed the harsh memory in defining him—he worked at a hospital, rising early in winter before dawn, my mother's coffee steaming the cold air. He would trudge, bent, on his way to clean the vestiges of death, bloodied towels, dirty corridors in the one place that had given him a temporary job.

Yes, and remember those times, recalled with smothering pity now, when he demanded that my sister, my mother, and I sit attentively to listen for hours to operas playing on the radio, and he was imagining himself again the conductor he had been, leading a splendid invisible orchestra. He would slice the air with an imaginary baton, up, down, up, down, goading the frenzy of the music, smoothing its lyricism. His face glowed with remembered honor, perspiration, and tears. As he worked at his relic of a desk reorchestrating his unwanted compositions, frantic sweat stained inked notes.

"I am known, I am respected! Wherever I go, I'm greeted with dignity!" he had often told us.

None of us ever questioned that. Out of work, he spent more time at the old courthouse building, a solid block of heavy architecture squatting across from a small park that could not compete with the building's ugliness. Along the hallways, he would walk with his newly acquired cane. Often he demanded I go with him, walking beside him, silent.

"Professor!" A judge would come out of his chambers to greet him warmly as we walked along the ugly echoing corridors.

"Professor Rechy!" Two lawyers would interrupt their conversations to note his presence, to chat with him.

"Professor Rechy!" Up and down the halls, I would hear that greeting. Perhaps, during those walks, he wanted me to be the witness of his claims, the implicit accolades—wanting me to remember them, as I did now, traveling to El Paso for his funeral on an indifferent rumbling bus.

What in me had aroused the extremity of his hostility? A hidden judgment on himself? Did he see me as the artistic child he had been?—detecting the origin of his failure in my own hopes? Was that enough for the reign of fear he created with masterful cruelty?

That was all I needed to allow forth memories long withheld, memories demanding consideration now. As night deepened into a cavern of darkness that the bus carved with its lights, I would not allow myself pity even for his tears because they were a prelude to his rages.

From the very beginning . . .

When I was a child, he would flail crazily with his fists at my mother, accusing her of all the filth he could summon, shouting, cursing her, extending the accusations to me as I rushed to her side, to hug her tightly, form a shield so that his blows would connect with me, not her. His threats escalated. He would set the house on fire when my mother and I were asleep, he told me in a soft whisper. When he threatened to leave us to cope alone, my mother begged me to go after him. With his clenched fist he pounded on my head, knocking me out. I lay unconscious on the sidewalk, then he knelt over me trying to resurrect me from the blow.

My sister Olga would scream with horror, at times beating at him with her fists.

Somewhere in the house, he kept a sword from one of his operas, an actual sword, unsheathed, that required a safety cover during performances. He would change its secret hiding place. We lived in fear that at any moment he would fulfill his threat to bring it out of hiding and slash at us. When he left, my mother and I and my sister Olga—Blanca was already married; Yvan and Robert were in the army—would scurry about the house, trying to locate the lethal weapon, to hide it where he would not be able to find it.

In moments of erupting blackness, he would inch toward me, closer, closer, his malevolent face threatening disaster, until he had cornered me. The more I shouted at him, the more menacing he became, until he had pinned me against the wall, his face so close to me that if there had not been the full intimation of violence, his action would have suggested the intimacy of a kiss. Directly in my face, he shouted:

"Say one more word and I'll smash your pretty face so no one will ever look at you." His fist clenched, ready to mangle my face. My sister Olga would try to pull him away; my mother begged him to leave me alone. For minutes, frozen before me, he did not budge.

On his desk he kept a piece of petrified wood. He would call me over, in a voice that seemed to be kind. In that same soft tone, he would say: "This petrified stone was once the hand of a child who raised it against his father."

I would try not to look at that stone whenever I passed it; but, always, my eyes would be drawn to it, as powerful as a curse, as powerful as the curses he repeatedly aimed at me:

"A father's curse is lasting, and I curse you to be miserable for all your life."

When he sat playing solitaire, deep into the night and in a voice that belied the monstrosity of his next words, he would say to me: "When you're asleep, I'm going to kill your mother, and you'll be left alone, to face me."

I would lie waiting for the door to the room he slept in to close, a closed door that contained every possibility of horror if it swept open. When I heard it close, I would rush up out of my bed in the back of the ugly house. My mother would get up from her bed in the room separated from his by the closed door. We would exchange places. I would then arm myself with wooden boards, whatever I could find outside, so that, on the slightest stirring behind that closed door, I would reach for something to ward off the threatened attack on my mother. As morning dawned, my mother would wake me softly—if I had managed to fall asleep. Once again we would exchange places, so that he would not know of our subterfuge and overwhelm it.

Days, nights, weeks, months, years of that, years, days and nights when I would lie awake, knowing that tomorrow, even that very night, I might face new violence.

After my sister Olga's wedding, we were preparing a picnic, my sister Olga, who was pregnant, her husband, my mother, and I. We would drive to nearby Carlsbad Caverns in New Mexico for a rare outing, leaving before dawn. The night before, my mother had prepared food to take. It was placed neatly on the kitchen table, rare treats she had managed to concoct: sandwiches, a salad, lemonade.

My father had neither agreed to go with us nor decided against it. When we had announced the trip, he had fallen silent. I prayed he would not come with us, marring the few hours we would be away. The night before we were to leave, he sat at his desk playing frantic solitaire, thrusting cards down as if each depicted his doom. Deep into the night, he went to bed and closed the door of his room.

I woke up, eager for our trip to begin, eager to be away from him. I ran to my sister's apartment a block away, to wake her and her husband, who was driving us in his car. I rushed back to get the food we were taking.

Entering the weed-ridden backyard, I saw my mother standing in the still dark morning, terrified. A few desperate stars remained in the sky.

"Don't go in!" she shouted at me.

I rushed past her, into the house, to grab the food, to make sure that our trip would happen. My father stood over the table, his face distorted. He was hiding something in his lowered hand. As I reached for the packed basket, he slashed at me with the kitchen knife he had been hiding.

Olga's husband, alerted by my mother, yanked me back before the knife could slice my stomach open.

We went on the short trip, rendered desolate by fear. What would we face when we returned? What we returned to were his racked sobs as he sat at his desk again orchestrating his abandoned music.

The Greyhound bus screeched. Several passengers were jolted awake. There had been a loud strange sound, a dull thud, dragging. "Everything's all right, folks," the driver assured us. "Must've hit something on the highway."

Something that had been alive . . . dead now.

As I walked with my father on a day of wind and tumbleweeds, he stumbled in the street, his cane spun away, twisting in the wind. He grasped at me for support. I dodged away from him and ran to the curb, leaving him there.

Through sheets of gray dust, I saw him struggling to get up, falling again. I didn't move. I heard a car coming, its fog lights on behind a sheet of dust, dirty yellow ovals approaching. I didn't move. The lights came nearer to where he was grasping for his cane. No, I would not move. The car braked, screeching, advancing closer to his struggling body.

I ran back to the street and I pushed him away from the path of the skidding car.

I picked my father up, carrying him across the street to safety, returning to snatch his cane as the dusty spectral car faded away into the sandstorm.

★　★　★

In the bus, I closed my eyes and longed for tears, held in abeyance by what I was still deliberately omitting from my evaluation of my father's life—and mine—what crouched always in my mind, murky, often a blur before clearing, what even now I tried to force away, deny, banish, a mysterious time when I felt loved by him, the only time.

(And even now, as I attempt to write about those memories, many years after that Greyhound journey to his funeral, I pull away, afraid of remembering, wanting to withhold, to camouflage, to lessen, but, now, the memories demand accounting though regrets may come later.)

I was six. My father's cronies would come over to the decaying house to play cards with him, or dominoes. There would be five of them altogether. At certain points in the noisy activity, my father would summon me over. He would say in a gentle tone, "Give me a thousand." I never knew what "a thousand" meant; I knew only what I was being signaled to do: I would jump onto his lap. He held me tightly, laughing with the others, holding me tighter. Fondling me?—perhaps fondling me. (I must reject this memory, withhold it even now as I set it down, shelter him from the monstrous accusation, disguise it with ambiguity.) Fondling me, his hand—I nuzzled against him, feeling warmth, moments, seconds . . . Then he gave me a penny or even a nickel. Still laughing— not meanly, no, not meanly, as if he was only playing a game (*and was he? Was that all, a meaningless game?*)—he would pass me on to the laps of the other men at the table, one after the other, holding me, squeezing me, laughing, their hands on me. They each gave me a penny or a nickel.

On the Greyhound bus, nearing El Paso, the city's lights winking into the night, I leaned back, my eyes closed; and I recalled the morning when I was leaving for the army and he had given me his precious ruby ring, which I now touched on my hand.

★   ★   ★

As if to affirm the truth of my father's asserted importance, telegrams addressed to my mother at the Western Union office came from important figures all over the country and Mexico, those who had ignored my father's slow dying. All the family gathered. What memories was each member evoking?

I faced my mother, faced again that she was still living in the projects in the poor neighborhood. With the allotment I had provided from my own salary for both her and my father, and with the continuing help of my brother Robert, she would be able to survive relatively well when I returned to finish my time in the army. My goal to buy her a house of her own seemed distant, so distant.

I remained in El Paso only for the few days of the required rosary, the burial.

I bought the stone for my father's grave:

Professor Roberto Sixto Rechy.

17

I returned to Camp Breckenridge, Kentucky, only to learn that my company had received orders to go to Germany. Having been absent, I would be put into a "holding company," disorganized groups of soldiers waiting for further orders. As deaths mounted in Korea, most recruits would be sent there. I was unprepared for war. Deliberately, I hadn't learned how to fire a rifle, how to use a bayonet, how to survive bivouac. Even if I had learned to use the tactics of war, I was sure I would not have been able to employ them.

Amid the needles of red dust and smoldering heat of Kentucky, we waited in the barren barracks, called to formation each time new orders arrived. We waited outside in fatigues—rows and rows of soldiers overseen by a lazy lieutenant who stood yawning in the shade of the orderly room.

Those who were called, their orders received, fell out of the ranks and marched off to prepare for their destinations. The rest of us continued to wait. Everything and everyone waited. New soldiers arrived daily. They waited with us, idling in the barracks, then were ordered to rush outside in formation to wait for possible orders. As we stood in the ranks, heated sand burned through thick boots. We waited in "at ease" formation—not quite at attention, feet slightly apart, hands clasped behind at waist level—for over an hour, as long as two hours.

As the endless roll of names was called by a sergeant, I located myself toward the back of the staggered ranks—and I read, a defensive tactic on my part to endure the interminable calling of names and orders, a risky decision but one made possible because of the large disorganized groups of troops, more than 100, 200, more as the ranks swelled. At the post exchange, I had found a paperback edition of Freud's *Interpretation of Dreams*.

Acting Corporal Bailey was pacing up and down between the rows of men. I had seen him before during these sloppy formations. He seemed always to want to look furious, his brows furrowed purposefully, his hands clasped tightly behind his back as he walked— no, marched, always marched—along the ranks; his thin gangly body angled as if to propel him forward. Also waiting for orders, but apparently stalled for much longer than the rest of us, he had been appointed acting corporal. The two stripes designating that title were pinned to his sleeve, a fact that made him often press them firmly as he marched, as if to assure himself that they had not fallen off.

A hand landed harshly on my shoulder. Too late to hide the book I had been reading.

"What is your name, private?"

"John Rechy."

As Acting Corporal Bailey stood before me, his feet shuffled angrily as if to stir dust, his mouth awry, I saw that he was younger than I had thought, perhaps twenty-three. Despite his contorted features, his face looked like that of a plain child. "Now, again, soldier, what is your name?"

"Private Rechy," I said, understanding.

"Private Rechy what?" he demanded. Others nearby in the ranks turned, alerted to something out of the ordinary, welcoming it as a break in the boredom. The awareness passed from one row to the next, more faces turning. In the distance, the lieutenant located himself at the edge of the shade he courted, closer to what was occurring. The sergeant reading today's orders continued the call of names until he, too, alerted to the mounting altercation, began to read slowly, paused, finally stopped.

"*Private* Rechy, address me as sir!" Acting Corporal Bailey demanded.

"Sir?" I questioned. The frustrations of the days past, the weariness, the unresolved sadness at my father's death, memories of my mother crying, memories of loss, these days of endless waiting, not knowing where any of us would be sent, all conspired to make me furious at this man who was interrogating me stupidly. I said recklessly for the others to hear: "You're not an officer, Bailey, not even a real corporal; I don't have to call you sir."

"Private Rechy," he barked, "you can be court-martialed for reading in ranks—and for disobeying orders." Forced to defend himself now that muffled laughter was floating among the ranks, he had raised his voice.

"What orders . . . sir?" I spoke the word with such obvious derision that those around me laughed. "I've been waiting for orders for ages—like everyone else here, like you." I knew that I was veering toward disaster, but I was propelled by surges of anger.

"Come with me!" he barked. He was about to take my arm to lead me, but I pulled back, and then followed, the book still in my hands. The lieutenant who waited in the shadows advanced, as if to take over the situation. It would have been he who had appointed Bailey an acting corporal.

I was in serious danger. Even if Bailey was only an acting corporal, the assigned position gave him the authority he was exercising. I had seen enough of the army to know that once the infernal machine of power was set into motion, even by an incident much less significant than this, it ground on of its own volition. I had become a candidate for a court-martial.

The lieutenant waited in the near distance now, as if to let this scene play itself out before he would move with authority.

Acting Corporal Bailey led me to the front of the ranks. Nearby was a large aluminum can, like a barrel. "Roll it over here, Private Rechy," he said.

Increasingly aware that I might now be involved in an unstoppable disaster, I tilted the large can and rolled it to where he was indicating, the cleared space where the sergeant had been reading orders—he had stepped aside as if to become only a witness in this odd drama.

"Set it upright, Private Rechy!"

I put the book on the ground and set the can upright.

"Pick up the book, Private Rechy!"

I did. Baffled by the ridiculous situation, attempting to dissipate the fear I felt, I joined the laughter issuing from the ranks.

"We'll see how loud you laugh now, Private Rechy," Acting Corporal Bailey whispered into my ear. "Get the damn book and stand on top of the can."

"You're joking . . ." Anger overwhelmed fear.

"Stand on it, Private Rechy!" Acting Corporal Bailey glanced at the lieutenant, as if for permission to proceed.

The lieutenant did not move, passively allowing what was occurring to proceed.

"Get on it, Private Rechy!" Acting Corporal Bailey said.

"What the hell?"

The troops were quiet, aware of the seriousness of the proceedings—they might be swept in. The muffled snickering died down.

"I said, get on it, Private Rechy!" Acting Corporal Bailey leaned over and muttered so close to my ear that I felt the quiver of his lips: "You're an inch from a court-martial. Don't take it, Private Rechy!"

I got on top of the can.

"Now read, Private Rechy!"

"What?"

"Read what you were reading in the ranks, Private Rechy! Aloud!"

The lieutenant retreated into shade, away from the rancid heat.

Fury allowed me to open the book, flipping pages, wondering when this would end, hoping it would end now, but it proceeded.

"Read, Private Rechy!" Acting Corporal Bailey commanded.

The absurdity of this calamity began to soothe me, as if I was being asked to perform in a play I had not rehearsed but must now invent. I skipped pages in the book to find a dream I had read the day before; about a megalomaniacal little man, trying to assert his wounded power.

I began to read.

A loud guffaw escaped from one of the troops. Then another. Another, more, as several in the ranks made the desired connection between the man in the dream and Acting Corporal Bailey.

I continued, feeling that I could perform in someone else's play by turning it into mine, no matter what would happen when the imaginary curtain fell.

"Get down, Private Rechy!"

"You ordered me to read."

"Get down, Private Rechy!"

No one attempted to stop the laughter. Even the sergeant who had interrupted the reading of orders was laughing.

The lieutenant marched authoritatively forward.

The laughter dwindled, was smothered. On seeing the officer, the sergeant called out: "Ten-shut!"

The company assumed the commanded position of stiff attention. Acting Corporal Bailey stood rigidly facing the lieutenant, his hand at his forehead in a stiff salute. I jumped off the can and took the required position. This had to stop; it had to stop; it had to stop.

The lieutenant leaned over to speak to Acting Corporal Bailey. I could not hear what was said. My ears were ringing, pulsing with tension and fear. The lieutenant marched away, to the orderly room.

"At ease!" the sergeant called out to the company, preparing to continue with the roll of orders.

"Lieutenant Howe wants you in the orderly room. *Now*, Private Rechy!" Bailey said to me. "Double time!"

My body was cold in the hot humidity, which was so intense that I hadn't realized I was sweating, perhaps trembling.

With Bailey behind me, as if I were under arrest, I walked into the orderly room.

A bored clerk was typing at a desk in the small room. "Go on in, private," he said, indicating a closed door.

I knocked.

"Come in, Private Rechy!"

I walked into the lieutenant's office. I saluted and said words I hated but had to say now: "Private Rechy reporting as ordered . . . sir!"

"At ease," Lieutenant Howe said. "Close the door." He was young, in his mid-twenties perhaps, a trim man.

I closed the door and stood before him in an at-ease position.

Lieutenant Howe said: "Do you think that"—he pointed to the book I still held in my hand—"do you think that's what's wrong with Acting Corporal Bailey?"

I still waited for orders in the jagged "holding company" in the dusty heat of Kentucky. For a short time—a few hours—the incident with

Bailey had transformed me into a hero among the soldiers, who slapped my back, laughed. They did not know, nor did I tell anyone, about the encounter in the orderly room with the lieutenant, especially not that I had stayed informally, sitting in his office, talking about where we had attended college, where I had studied, what I had majored in. All that the others in the company knew, what they were reacting to, was that I was back in the holding company, not arrested, not put up for a court-martial.

Everything settled into the same routine. I did not read in the ranks any more, realizing how foolishly I had put myself in peril by heckling Bailey. If any officer other than the lieutenant who called me in had been involved, I would now be awaiting a court-martial, perhaps waiting to be taken to an army prison.

It was now the weekend after the incident. Since no one was granted a pass in a waiting company, most of the men rushed to the post exchange after the last reading of orders, trying to break the tense monotony.

I was alone in the barracks, lying in my bunk, my eyes closed, trying to relax the tension about pending orders. Europe or Korea? Korea was mounting deaths, burned villages, bloodied bodies.

I opened my eyes.

Standing by my cot was Acting Corporal Bailey.

I sat up, apprehensive, certain he had come to extend the earlier conflict. "What the hell do you want, Corporal Bailey . . . sir?" I had added the last word to obviate a reason for his planned confrontation, hoping he would not interpret it as sarcasm.

"At ease, Private Rechy."

Still tensely, I leaned back on the cot. He sat down near my feet.

"You don't have to call me sir," he said. "I'm not a real corporal, just like you said out there. These stripes are pinned on." He touched the stripes, they were loose.

I didn't relax. Would this passive mood shift into abrupt anger?

"What I did out there, to you, it wasn't right, it was—" He shook his head, baffled.

"It's over," I said.

"Not for me."

In siding with me, had the officer censured him? That wouldn't have been fair. The lieutenant had allowed the scene to play out. Had he done so to humiliate Bailey?

"Heck, I'm no one, no one at all." He seemed to be speaking to himself. He placed his hand on the cot. He looked so sad, so tired, as if feeling the weight of his harsh judgment on himself.

"That's not true," I said, "you're—"

"Private Rechy—"

"Corporal Bailey?"

Silence.

I was tempted to touch his hand, so close to mine, to bring about some release from whatever he was feeling, trying to say.

He stood up abruptly, looked down at me. He reached for the pinned stripes on his sleeve as if about to tear them off. Instead, his hand fell, unable to finish the gesture.

"I just came to say good-bye. I'm leaving tomorrow," he said. "I got orders for Korea." He marched out of the barracks.

I never saw Corporal Bailey again.

My mother wrote to me every day, praying for me, blessing me with familiar prayers. I cherished Wilford's long letters. He was directing Brecht's *Mother Courage,* back in Urbana—"Keep writing, you're very talented, Johnny."

My sister Olga wrote, too, her letters full of love, memories we shared—and gossip. I welcomed the distraction of another world.

I would sit on my bunk, propped up as comfortably as possible and read her long letters.

"Alicia Gonzales is living in San Francisco!" My sister began today's letter dramatically with that announcement." Tina had given her daughter a long-distance farewell and blessing, she informed me. "She's not my daughter anymore," she had told my sister, "I commit her to the hands of the Holy Mother." My sister went on: "Maybe she'll return for her mother's funeral and regret being such a cruel daughter, watching her coffin proceed to the cemetery."

I couldn't help laughing aloud in the barracks at my sister's projection of Isabel's regret when her mother would die. The scene clearly came from one of her favorite movies, *Imitation of Life*.

Isabel Franklin had left New Orleans. What had she prepared for there before her move to San Francisco? What would she look like now? I tried to picture her as I had seen her last, in my uncle's Cadillac . . .

Then the hand with the cigarette drifted away from her face, was lowered . . .

My memories of Isabel had instead evoked Marisa Guzman.

"Private Rechy! Report to the orderly room."

It was the booming voice of a sergeant entering the barracks. After all the time I had waited in formation sweating under the Kentucky heat, my orders had come in separately while I was in the barracks.

I rushed to the orderly room. My pulse was beating with dreaded anticipation. Korea?

The clerk in the orderly room handed me my orders, cluttered with army language that I skimmed, urgently wanting to find where I was being sent.

Germany.

Back in the barracks to prepare to leave the very next day for New York, from where those of us going to Germany would be transported overseas by ship, I looked around at other soldiers also packing. I could tell from their faces, dejected, which ones had received orders for Korea. How many would return?

How many would not return?

Corporal Bailey . . .

Before, I had not felt political in a strict sense. I had detested the army for its dull routines and arbitrary strictures; now I detested it for its seizure of lives, the terrible power that could control individuals indifferently, with lives destroyed for a cause not their own, men executed.

My mother wrote a saddened letter—we were going to be separated by a longer distance now. Still, despite my hatred of the army, my sense of freedom from El Paso grew as the USS *Upshur,* the ship that transferred my group to Germany, plowed through the ocean for five long days of weariness and nausea.

Our group was sent to Frankfurt—we saw only fleeting glimpses of the city through windows blurred by foggy snow. At a camp that looked like all the others, we were processed again, with more humiliating physical examinations, more needles shot carelessly into our arms, more paperwork.

On my first free day in the Frankfurt compound, I walked through dirty, icy slush to the USO club. A band was playing there that night. As I was about to enter, a Negro soldier ran out and smashed his fist into my face. There had been a race riot. I must have been the first white-looking face he saw after he fled.

Still attached to the 101st Airborne Infantry Division, I was placed with others of my unit in another holding company. Here, we were organized into squads as we waited again for more permanent assignments. The barracks were sturdier, built for German soldiers, taken over now by American troops. Shabby German men and women cleaned the barracks and the other buildings in the camp. Some of the German workers fawned on us, hustling for American cigarettes that they would sell in the hot black market. Sometimes ragged children jumped over the wired enclosures around the camp, sneaking into the barracks, pleading to be allowed to shine shoes and boots in exchange for money or cigarettes.

Although we did not fly or jump out of parachutes, we wore the uniform of the 101st Airborne Infantry Division, a uniform I liked: olive pants bloused over boots, Eisenhower jacket with the Screaming Eagle emblem, a sky-blue scarf, blue-bordered cap. I wore it the first day we were allowed off the base.

In the city, I wandered the wintry cobbled streets, past old stone buildings that had survived the bombings, past new glassy structures going up alongside the Rhine River—arced bridges, barren trees speckled with frozen snow. Years after the bombings, there was a sense of unresolved defeat in this city that had not been attacked as fiercely as others. Reminders remained, buildings left to crumble in cascades of dusty bricks.

Because of the cold, only a few people walked along the banks of the frozen river, isolating me and them. The scene was peaceful, the city humming with silence. As I lingered along, a man in a heavy overcoat stepped in front of me. I halted. He raised his chin, mumbled something in German, and walked away. I was jolted into the realization that I was in a country in which I was the enemy, in a country that had not long ago turned savage.

In the camp, the tedium was the same—roll calls, waiting for orders, minor duties to be performed, redundant training exercises, and the most dreaded chore, especially in winter in a foreign country: guard duty.

For twenty-four hours those assigned to guard duty were driven by army trucks to outposts on the base, often an unused building, a lot for retired vehicles, desolate abandoned places chosen for added drudgery. There, each sentry would slow-march for two hours, back and forth. Every two hours all guards were relieved, driven to a barracks to sleep for four unsleepable hours on bare cots before being returned for another cycle until a cadre of new sentries were sent as replacements to begin their own isolated marches.

I had begun my first cycle at two AM. It would extend until four AM. The cold night was illuminated only by the whiteness of yesterday's snow turning into ice, graying steadily. In the moonless sky, a few scattered stars attempted to shine before being snuffed out by roiling clouds.

I was assigned to walk about a vacant building, once perhaps a commissary. There was nothing nearby, just slushy gray ice on the ground piling against the base of the mesh wire fence that enclosed the entire base.

With my M1 rifle slung on my shoulder, I paced back and forth, willing time to move, not crawl, second by second.

"GI, over here, GI!"

Automatically, I took the required alert position with my rifle. Although no one truly expected any trouble in these outposts, officers often roamed to ensure that soldiers on guard duty performed exactly as demanded. I pronounced words drilled into us—words we had to speak or risk company punishment, words that I found ridiculous and that I now spoke by rote.

"Halt! Who goes there?"

"Over here!" Again the whispered voice came out of the foggy darkness. An officer checking up on me? I tried to tell myself that was the source of the urgent voice. But, no, the voice had come from the frozen darkness beyond the compound, along the wired boundary, outside it.

"Over here, GI, by the fence, GI!" It was the voice of a woman with a German accent.

I approached the smothered darkness, my rifle now truly ready for whatever would occur.

"Over here!" the voice persisted, a loud whisper.

Glimmering flakes of snow were stirred by rustling feet crunching ice.

"GI, over here, over here!"

The words were echoing unevenly, as if spoken by other voices, more voices, more distant.

"Over here!"

Not echoes, no—there *were* other voices, whispers, outside the fence, a hissed chorus of the same words, some coming faintly from where the soldier on guard duty in the post next to me would be, a distance away.

The shuffling of feet grinding the icy snow grew more urgent, shifting from one place to another beyond the fence, then returning, running in place.

I neared the fence.

Behind the mesh of wire was a dark silhouette. Now I could see the outline of a face. Whoever was there was kneeling or squatting—the face was situated low.

The voice from the outpost next to mine faded, was throttled with a loud gasp by what seemed the night itself.

"You want same, like that, GI?"

I could now make out the crouching form against the frozen night.

"Blow job, GI. I give a good blow job to GI. Cost very little."

A woman was kneeling on the other side of the fence, on the blanket of ice, knees shuffling for some warmth. Her voice might have been disembodied except for the puff of chilled breath that rose with it.

"Open your pants, GI, come on, through here, through the hole in the wire—get a good blow job. Keep you warm, GI. Only few marks. Whatever you got."

My eyes adjusted to the deeper darkness, and I saw the source of the other smothered footsteps. Shadowy forms were spreading about the periphery of the fence, seeking other soldiers on duty along the rim of the compound, moving away from one, rushing to another.

"GI, GI! Push your cock through here. Pay me few marks for blow job. OK, OK, GI?"

Fingers reached out through an opening in the wire widening a hole there.

I strapped my rifle about my shoulders. I dug into my back pocket for money already converted into German marks. I took out whatever I could grasp. Through the hole in the wire, I held out the money to the ghostly presence, and quickly pulled away from the bleak form. I heard rustling feet on the frozen ground scurrying away in the darkness to another site.

My guard session ended, an eternity of stopped time. The officer on duty that night pulled up in a truck to pick me up and take me back to the waiting barracks for a sleep break, four hours before another guard session would occur.

Echoes of the persistent whispers, the rustling of feet crushing ice—the image of the hand pushed through the fence—persisted, mouths open breathing out the frozen cold.

I jumped into the back of the truck swiftly, wanting to leave this nightmarish incident behind if only in distance. The truck had already picked up two other soldiers from their posts. They were both laughing.

"My fräulein hardly had any fuckin' teeth left," one of them said. He was a pimply young man, perhaps nineteen years old, with a Southern accent. "Man, that fräulein blew me right up to my balls."

"Fuck, I wish she'd a blew me," said the other soldier, a gangly black young man, rubbing his groin as the truck moved on to pick up another sentry. "My fräulein was all teeth."

"Did you pay her?"

"Yeah."

"You shouldna," said the redneck. "I didn't pay my fräulein. When I came, I pulled back and left the kraut bitch to freeze."

18

I was sent to Fulda, an hour away from Frankfurt by train. In the new camp, again dreary time stretched into drills and marches without a goal; again we awaited company assignments supposedly based on qualifications; again there were bad meals in the mess hall, and forced camaraderie among the soldiers, a camaraderie I tried to share but could not. Again, endless days would elapse before we would be allowed to go into the town itself. On the base, I spent most of my off time in the library, reading.

An older soldier, a sergeant of about thirty-five, followed me out.

"How're ya doing?"

"OK. You?" I answered.

"Hard to find anything to do when you first get here, isn't it?"

"Sure is."

"Wanna come over? I got a barracks room of my own. I got some booze."

"No, thanks, I'm kind of tired," I said.

He looked at me, smiling, but not in a friendly way; it was a nasty smile.

★　★　★

There were in the army small groups of soldiers who after hours became effeminate, exaggerating their gestures, pitching their voices high into mirthless shrieks.

I was not a sound sleeper. At night, when the lights were out, I would hear footsteps moving toward the showers. The footsteps would not resume, coming back, for some time. Here, too, I waited to shower; if I was not alone, then I would shower when there were few others.

After hours one afternoon, I saw the man who had followed me out of the library. He was in a group of soldiers outside the barracks. When he saw me, he said something to the others. They all tittered. I heard the word "cute."

I turned back, paused, smiled, then hurried on. After that, I avoided them entirely.

The day arrived when we were allowed to leave the camp and go into the city. Pretty, quaint, archaic, Fulda was a small town of steepled churches—mostly Catholic—and crooked stone streets. It had been spared the bombings of World War II that pocked other German cities. There was about it a sense of a city abandoned from another time, intact.

Impulsively I went to Mass in the largest church in the city. The church was old-fashioned, with several steeples, and a statue of Christ on the lawn in the center of a fountain, now idle, icicles clinging to the spouts. Inside, the church reminded me of the churches of my childhood, although it was not as gaudy. Still, there were painted saints, confessionals of carved wood, candles glittering in squat red glasses, alcoves dedicated to various saints on decorated altars.

As I was kneeling to light a candle before the Holy Mother in honor of my mother—I did this whenever I entered a church—I saw a pretty girl next to me smile, then look away.

After Mass, I waited outside. I saw the girl hurrying out, alone, although inside the church she had joined a group that I assumed to be her family.

"Hello," I said as she passed by, slowing.

"Hello," she said. Then she pointed to the blue scarf of my uniform. "Pretty," she said.

To show off the good-looking uniform, I had not worn the allowed cumbersome overcoat. I pointed to her sweater. "Pretty," I said, enunciating carefully.

"I understand English," she said, with an accent.

"That's great."

"Cold, yes?" she said, rubbing her gloved hands.

"Very cold . . . Uh, would you—?" I was about to ask whether she would like to have coffee with me in one of the nearby pastry shops, but a stolid man and a square-shaped woman, both dressed in gray suits, emerged out of the church. They said something in German, sharply, to the girl. The man stood before me and her.

"Sir?" I said.

"Keep away from us, filthy American scum!" the man said.

Was it possible that he felt his faction had been right in its lost cause? Not itself filthy?

Without turning, the girl walked along with them.

On the front in Korea, more soldiers died daily; among them would be some of those I had bunked with during basic training. All we had to cope with here was boredom, broken by an occasional sortie into the placid town. I was haunted by the memory of Corporal Bailey, so forlorn that day, bidding me good-bye. Through the happenstance of assignments, I was here, and he was there.

I now had even less money to spend. After months of being paid dual allotments, for my mother and father, and months before my farther's death was taken into consideration, I learned that I owed the army for all those months of extra pay. A sum was deducted monthly; I retained fifteen dollars a month.

The boredom grated on me. I spent hours at the library reading. Sometimes I started a book, stopped impatiently, moved on to another: *Billy Budd, The Ambassadors,* John Donne, James Thomson, *A Portrait of the Artist as a Young Man.*

Because of my proficiency in typing and my degree in English, I was assigned to record company-level courts-martial, proceedings held for petty offenses—being late for formation, talking in the ranks, charges so insignificant that the hearings were recorded in longhand from notes made as I listened to the petty transgressions blown up.

I looked forward, like all others in the army, to mail. I would separate myself from everyone else so that my letters could pitch me, at least for a short time, into other worlds. Wilford wrote to me almost every week. He was directing a new musical play he had written, *Trapdoors of the Moon,* based on stories I had told him about my family, all converted into a poignant comedy—a feat, I thought, of major proportions. He was trying it out in Urbana, intending to move it off-Broadway. How great, he said, if I could be there to see it with him.

My brother Robert wrote to me expressing the hope that I would return to college, after the army—"You're going to make something of yourself, Johnny," he wrote. I could rely on the GI Bill for education. Whatever else was needed, he would provide, he assured me.

My mother continued to write almost every day, long letters, full of blessings, endearingly without any punctuation whatsoever. I smiled to think that she had that in common with the later James Joyce.

My sister Olga wrote to me regularly—often sending her letter in the same envelope with my mother's prayers and benedictions. My sister's letters always began with concern that I be well and enduring the "damn army." Then they roamed quickly—I welcomed this—to gossip tinged by her with hints of movie catastrophes.

In today's letter, and without introduction, she wrote: "She's looking for a rich husband!"—of course, she meant Isabel Franklin. That information came from an item written in a gossip column by a famous magazine writer often called "Mr. San Francisco" (not, my sister added, "because of his physique"). Someone had sent the item to Tina, and Tina had sent a copy to my sister. This was the copy I was now reading:

> A beautiful young woman has become quite a presence in San Francisco, often seen glittering at the opera. The mystery woman is from New Orleans, from a family in Spain, an exile alone in the country.

Was the unnamed mystery woman really Isabel Franklin?

I was sent for a few weeks to an army school in Berchtesgaden to learn shorthand so that I might record court-martials verbatim as a sworn court reporter.

In the midst of forested greenness and steady drizzle, the small city bordering the Bavarian Alps had been one of Hitler's places of respite, an aerie that commanded the highest mountain, frozen now although spring had come.

In my uniform—I couldn't afford to buy civilian clothes—I took a cable car up to the top of the mountain. There, I entered a restaurant that seemed to have been pulled out of a movie set in Bavaria, with oak panels, decorated mugs on wooden shelves, and a waitress wearing an ornate headband, a decorated blouse, and a pleated skirt. Seated at the scattered tables were German men, talking loudly, laughing raucously, some dressed in lederhosen, short leather pants. Almost all were drinking from frothy mugs of beer. When I entered, the laughter stopped. I sat down. As the waitress walked toward me, one of the men put out his arm, blocking her advance.

I waited, not wanting to retreat from the type of men who, I was sure, had been part of the events that had set the world on fire. All talk had died down.

I walked out into the cold mountain air, realizing only then that my breathing had become irregular with fear.

The *Ring* cycle was playing in the grand opera house in Munich, not far by train. Along the wintry streets of that city, one of the most devastated, vestiges of gutted buildings remained. Blessed now by snow, some of the rubble had become jagged ice sculptures.

A huge, imperious creation, the opera house had survived or been allowed to survive. When I walked in for the performance, the lobby was crowded with German men and women dressed in threadbare formal clothes. I sat down quickly so that others would not have to get up to let me pass into my seat.

I was tense, although I had detected none of the strident hostility of the men in the Alps. The opera seemed endless. The music was not like the lyrical romantic operas my father had loved. When the first act ended, people in the audience pounded the floor with their feet, rapidly, steadily—their form of ovation. Then they rose, applauding wildly, calling out passionately, shouting, stomping. Men and women all around me were crying unabashedly for Wagner and his vision of supermen.

I left before the opera ended.

I wandered about the cold city—surely a beautiful city before it was battered—now a scarred beauty, a city in mourning. It was late when I went to the station to take a train back to the school.

Women, heavily painted, roamed the cavernous building so-liciting soldiers; they pleaded openly, chided, demanded, bartered like the women who had sold their mouths in the darkness of the outpost in Frankfurt.

In the restroom, a soldier facing away from the urinals was being blown by a squatting woman. Other soldiers watched or waited their turn or continued to urinate.

Back in Fulda after completing the course in shorthand, I became increasingly restless. I hated the guaranteed convictions meted out by a panel of stiff officers to recruits in trouble, recruits who were most often professional army men looking their shiny best to be adjudged "good soldiers" by the officers. The only way I saw to shake time loose from its entrenched stasis was to keep transferring from city to city. In the office where I wrote reports, I typed out an impeccably worded and formatted letter to Fifth Corps headquarters in Frankfurt. Using words and phrases I knew would impress, I asked for a transfer. The transfer came through, contin-gent on my agreeing to extend my time of enlistment another year. I agreed, although I had no intention of doing so. The offices I worked in were in the Farben building, a luxurious glass building that had been occupied by Hitler's elite. Still a private—I had not stayed anywhere long enough for a promotion—I was assigned to be the personal aide of a gentle old officer, a colonel. My main function was to report to him weekly, from an issued list, how many other high colonels were ahead of him to be promoted to generals.

Eventually—and here, too, everything turned into unbudg-ing drudgery—I earned ten days of leave.

19

Taking with me Levi's and T-shirts I had asked my brother to send me, clothes I had left behind, I turned up in uniform at an army airport and hitched a ride on an army plane. I landed at Orly field in Paris with thirty dollars in my pocket, the amount I had been able to save out of my salary.

I rented a cheap room in the first hotel that seemed affordable. I quickly changed to the casual clothes, and I plunged into the city with an excitement I had never felt before, the excitement of a new world of freedom, in another country, away from the army—and in civilian clothes.

I was instantly infatuated with the city. In the following days, I explored it relentlessly, rejecting sleep. I climbed Montmartre, to Sacré-Coeur, the white church so grand, so elaborate, so gaudy, like a huge wedding cake at the top of the hill. I lit a candle for my mother and rushed out quickly to experience more. Once, an American tourist, consulting a booklet, asked me directions in mangled French. That pleased me, because, looking around, I saw so many wondrous beautiful people.

Everything about the city entranced me—its flowery parks, its edifices from decades past, its ubiquitous statues, the wide boulevards, the crooked squeezed streets and alleys. All of that aroused in me a euphoric mood I could not entirely identify beyond a feeling of new freedom; that mood contained within it a sense of grand possibility beckoning, something that lingered with me as I roamed about the gardens of the Louvre and then the museum itself, startled to actually be looking at fabled paintings. It was aroused, that exhilaration, like a sweet powerful scent, as I responded to passing glances, smiles I seemed to be courting, from attractive young women and men everywhere, at times looking alike; a sustained sense of exhilaration that I carried with me into the small cafés where I ate the day's only meal, and along the banks of the Seine, where I bought fruit for lunch. But along with the feeling of something ineffable about to happen here, in this city, there was, but only in brief moments, a tinge of fright.

I had walked and walked to the outskirts of the city, without realizing it. It had grown dark. There was a party going on nearby, a combination party and carnival alongside one of the small streets. Young men and women, some tipsy, were dancing. A girl drew me in, and we hopped around with the others, and then a young man joined us. Soon, the girl had spun away to another group, and I was dancing with the young man—not really dancing, more, just moving together and laughing.

It was deep night when I left. The subways were closed; I discovered that only then. I would have to walk a distance to return into the heart of the city, where I was staying. I didn't mind. I was intoxicated with the sense of extravagant welcome I had experienced in the gathering I had just left—or was it, now that I was away, a sense of foreboding?

Exhausted, I reached Saint-Germain-des-Prés, the stretch near an old steepled church across from the Café de Flore, where, I had read, Sartre and de Beauvoir had congregated. I had wandered along this street in the daytime—yesterday?—when it had been buzzing with people of every sort. Upon entering the area at night, I detected an entirely different atmosphere. It must have been as late as two in the morning, later.

The night was tinted only by distant lights; trees were dark silhouettes; there was the pervasive sound of footsteps, slowed, halting, resuming. Figures along the twilit street seemed to be floating, singly, then together, separating or moving away together.

There were only men here now.

The street was touched with a warmth that seemed to have been hiding within the coolness of the night, within which, occasionally, laughter, softened but pitched into mirth, broke, but only somewhat, a mesmerized silence.

My exhilaration and apprehension heightened even more. Was it here, still not fully detected, not fully identified, that the excitement of days was finding its origin, the stretch of blocks its sudden center?

I stood near, but not within, the muted, slow procession of men, watching intently, studying it all, until, now—but exactly when?—I realized I was moving in to join it, responding to what felt like a summons, issued when? How far back? Only now? Only here? As far back as—

I entered the slow current, so slow that it was as if I had walked into a dream, a dream shared with others here, a dream that stark motion or sound would banish. No, no, not like that, no, not at all. It was as if I had suddenly *awakened* from a long, long dream and into reality. What surprised me most during that confusion of contradictory feelings was that I was drifting into this reality so easily, as if unknowingly having rehearsed it, assuming the same rhythm as the others, pausing as if to glance into a window, moving into a new reality.

"American?"

Until he spoke, I had not noticed the man who had approached me, walking slowly toward me—no, I *had* noticed him, I had paused to be met by him. Had I?

"American, yes," I said. I was not annoyed that he had recognized me as an American even out of uniform.

"GI?"

That did annoy me slightly, that despite my clothes, this had shown through. I mumbled, neither no nor yes, an ambiguous sound.

"Cigarette?" he offered.

No! "Yes." In the last few months in the army, doing anything to ward off the monotony of waiting, I had taken up smoking, especially when I was reading in the barracks, but I had stopped a few days earlier. Now I took the proffered cigarette and looked at the man directly as he snapped a match to light my cigarette.

He was young, no older than twenty-five; he was handsome, yes, with an angular face, like that of a fashion model. The latter perception was strengthened by the fact that he had longish hair—black, no, brown—combed back. That emphasized the keen features. He was slightly taller than I, slender, with a swimmer's body.

I continued walking in the direction I had been headed; he joined me, silently. We were both smoking, the smoke becoming a part of the hypnotized night. Others glanced at us, glances skidding from me to the man I was with. The slowed activity on the street assumed for me a sense of ritual, of performance, of instinctive choreography, ghostly dancers.

"You speak French?"

"A little." I had taken a course in French in college.

"*Voulez*—?" he started.

I shook my head, no. "I don't speak it well enough to understand." Yet I had inferred what would follow—did I?—and it did.

"Would you like to visit my apartment?" he said, with an accent.

Did I? Would I? He had thrust me out of the dream, into the former reality. I felt like walking away, even running. "Sure, yes," my voice said.

He smiled. "Good,"

"No."

He frowned.

"I have a room nearby; you can come with me." I had spoken those words.

The frown eased into a smile. "*Bien.*"

As we walked away from others still drifting, I no longer wondered whether I had wakened from a dream or into another.

I was simply walking to my rented room with a man I had just met.

We reached the small hotel. I had hardly used it throughout the frenzy of my infatuation with the city.

I had a key to the front entrance. As we entered, a woman—I recognized her as the person I had rented the room from—peered out of a door. When she saw us, she did not retreat; she kept staring at us, the door more ajar now, as if to call further attention to herself.

"It's all right," the man whispered as we proceeded up the stairs. "French hotel women are always curious."

I hadn't been aware of indicating trepidation.

We walked quietly up the steps, to the third level—there was no elevator. We entered the barely furnished room, where my army clothes lay on a chair. He glanced at them, smiling, probably confirming what he had suspected, that I was in the army.

I had left the bed unmade from a time that I had returned to doze, only to awake, aware that I was wasting time sleeping in this city of mysterious clarity. I moved away from the bed.

I turned on the light, to chase away the darkness that seemed too intimate. I drew apart the drab curtains—more like stitched panels of cloth—to allow in even more light from outside, from another world that this room was expelling.

The man reached out, drawing me toward him, bringing his body against mine, his lips parting. One hand slid down, locating the buttons of my Levi's, his other hand fumbling with the buttons of his own pants.

"You'll have to leave."

"What?"

I had pulled back from him. "That woman downstairs; she runs the hotel; she warned me that I couldn't bring anyone to my room," I lied. "She's capable of calling the police."

The man laughed, without humor. His smile turned into a smirk. "That's a lie," he said.

"No, it's true, I—" I raised my hands before me, prepared to push him back.

The smirk turned into contempt. "You are mistaking yourself, American, but no one else."

He walked out.

The man's words echoed in my mind throughout the next day. I knew what he had meant. "You are fooling yourself, but no one else." I repeated the words in my mind, exploring them, hearing them again, denying them.

In the few days left of my leave, I went to more museums, art galleries, churches, the Folies Bergère, roamed in more parks. I saw Jean Cocteau's *The Infernal Machine* with the writer as the prophet and Jean Marais as Oedipus. Jean Marais! The man Baxter Polk had shown me in the disturbing photograph long ago. On the stage, the beautiful man did not act; he moved from pose to pose to pose, a performance of postures.

The memory of the searchers I had joined that one late night recurred. I would not seek the area out now, although I knew that, on that night, I had stepped into another world that I must have known long ago existed. Whatever necessary subterfuges I might have to concoct to live within it, I would not be able to abandon it.

Into my contradictory thoughts, the memory of the kept woman floated into my mind . . . *as she reached again for the cigarette on the ashtray and looked up and smiled, definitely smiled.* Assertive, elusive, that memory, soothing—no, no, disturbing.

20

I had overstayed my leave by several days. I was technically AWOL, exposing myself to a court-martial. I turned myself in at Orly field, and was "arrested"—a mere gesture I had counted on so that I would be flown back to Frankfurt quickly. I had also relied on work's having piled up in the office to an extent that the kind colonel would welcome me back without charges.

He did.

Time crawled before I began edging toward the end of my required term in the army, a term I had agreed to extend by one year to effect the transfer to Frankfurt. I had already taken steps to circumvent that by applying for early release to attend graduate school. As I waited for the official granting of my application for early release, monotonous days piled on monotonous days. When the application was granted and I told the colonel I was leaving, he was wistful, especially because he was still a few rungs from being promoted to general; as he had seen in the listing I had just compiled for him, half a dozen colonels were ahead of him for promotion.

My mother's last letter to me before I left Germany—"I'm counting the days before you're here, *m'ijo*"—included a hastily added sheet of news from my sister Olga. The envelope had been opened and then resealed, and even the paper on which she wrote, torn somewhat jaggedly, seemed to gasp:

"Alicia Gonzalez is engaged to the famous magazine columnist in San Francisco. I bet she won't be when he finds out who she really is."

As I prepared to return to the states, there were these considerations: I would have to return to El Paso, a cemetery of cruel memories, and cherished ones; a place of endless windstorms and enraged tumbleweeds, of hot desert and a beautiful azure sky like no other I would ever see, and of the grand mountains I had climbed. In El Paso, I would have to face my mother with the news that I would be leaving again, after a brief stay. I would have to harden myself against her tears, and perhaps even more so, against mine. I would again leave her in the projects—where, I reminded myself without washing away the sense of impotence, she lived proudly. I would give her my separation pay, and that would pull her through until I could send her money again. I intended to work while I went to school on the GI Bill—in New York. I had applied to Columbia.

Wilford would eventually be there. Even with the knowledge I had gained about myself in Paris, I would not—could not—pretend to reciprocate his feelings. I loved him, yes, but, I knew, he had been in love with me. Would what I could give him, the love of friendship, be enough?

It took five days to return by ship to New York, from where, with only a glimpse of the city viewed out of the windows of waiting army buses, all released soldiers were taken to Camp Chaffee, Arkansas, for official discharge. Again, the forms to fill out, the equipment to return, the desultory formations to keep. Soon, soon, it would end.

The day I was to be discharged—that would happen in a few hours—there was only one more office to stop at for final papers, and I was on my way there now. I was feeling so recklessly free from the army already that I opened the top two buttons of my khaki shirt. I placed my cap askew, I—

"Hey, soldier!" A jeep had screeched to a stop beside me. A sergeant was driving. A lieutenant sat beside him.

"What the hell do you think you're doing going around like a tramp, soldier?" The lieutenant jumped out of his jeep, standing before me only inches away. "Are you drunk, private?"

"I'm discharged," I said. That would be true in less than an hour.

"You're still in uniform," shouted the lieutenant, who was only slightly older than I, "and as long as you are, you belong to the army, private, and that means you wear the uniform proudly!"

The fact that I was almost free and that this stupid lieutenant could still assert his authority over me made it difficult for me to breathe, to form any words.

"I can have you court-martialed!"

The sergeant jumped out of the car, standing behind me, ready to execute whatever orders the lieutenant might issue.

"You understand, private?!"

Of all the times of defiance, this was the most dangerous. In a moment this lieutenant would order me arrested, handcuffed, taken to the brig; would charge me with insubordination—and this petty encounter would grind on toward a court-martial. I wanted to resist, needed to resist, had to resist.

"*You understand me, private?*"

I breathed deep. I formed the words I would aim at him, whatever the result, including the word I would use now for the first time in my life: Fuck you, son of a bitch!

"Yes, sir," I said. "I understand."

Hurriedly, I adjusted my shirt, the tie, the cap.

"That's better, private," he said, and hopped back into the jeep with the sergeant and rode off.

I was breathing again, with relief and rage, relief because I had guaranteed that in less than an hour I would be out of the army, rage that I had acquiesced in one last despised order, that I had compromised my cherished defiance.

★ ★ ★

Discharged, I got off the bus in Dallas. I would stay there for a couple of days at the YMCA. I wanted to go home looking relaxed, not worn down by the last encounters in the army. Too, I wanted to advance toward El Paso slowly, to enhance the awareness, with distance, that I was leaving behind those years in the army that were already blurring for me, a period of my life I would soon be able to separate myself from, as if all of it had happened to someone else.

I stayed at the main YMCA in a city of tall buildings, slurred accents. It was hot; very hot; very, very hot. Fat clouds roamed the sky promising rain, bringing only humidity. It clung to the streets, waves of heat radiating visibly.

I went to the sundeck of the Y. There were about twenty men, twenty bodies; some looked naked in tiny bikinis like posing straps. Most were young. A few older men roamed about as if to find an elusive place to take. I placed a towel on the concrete ground. I took off my shirt, socks, and shoes. I lay back. A man moved over next to me. I shut my eyes, aware of the same muted currents I had located in Paris.

When I had had enough sun, I picked up my towel and clothes and returned to my room. Still in his trunks, the man who had lain next to me on the sundeck was following me.

I left the door to my room slightly ajar.

"Can I come in?" he asked.

"Sure."

I sat on the small bed. He sat next to me. He placed his hand on my groin.

I pulled back harshly.

"What the hell—?" he said.

"I'm too tired."

"Fuck you, creep. You're not all that hot, punk."

I welcomed his disdain. I deserved it. Why had I done this again!—encouraged only to reject. I did know this now: What had presented itself, in Paris and here in Dallas, was not what I was looking for, at least not yet. But I had taken another step into the tempting world of men, only men. What essential step was next before I joined it?

I returned to El Paso.

"*M'ijo!*" my mother cried joyously, opening her arms to welcome me, instant tears covering her face. She looked lovelier than ever.

"Mama!" I said, surrendering to her embrace, enclosing it tightly with my own.

"I've missed you so much, *m'ijo,*" she said.

"I've missed you very much, too, mama."

"But now you're back home; the Holy Mother has heard my prayers."

"I'm home now, mama, yes."

That night, with my brother Robert, divorced for the second time, we had dinner. In anticipation of my arrival, my mother had ordered from the butcher the best cut of filet mignon. Robert topped it with hot chili.

I went to see my sister Olga.

"Sister!"

"How handsome you look, little brother! I've missed you so much."

"I've missed you, too. How beautiful you are, sister!"

"I know," she said, "more beautiful—no?—now that there's more of me."

She had learned how to cook—soup.

We talked about what had occurred since I left—her husband had a better job; Louie, her boy, was enrolled in school; and she was pregnant again. She asked how I had been able to overcome the army. "You, so finicky," she said. I told her good things only. "I went in a private and I came out a private," I said, with the curious triumph that this gave me, a testament to my maneuvers to keep moving from place to place.

"Well . . . Oh, why pretend?" she said, "I know you want to know about Alicia Gonzales."

"Isabel Franklin."

"Alicia *Gonzales*. She is crueler than ever. No matter how Tina tries to contact her—"

"You told me Tina had given up, didn't care."

"How can a mother stop caring?"

I smiled; the tomboy who had protected me had become a mother.

"Go on, then," I said, expecting that she would decorate, with grave emotion and suspense, what had occurred.

"That man—isn't he a gossip columnist?"

"Yes." I knew she was talking about Bert Schwartz, the man who had in his magazine column referred to the "beautiful mystery woman" from New Orleans by way of Spain.

"Don't you think he'd know what everybody in El Paso knows?"

It did seem illogical that the columnist who often unearthed deceptions would not know who Isabel Franklin really was. What I didn't understand was why my sister thought it should matter so particularly now to him.

"She married him," my sister said.

My brother Robert lent me his car, a Ford. He had become foreman at the factory where he worked. He had been elected president of his union three times, by acclamation. "Whatever you need, brother," he reiterated, as he had from my earliest years.

I visited with my brother Yvan, always, for me, a stranger I was fond of, felt warm toward, even loved. I visited my sister Blanca, and we remembered how she had coached me to sing—"in case she answers"—after I had written Shirley Temple offering to partner her, but the little bitch never answered.

I parked my brother's car and got out, to walk familiar blocks. In reaction to the army, I had not shaved for a couple of days. I had unbuttoned my shirt, three buttons now.

"Hey, boy!"

I couldn't believe it—the tone of the lieutenant in Arkansas who had threatened to court-martial me on the day of my separation from the army.

A squad car—the El Paso police—had stopped as I had been about to cross the street back to my brother's Ford, to drive to the mountains I had so often climbed.

"Yeah?"

They hopped out, hands on their holsters. An Anglo and a Mexican—the latter startled me. Not too long ago, a Mexican cop was rare.

"Where you from? Whatcha doing in El Paso?"

My appearance had branded me an outsider, a potential troublemaker as they saw it.

"I live here," I said.

"You live here?" one challenged.

"Yes."

"Where?"

I told them.

"You don't look from here," one said. But they had removed their hands from their holsters.

"You working?"

"I just got out of the army."

"Not working," the one said to the other. "Hustlin' your way to Los Angeleez, huh?" he sneered at me.

"Vagrant," the other said. "No visible means of support," he recited.

I knew what they were plotting. Generalized vagrancy laws were used everywhere, whether the details were legal or not.

"What's your name?"

"John Rechy."

"Rechy?" said the Anglo.

"You related to Yvan and Robert?" the Mexican cop asked.

"They're my brothers."

"Professor Rechy?—he's your father?" the Anglo asked.

Professor Rechy; yes, that was what everyone still called him. "Yes, he was my father."

"Sorry, kid," said the Anglo cop. Both smiled at me. They walked back to their car.

"Stay out of trouble."

"And get a shave."

Despite the quick anger that would always be aroused when I was confronted by arbitrary authority, I had discovered this: I could look like a transient, an attractive transient.

I could barely face my mother when I told her that I was going to school in New York. We were sitting on the couch in the small living room where I slept while I was there.

"I love you so much, my son," she said, "I miss you so much. Couldn't you go to school here?"

"And I love you just as much, mama, and miss you a lot. I need to go to a better school. I want to be successful so I can give you what you never had, what you deserve for giving me so much."

"I don't need anything more," she said staunchly.

I felt myself wavering. Yes, I could go back to school here, I could—No! I had to leave.

She moistened one of her fingers with her saliva.

"Remember when I used to curl your eyelashes?"

"Yes, I remember."

She touched my eyelashes with her finger. "That's why they're so long and curled now."

Under the GI Bill, I qualified for full college tuition. Anticipating acceptance, I applied for a writers' workshop taught by Pearl Buck, only as a possible way to connect with someone or other who might help me toward publication. She required a sample of work for admission. I had already sent her the first chapters from *Pablo!* High on Wilford's enthusiasm for it—I kept putting off plans to connect with him again—I had no doubt she would welcome me. I was waiting only for the official notice.

The dreaded time arrived for more painful good-byes. My sister Olga's stomach was full with her new child. She still looked beautiful. After agreeing to forward immediately any notice from Columbia, she reminded me: "So long, remember? Never good-bye, little brother."

I tried to kiss her; her full stomach interfered. I manipulated the kiss sideways. "So long, beautiful sister."

With my duffel bag containing all the clothes I thought I needed—and with the typewriter my father had given me—I waited outside the government projects for my brother to drive me to the bus station. I hoped I would never return here to see my mother still in the projects. Now she stood next to me. Robert honked for me.

My mother blessed me. "*Que Dios te bendiga, m'ijo.*"

★   ★   ★

With the fifty dollars I had kept from my separation money, and the priceless ruby ring my father had given me, I took the bus to New York. Not yet there, in Urbana—where Wilford was when he had last written to me—I impulsively got off. I would contact him!

No, not yet, not when I was just drifting.

I wandered about a well-kept neighborhood. I passed a lawn overgrown with grass, despite the elegant house it was a part of. I knocked at the door. A coifed lady came to the door. If she had a lawn mower, I would mow her lawn, I said—or I could clean her garage.

"Are you a student at the university?"

"Yes, ma'am," I lied easily.

She hired me to do both chores. I was twenty dollars richer. I asked whether she knew someone else I might do similar work for. She called a neighbor. For the neighbor, I mowed the lawn and pulled weeds. When I left Urbana, I was fifty dollars richer, with tips.

When I stepped out of the bus at the Forty-second Street Greyhound station in Manhattan, I was overwhelmed by terror. Where would I stay? What was I doing here? A newspaper headline warned that a rare hurricane was threatening the city. Rain was already pounding against the windows of the station. A cop there kept staring at me ambiguously, perhaps misinterpreting my obvious bewilderment.

"Can you recommend some place for me to stay?" I asked him, to dissipate his unease about my intentions.

"Try the Sloane House YMCA," he said, pointing. "It's just down the street, kid. You won't even get wet."

21

I checked in at the Sloane House YMCA, paying a week in advance for a room. From a public telephone in the lobby, I called my sister Olga, to give her my temporary address and to connect with a badly needed friendly voice.

"Little brother!"

"Beautiful sister! Is my mother OK?"

"Yes, sure, don't worry, we're all watching over her. Little brother, you received that letter you were waiting for, from that Chinese woman."

I was too eager to hear about Pearl Buck's acceptance to laugh at my sister's confusion. "Please open it; read it to me."

I heard her tear open the envelope. There was a puzzling pause.

"Little brother—"

"Sister?"

"Little brother, she says—uh—let me read it again. I think she says—"

"She turned me down?" There was only that one reason for her hesitation. I accepted the awful fact immediately: Bad news becomes assertive the moment it is spoken.

"I think so, but—" My sister read to me: "I have no doubt you're talented, but from the sample you sent me, I don't believe I could help you in your writing. I wish you the best."

"Fuck her," I said.

"Little brother!"

"Sorry, sister. I don't really care. I wasn't going to take her class anyway. She's not a very good writer, you know."

I managed more small talk, interspersing it with questions about whether my mother was really all right.

Now what? In the tiny room I had rented, I lay in my shorts on the small bed, not moving, trying to cool off. Now what? I felt lonesome, afraid. Shoved harshly every which way by the wind, heated rain pounded the windows. Now what?

It pleased me to remember that I had never read anything by Pearl Buck and hadn't even seen the movie made from one of her books. That provided a few moments of respite.

Increasingly hot and unnerved, in my shorts and with a towel, I made my way to the showers, hoping to drench away some of my growing anxiety and sadness. I told myself that the strange content of my novel—overtones of incest, narcissism, rampant witchcraft, an old man obsessed with a boy—had frightened the woman away. Besides, whom did I trust, Wilford or her?

I walked along the hallway past a half-open door; someone was inside. In the shower, I welcomed the cold water on my body. A rough-looking bulky man entered. In a glimpse, I saw tattoos on both his arms. The man removed his towel and got under the shower next to me. I reached for my towel, to dry myself and leave.

"Hey!"

"Hi."

"Take you out to dinner—how about that?"

I was almost broke—I hadn't even let myself check how much money I still had.

"Come to my room when you're dressed," he said.

I returned to my room. Taking my time so that the man would not think I was anxious, I dressed in jeans and a T-shirt.

"Come in, kid," the man responded to my knocking at the designated door, the room I had walked past earlier; he had probably seen me. I went in. Dressed, he sat before the small table provided in every room. Before him was a bag of food, recently delivered, I could tell, from the smell of hamburgers and french fries. Next to the two bags were bottles of Coke. My stomach turned at the assault of mixed odors.

"Thought you'd like to eat here, real quiet, and we can relax."

I didn't want that, no. Nor did I want the hamburgers, which as he took them out dripped with grease.

He saw my apprehension. "I'm kinda low on cash now," he explained. "Otherwise, we'd go out to dinner, like I said in the showers. Stick around and we'll go out tomorrow. I'll be loaded," he added when he saw me hesitating. He bit into a hamburger, limp pieces of lettuce and tomato dangling from his lips. "I sure wish you'd a been at Mary's Bar in the Village last night—that's a hustling bar." His eyes were probing my reaction.

A hustling bar . . . a phrase, foreign to me . . . no, the cop in El Paso had used it. I moved farther into the room.

"Yeah, last night I woulda taken you out to a real fine restaurant— and you'd a been fifty bucks richer."

Fifty bucks richer. Pieces of a puzzle about to be solved. Solved or found.

He laughed. "I know, I know, seems like a story. Fifty bucks!—when the going rate's five, maybe ten. I was drunk, hot for the guy, and I'm real generous when I'm flushed. Let me tell you, kid, he wasn't near as good-looking and sexy as you are. You're a beaut, kid. Come on, sit down, we'll figure all this out. We'll just eat this stuff now and talk. Tomorrow I get my paycheck—I'm a merchant marine, get paid good—and we'll do the town up. How's that?" He slurped the Coke.

I shook my head, feeling conned, pegged as green. "I'll see you around tomorrow." I was almost out of the room.

"Hell, kid," he said to me, forcing, I was sure, a yawn, and I realized he'd spiked the Cokes; a sour smell mixed nauseatingly with the odor of greasy burgers. "If you're really hard up for ready cash, go to Times Square, always good for ten—good-looking guy like you; just stand there—"

Hustling . . . I had looked the part . . . fifty bucks, ten . . . Times Square.

Rain slashed in sheets at the city; tall buildings were under assault by waves of water. Yet Forty-second Street was crowded; people were hurrying along with umbrellas, suddenly upended by rainy wind. Although it was still afternoon, the day had turned a dull gray.

At the desk at the Y, I had inquired where Times Square was; the man there had smiled knowingly. Now I stood on Forty-second Street without shelter, allowing the rain to drench me, feeling my body soaked with wetness as if I was naked.

I stood there until the rain abated, became only steady. A pale sun was struggling out of entrapping clouds. The city glistened, for startling moments. The electricity of the storm had made the approaching dusk hotter, steaming up the streets.

For the first time I noticed a sign blinking over an arcade across the street.

F*A*S*C*I*N*A*T*I*O*N

It seemed like a powerful invitation I had already accepted. Looking about the grimy street—of blinking neon lights and pinball arcades, scruffy movie theaters, the open mouths of the sub-way spewing out people; cars crowding the street, inching along in traffic, horns protesting—I saw young men lolling about, standing out even among the surging crowds. They would pause briefly, swagger on. I spotted them easily, studied them, their stances, their slouched poses as if uncaring; but their heads turned often, toward mostly older men, some in business suits, who walked along at a faster pace—as if determined to convey that they had a definite destination while really only scouting. One or another would pause, exchange a few words with a loitering young man. The two might move away together, or split up, moving to others.

I recognized the dance of the streets, but it was not as slow here. This was an extension of the world I had entered in Paris, yes, but another avenue, a territory I felt now I had been waiting to enter. The earlier interludes, in Paris and Dallas, were only the first steps into it. Easily, I assumed the studied posture of the others, the posed unconcern, the slouch.

Then all the anticipation that had led me here breathless, and had kept me here through the rainstorm, was washed away. I could not remember when I had felt this alone, this afraid, this lost, this bewildered—lost, longing to return to the safety of El Paso, the warmth of my mother's love, the comfort of my brothers and sisters. l would rush back for my duffel bag and my typewriter at the Y, buy a ticket back to El Paso, I would—

"I'll give you ten bucks, and I don't give a damn for you."

A short man, compactly built, perhaps in his middle forties, had stopped before me, hat slouched, posture cocky, looking me up and down knowingly.

"What?"

"You heard me."

I had, but I wanted to hear the thrilling words again, although I knew exactly what he meant.

"Well?"

"Yeah, sure," I said.

"You eaten yet?"

"No."

"I'll buy ya dinner, come on," he said.

He dashed into the street and stopped a cab that was shifting to pick up another man. He jumped in, motioned me in, and closed the door quickly, exiling the other, protesting man. "Gotta keep on your toes in this fuckin' town," he laughed.

He took me to dinner at a good restaurant—"the best we can go to, with you dressed like that." We took another cab to his apartment, well furnished, nothing fussy, solid furniture. He led me to his bedroom, a large bed, neatly made up. He put a ten-dollar bill on a table. He went to another room and returned wearing a robe.

Coaxing me back onto the bed, he took my clothes off. He stood looking at my naked body. He touched my body, his hands moving slowly along my thighs, my chest, my arms. I felt as if I would explode, with excitement—or fear—both. He bent his head over my groin. He licked my aroused cock. I twisted away, holding my breath audibly. My body relaxed.

He blew me until I came, gasping with a force I had never experienced before, as if in those moments I was pushing out, into his mouth, not only my come but all the fear with which I had begun this welcome initiation.

He gave me twenty dollars.

"My name's Klein," he said with braggadocio. "*Mister* Klein," he emphasized as if grabbing for something he felt he had compromised.

"Johnny," I introduced myself.

"See you again, Johnny."

"Sure, Mr. Klein."

"Call me Ed."

"Sure, Ed."

"Library steps, Fifth Avenue, tomorrow seven o'clock. Be there, kid, OK?"

That encounter was the beginning of the birth of a new person, myself, another self, the first step I took to live a life that, years later, I would write about, although at the time I had no intention of doing so, in a novel titled *City of Night*.

22

I returned to the rented room at the Y. I slept and woke startled because I had gone to sleep with the sound of the rain, to its rhythm, and had been wakened by its absence. I had placed on the table the twenty bucks Mr. Klein—Ed—had paid me last night. "I'll give you ten bucks and I don't give a damn for you"—those words returned like a mantra. This was the world I had been seeking in its periphery. It was a world in which I would be desired and not be expected to desire, and I would be paid in confirmation of that powerful fact.

Until I was at the library on Fifth Avenue, I wasn't sure I would turn up to see Mr. Klein again. Still undecided, I had walked through the library toward the Fifth Avenue exit. Through glass doors, I saw him waiting outside for me on the steps, between the two stone lions there. His hair was trimmed. He wore a sport jacket fitted trimly to his stocky body, probably tailored. He was trying to look his best for me. What he expected from me, I would not be able to give; that was not allowed in the world I was choosing to live in, indifferently. He was too kind to deserve my indifference.

I turned back into the library and walked away from him.

★   ★   ★

When I went to the apartment of a man who spoke only the words needed for the proposition—what was involved, for how much—I learned more rules for existing on the street.

Next to the man's bed was an open book by Colette. I leafed through it.

"You read much?"

"Yes."

"Colette?"

"Some—yes."

"Here." He paid me. "I don't want you, I want a tough man."

So, like the others on the street, I would be street-smart but not smart, tough but not smart.

I moved out of the YMCA Sloane House and rented a room in a huge gray building on Thirty-fourth Street. On one corner, where Park Avenue declined into Fourth Avenue, an old army building, the Armory, squatted like a medieval fortress; on the other corner was a building known then as the Casbah.

The building had the look of something abandoned from long ago—five stories, six wings, creaking elevators. Once, the various wings had been spacious, elegant apartments. Now each wing was broken up into rooms, united by long dark corridors, with a community kitchen and two bathrooms in each branch. I paid eight dollars a week for a small room whose single window faced another room only a few feet away in the neighboring wing. I opened the case with my typewriter and placed it on a table.

Although several of the tenants were young semitransients undisturbed by the ghostly quality of the place, it was occupied, permanently by older people: a menagerie of the rejected, the banished, existing in the tenebrous rooms.

"Lambie-pie, my name is Gene de Lancey."

A woman of about sixty had pushed herself into the hallway to introduce herself. A haunted presence, she had moved soundlessly, barefoot, into the corridor, as if not to call attention to herself until she spoke. She wore a bright silk kimono, now faded, and an artificial flower in her hair. In the murky light of the corridor, she postured before me, shifting from one pose to another, raising her chin often as if about to be photographed, choosing the best angle for her heavily made-up face.

"Lambie-pie," she said, "I'm glad you'll be our neighbor. Steve and I—he's my fourth husband; my first was a count—we entertain often, we play roulette and you'll be welcome, lambie-pie." She spoke in a refined tone.

"Thank you."

As noiselessly as she had appeared, she disappeared along the corridor. I wondered who would come to play "roulette" in her cramped apartment.

Since the time with Mr. Klein, I had hunted Forty-second Street nightly for paid sex, each time feeling a rush of fulfillment that lasted until the next paid encounter, a higher rush that, too, needed to be sustained with more. When—once or twice—I saw Mr. Klein picking up one of the other loiterers, I felt a pang of sadness, regret; but I avoided him. The initiatory interlude with him had provided all that I would allow it to. A rigid set of requirements was evolving for my life on the erotic streets, and the main one was this: to be desired without reciprocation.

Late one night, as I walked into the lobby of the Casbah, which still boasted a sleepy Jamaican doorman, I encountered a reed-thin man, about seventy, and a woman even more frail, who leaned on his arm so that both walked askew. He wore a frayed tuxedo, she a gauzy dress with a patched train. As I waited for the elevator, two more couples as old as the pair in the lobby were exiting. One woman wore an old tiara; the other carried a sequined fan. The men wore mothy tuxedos. They had to be Gene de Lancey's guests.

The party had broken up. As I walked to my room, wanting to pass by Gene de Lancey's rooms unnoticed, she slunk out in a gossamer gown, her face painted even more outrageously than when I had first seen her.

"Lambie-pie! Please come in. Please, please, *please!*"

"I'm—"

"Please!" she said, desperate.

I went into her apartment and saw what I thought was an odd, complex toy. It was a miniature roulette set. Around the apartment were remnants of what must have been an attempt to create a grand party: flowery paper cups, bottles of cheap champagne. The apartment was suffused with wilted desolation. On a couch a man snored. "My fourth husband," she dismissed him. "Lambie-pie, please sit down, please."

"OK, for a short while, I'm—"

"For a short while, yes. Only a short while."

Noiselessly she glided away to a shelf in the room. Noiselessly she returned, holding before me an old magazine, *Vanity Fair,* from decades ago. On the cover was a drawing or a photograph of a beautiful woman, her chin up, her eyes half-lidded, lips glowing, parted. One hand touched her cheek.

I looked up and saw Gene de Lancey, her chin up, her eyes half-lidded, lips glowing, parted. One hand touched her cheek. "Who?" She pointed at the illustration.

"It's you," I said. "Of course."

She closed her eyes, her hand at her throat. Tears squeezed out. "You recognize me? I haven't changed?"

"It looks exactly like you."

She bent over me and kissed me. "Lambie—"

I stood up. "I'm tired, really tired, I've been up all night. I'll visit another time."

My room in the Casbah was so hot that, despite the fan I kept running, I left the door open so that air might be able to enter through the space that separated one wing from another. The typewriter remained dormant on the desk.

"Lambie-pie!"

I sat up.

Gene de Lancey was at the open door. She reeked of alcohol although it was, perhaps, ten in the morning. She was wearing one of her kimonos and was barefoot as usual; her face was already starkly made up, like a mask of someone who had died long ago. She was holding an offering toward me, a candied apple.

"Thank you, Gene." I took the apple.

"Lambie—"

"Yes."

"We never know—do we, lambie?—what we will become."

Talking to herself? She had assumed a vague look. She shot up, rigid, her face so livid her mouth seemed to be bleeding red. She gasped, uttered a cry, fled.

During the time I remained in that building, I did not see her again, although, one night I heard the sounds of the miniature roulette wheel and the players in her rooms and a voice—trilling laughter, hers—over it all.

The cigarette remained touching her lips as if reluctant to separate . . . that memory of the kept woman . . . seeking connections . . . hinting of an essential discovery before evaporating.

★ ★ ★

I began extending my hunting turf, sometimes only exploring. I hung around the Village, the fountain. Queens lined some of the ledges, camping, screeching, commenting on passersby. If someone insulted them, or if they perceived an insult, they would lash out with the precision of expert swordsmen, uncannily locating the most vulnerable targets, a suggestion of sexual doubt masquerading as hostility. Made-up as stridently as possible under the law, painted eyes scouring the streets restlessly, living on the edge—they had nothing to lose.

I explored Central Park at night. Along the edges of the park, men idled into the late hours, a shadowy silent choreography of exile courtship, the same slow, silent, universal dance I had witnessed in Paris. Although I knew this was not hustling turf, I would sit on one of the benches for hours watching attractive men moving in pairs melding into the shadows of the park.

My sister Olga forwarded a letter from Wilford, asking where I was now, telling me where I could reach him in New York. But I didn't want to contact him, not yet; that close friendship from a different past would fit awkwardly in my present life on the streets.

My mother wrote as often as before. So did Olga. She and her husband, now with two children, were moving to Los Angeles. Her husband had a good job lined up in an airplane factory. Now my mother would be even more alone. The separation money I had left her would be exhausted; Robert would, as always, take care of her. I would not—nor did I ever—send her street money.

I took a classified advertisement in the *New York Times*. I listed brief credentials from my army jobs. I received several calls at the public telephone in the hallway of the Casbah. The ringing annoyed the tenants after some—a few I had never seen before—poked their heads out of their rooms to ask, "Is it for me?" Being told no, they slammed their doors.

A man on the telephone invited me for an interview in his office on Fifth Avenue.

The lettering on the wide oak door of a glistening tall building identified a publication whose name I didn't recognize. In an impressive suite, a secretary led me into an inner office. Behind an imposing desk sat a man, heavy, with dark hair, thick glasses, about fifty; he looked like a giant toad.

"And what is your real goal?" he asked me after I had recited my army credentials.

"To be a writer," I was glad to say, since he was involved in publishing.

"Have you written anything?"

"Yes. A novel. It's called *Pablo!*—with an exclamation mark," I emphasized. That was significant to me, since only once in the novel was a character's name announced, in an exclamation.

"Oh—and it's about—?"

"A boy, a narcissistic boy who wants to be a dancer."

He removed his glasses, as if to see me better, closer up. "I like that, I like that."

I was thrilled. This seemed inordinately lucky, that on my first interview I would connect with someone who could help me artistically. Also, a job would allow me to call Wilford with confidence.

"Will you show it to me?"

The luck became unreal. "What about the job?"

"With your impressive army credentials?" He spread his hands to indicate how impressive. "Let's discuss it all later—and bring your novel."

He gave me a card and an address. We agreed on the time.

I turned up at another building, on Park Avenue, not far from the office I had been to, another glassy building. I assumed this was another office, perhaps that of someone else who would concur in my being given the job and, too, would be asked to read my novel, which I had brought with me excitedly.

"Is Mr. Taub expecting you?" asked the doorman.

"Yes."

"Your name?"

"John Rechy."

He scrutinized me before he called up, nodded, and led me to the elevator, providing me with a suite number.

I rang. Mr. Taub appeared. He was in a robe that swished audibly.

I hesitated. I had not expected an apartment.

"Oh, your manuscript." He held out his hand when he saw that I was carrying it; he eased it out of my hands. He glanced at the title. "*Pablo!*—yes, with an exclamation mark. Excuse"—he brushed his hand over his informal attire—"I like to relax when I come home from the office."

The apartment was large, luxurious, two stories.

I followed him into the living room—all soft, plushy furniture. I followed him upstairs. Rather, I followed my manuscript into his vast bedroom. He placed my manuscript in a drawer next to his bed, which looked like a tasteless king's—gathered drapery in back, held together by a large gold ring at the top.

"Sit down; let's be comfortable." He sat on the huge ornate bed and patted the mattress beside him.

I did not move from the door. "You said we were going to talk about the job. What is the job and what is the salary?" I could excuse myself for having withheld those questions earlier because of his eagerness to see my novel, and because of my anticipation.

"The job? Easy—for you. The salary? That will be up to you, how well you perform." The smile on his face was authoritative, knowing, a sneer.

"Let me have my manuscript back," I said.

"Oh, why? I want to read it. Now sit down."

He had adopted a commanding tone.

"Give me back my manuscript."

"I told you I'd read it, and I will. I'm sure you realize I have contacts with many agents, editors." That smile. He looked even more like a frog now.

"I want it back," I said firmly.

"Go ahead and leave if you want to," he yawned.

"Not without my manuscript."

"I'll read it—and then you can come back. I'll give *Pablo!* . . . with an exclamation mark," he smirked; "I'll give it back to you then. Now why don't you sit down with me?" He reached over and pressed his hand against the drawer where he had placed my manuscript.

Crazily, I thought how disappointed Wilford would be with me, that I had given the book he had praised to this man. I moved swiftly into the room, to stand close to him, assuming a tough posture learned on the street; it came easily. "Give my manuscript back to me, fucker."

He didn't budge, didn't wince. "Oh, come on, young man, don't make such drama out of it. You're here willingly, aren't you? And you did put that ad in the paper, didn't you?"

"For a job, yes!" I said, wondering if I had lost the tone of menace, if I was pleading. "Motherfucker—" It was the first time I had used the word that had shocked me in the army, a word other hustlers along Times Square used randomly. "You never asked my age, did you, Taub?" On the streets, I passed for someone younger.

The smile froze. "What does that mean?"

"That I'm underage," I lied. "The doorman asked me how old I was when I said I was coming up here, and I told him."

He opened the drawer and handed me the manuscript.

Outside, as I passed the doorman, he looked at me with clear contempt. I didn't care. New street cunning had come easily.

I did get a job, in a public relations office across from the United Nations building, with a political organization I knew nothing about, with the fancy name of American Heritage Foundation. I worked for a kind old-time journalist, drunk by midday, who wrote news releases about the foundation that was, now, sponsoring something called "Crusade for Freedom." That meant little to me. I sat at my own desk, typing form letters individually to various people across the country, explaining that their donation would allow a "freedom balloon" to be launched over the Berlin Wall by a group of patriotic citizens. I was then unaware of the political implications of what I was typing out by rote.

I sent my mother money regularly.

Every day I rushed to receive my mail from the Jamaican doorman at the Casbah—my mother's long-distance unpunctuated blessings, with notes from my brother Robert—"Need anything, brother?"—appended to her letters.

There was a long letter from my sister Olga. In anticipation of all her news, I didn't read it until I was lying down in the small bed in my room in the Casbah. Their move to Los Angeles had been delayed by expenses. Robert was going out with "a real horror, a weird woman" who powdered her face heavily in order to look white, not dark.

Then this:

"Marisa Guzman was in El Paso. She came to visit her mother, who's been sick. Marisa brought her lots of presents. Tina was there, too, to visit her sister. Señor's wife asked Marisa if she was still de Leon's kept woman. Marisa said yes and that she was happy. Señor's wife rejected the presents. "'They're bought with tainted money,'" my sister quoted her angrily. "She even blamed Marisa for Señor's death by returning for my wedding. She told her the least she could have done was to disguise herself so no one would have recognized her."

I remembered the spry old woman who had appeared to be free of Señor. His curses on his daughter must have festered within her during all those years.

At the bottom of her letter my sister had written, obviously hurriedly, probably having heard the news just as she was about to seal the letter:

"I'm sure now that the columnist Alicia married doesn't know who she really is! How is that possible? More later."

I put the letter aside and closed my eyes, remembering Isabel—no, it was Marisa as I had first seen her, the elegant, poised outcast, smoking, alone.

Me during the Vietnam-era protests. *City of Night* original cover.

Los Angeles, early seventies

Right after *City of Night* was released,
New York City

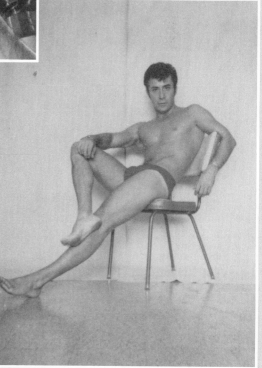

Me as Johnny Rio, Los Angeles

Me as Johnny Rio, taken in the desert, El Paso

Griffith Park, cruising, early seventies, Los Angeles

Late nineties, early 2000

23

I left my job at the American Heritage Foundation, finally aware that it was a right-wing group that stood for everything I was growing to detest. I gave notice, saying good-bye to the kind alcoholic man who had hired me. I took the elevator down. On another floor, the door slid open, and there stood—

I gasped. Was it possible? Yes, but if so, why wasn't everybody else gasping? There stood—

Eleanor Roosevelt!

Noting my reaction, she smiled down at me—I had never seen anyone so tall and imposing—and said, "Good morning, young man."

I was so overcome with awe that I wasn't able to answer.

She had been a hero of my father's. Another revelation: The man committed to liberal, even radical, causes was the man who had turned into my enemy, a wounded enemy.

When the elevator landed on the floor of her office and the grand lady exited, I shouted after her, "Good morning, Mrs. Roosevelt!"

The interlude on the elevator was an appropriate ending to my stint at the right-wing foundation.

★   ★   ★

I moved out of the shadows of the Casbah. I rented a room in an old, elegant building on upper Riverside Drive. Outside my window was a strip of park that ran along the river. In the late afternoon, a splash of sun on the water reflected into my room. I chose the room because of that.

I began a pattern. Because of my experience with courts-martial in the army, I could easily get a temporary job with lawyers, through a specialized agency that had responded to my earlier ad. I would work a few days, then stop. I returned to the hustling turfs. Progressively, even while I was working, I would hustle. I did not need the money. I needed only sex money, the uncommitting admiration that it affirmed.

I called Wilford. He was delighted to know I was in New York. Yes, yes, we would get together.

I wanted to do something special for him, to re-establish our friendship, to establish it firmly, on what I wanted to be a new level. There was a communal kitchen in the wing I lived in. I did not know how to cook—my mother would have shooed us out of the kitchen if we had attempted to cook. I had seen in a grocery store nearby, cans of "chicken à la king." There was a recipe on each can; all it required was buttered toast points. I bought three cans and a loaf of wheat bread. I bought three avocados. I bought a bottle of white wine I chose because it seemed expensive. I bought a salad dressing that looked pretty. I invited Wilford to dinner.

Before he arrived, I hastily heated the cans of chicken à la king in pots, scrubbed thoroughly, provided in the community kitchen. I toasted the bread and cut it into triangles. I cut the avocados into wedges. I borrowed some dishes and a corkscrew from a man who lived across from me and would always open the door when he heard me. "Who's the lucky party?" he asked me.

I showered and dressed, making sure I looked terrific.

"Wilford!"

"Johnny!"

We hugged. There was catching-up talk, rushed. Was I going to Columbia? Had his play gone well in Urbana? Would it come to New York?

"You look great," he said. "As vain as ever?"

"More than ever," I said. "You look fine, too, Wilford. It's wonderful to see you."

Then it all became strained. It was time for dinner.

I filled the plates in the kitchen and brought them into my room, pretending—though I didn't dare claim it—that I had cooked. I arranged everything on a small desk, part of the furnished room.

"It's all awfully good," Wilford said. But he wasn't eating.

"I love chicken à la king," I told him. "And avocados."

"Johnny—" Wilford smiled. "You didn't have to do this, you know."

"Do what?"

"Uh—cook."

"I didn't really cook anything," I confessed what I suspected he must have known.

"Oh." Then he burst into laughter.

I joined him. He pushed his plate away. "I can't stand chicken à la king, and I hate avocados. Let's just have some wine, OK?"

I was relieved. Even to me, the meal had been awful, parts of the saucy mixture—hardly any chicken—tasting cold, others only warm.

I sat on the couch, which was the bed when it was opened and pulled out. Wilford stood up from the desolate table and sat next to me. He moved closer. He placed his hand on one of my legs, just inches from my fly. I closed my eyes. I would force my-self to cope with whatever happened now. My body refused.

"Johnny—"

I stood up quickly. "Wilford, I—it's just that—"

Standing, too, he smiled at me. "I understand, I really do," he said. He looked at his watch. "God, it's late! I have to go. Dinner was great."

We both laughed.

"We'll stay in touch?"

"Oh, yes, of course."

I never saw him again; neither of us ever called again; we never wrote again. Eventually, he became one of the most respected directors on Broadway. I delighted in the triumphs of this man who would remain one of the most important, and loved, people in my life.

I was twenty-three, still able to pass as someone younger; but each day, it seemed, new drifters appeared on the hustling streets, picked up before the rest of us who had become familiar. We avoided looking at each other when the time without connection stretched out.

With my duffel bag and my hardly used typewriter, I impulsively left New York in September, before it would turn cold. The day I left, the city I had grown tired of looked uncommonly beautiful, the leaves still green, fluttering in a cool breeze but turning yellow.

"*M'ijo!*" My mother's arms engulfed me.

Mine engulfed her.

My sister Olga, packing in preparation for their move—finally— to Los Angeles, had gained a few more pounds after giving birth to a girl, but she was as beautiful as ever, and every bit as much the gossip. After "catching up," she launched easily into how she was sure the columnist didn't know who his wife really was.

Tina—who, apparently, still cared about her daughter despite her frequent declarations otherwise and her relegation of Isabel "to the mercy of God"—had been informed by her contact in San Francisco, "a true friend," that the columnist continued to write about his "Spanish wife from New Orleans."

"What I'd like to know is how she's kept the truth from him," my sister said, verbalizing the recurring consideration.

I wondered about that, too, though it was possible that the columnist might be withholding his belated discovery for reasons of public embarrassment. I remembered the pretty young woman who had cried that night in my uncle's Cadillac when I had attempted to light her cigarette and had seen her hands trembling.

There was something I had to do, here in El Paso.

I returned to "Alligator Plaza," San Jacinto Plaza, where the laughter of queens had floated lazily into the summer night when I was still in school. Had I been courting their attention, years earlier, when I had gone out of my way to pass by them? They were gone now, the painted ones, the wonderfully brazen ones. They had been replaced by men sitting alone, walking about idly, talking softly to someone, then moving on.

I leaned against the stone railing around the fountain; the sleepy alligators that once lingered there were long gone. An older man sidled up to me. "Hello, young man."

I turned to face someone whom I thought for a moment I recognized. No, not at all.

"Hi."

"You traveling across the country?" he asked me. His voice quivered.

"Yes," I pretended.

"You must be broke," he said, trying to sound friendly, his voice forced low, speaking words I knew he had spoken before in this very plaza.

"Yeah, I am, I—" The role I had adopted on Times Square played itself.

"I would be happy to help you out if—"

I recognized him. He was my high school math teacher.

My pose shattered before this lonely man from my boyhood.

"It was nice to talk to you," I said, surrendering the pose, even the tone of my voice—and now grasping for the right words that would hurt him least, disappoint him least. "I lost track of time— I'm leaving on the Greyhound bus in less than an hour. Really good talking to you, I really mean it."

He drifted away.

I had not succeeded in my intent, to test in El Paso the person I had become in Times Square.

My sister Olga finished the arrangements for moving, and with her family, she left El Paso. "Come to Los Angeles, little brother," she told me. "You can stay with us as long as you want."

Los Angeles, yes.

Once again I carried my mother's departing blessing with me— each parting more painful than the last—as I traveled to Los Angeles with my duffel bag and the Royal typewriter after a few more days in El Paso.

In the Greyhound bus as it traveled across the New Mexico desert, I dozed and woke up startled to look out the window and see giant stone formations like prehistoric beasts advancing along the highway.

In the morning, and on a yellow-gray plain out of which cactus bloomed, the bus arrived at the border of California. A small square building the color of dirt indicated an immigration checkpoint.

A hefty immigration officer entered the bus, the whoosh of its doors seeming to suck him in. He walked along the aisle, glancing right and left at everyone.

In the back row of seats, a Mexican family, a man and a woman with a little girl, sat rigidly. They had been so quiet since we had all boarded that I hadn't noticed them until now.

"Get off, *amigos*." Without explaining why he was taking them off—because they were clearly migrant Mexicans—he marched them off the bus. I looked back as they all disappeared into the interrogation site. The bus rolled on into the desert. A sign proclaimed:

CALIFORNIA

24

The bus depot was in the center of downtown Los Angeles. It was bustling with people, seething with activity. I left my duffel bag and typewriter in a rented locker and walked out. I wouldn't call my sister right away. With the instinct I had developed for picking up signposts—the bus station was one—I knew I would find, nearby, an extension of the turf I had left in New York.

I crossed the street, one block, two. Fifth Street. Main Street. There it was—a row of sleezy bars, all-night movie theaters, fast-food stands.

Harold's bar. A long bar with ratty booths, faded drawings of beach scenes on the walls. A bartender swishing and giggling with men at the counter. Two factions I recognized immediately: young men—a few tougher-looking here—and those looking for them, some wearing jackets, loosened ties, as if they had just left office jobs.

"Oh, my God, look what just walked in! Hold me, girls, I'm going to fai-aiaiaiai-nt!"

It was the swishy bartender screechingly welcoming me to Los Angeles.

★ ★ ★

Instead of calling my sister to pick me up, I took a cab to her address, to surprise her. She lived in a pretty bungalow in a court with five units. Flowers bloomed in a small courtyard with two grand palm trees.

"Little brother!"

"Beautiful sister!"

Gorgeous as ever, perhaps even more so, my sister had lost her excess weight, a fact she exhibited by whirling around before me. I accepted her invitation to stay with her; her husband had agreed. I would sleep in a small room off the dining room. I got along with her two children, the boy I knew and the new daughter. I sang them the song my sister Blanca had taught me in anticipation of an invitation from Shirley Temple, in response to my offer to join her: "Come along and follow me, to the bottom of the sea."

To be sure that I would be allowed to pay for groceries during the few days I would stay here, I went with my sister to the nearby Safeway.

An Anglo woman, leaving the store, glanced at us, detoured, and hurried back breathlessly to approach us.

"You're—!" the woman began in awe, addressing my sister.

My sister waited, courting some marvelous comparison, I knew. It came.

"—You're Ava Gardner, aren't you? But what are you doing in this part of town?"

My sister laughed her terrific, delighted laughter. I wondered whether she would playfully tell the woman that she was the movie star, and make up a story about why she was shopping here, borrowing from some movie or other for dramatic effect.

"I love this part of the city," she told the woman and smiled warmly. "No, ma'am, I'm not the movie star. I'm Olga Guzman."

Had she said that before, in front of me? When? I tried to remember. *I am* . . . When, before, had that occurred? The memory eluded me in a disturbing way.

★   ★   ★

The Korean War was over; more than fifty thousand U.S. soldiers had died among countless more Koreans. For what terrible reason so much devastation?

Had Acting Corporal Bailey survived?

After a few happy days with my sister and her family, I rented a room in a hotel in downtown Los Angeles, on Hope Street. The building was a few blocks away from Pershing Square and Main Street. One side of it faced the tall YMCA residential building.

Not since I had reacted so powerfully to Paris had I felt the exhilaration I felt in Los Angeles. I embraced the warm days, the cool misty nights, the sight of palm trees everywhere, tall, indifferent, elegant, strung along the streets in regal rows, shifting away from sea breezes. Every block in the city burst with flowers—flowered shrubs, flowered trees, flowers everywhere, every color, some like colored butterflies, others like birds—and roses, roses, all colors, roses even in abandoned lots. And beyond it all, the ocean, land's end, the edge of the country, the last stop before the sun set, golden-red.

And Pershing Square.

The size of a large city block, the square was green with velvet grass, lush with trees and flowers along several paths that led to a fountain in the center, silver strings of water spouting out in shifting arcs. At one corner was a bold statue of Beethoven covered in a mossy patina. All about, preachers thumped their Bibles; evangelists tinkled their tambourines and sang out "Hallelujah!" Neatly dressed office workers took a break at midday from the surrounding offices, sitting facing the sun along flowered curbs. Male hustlers loitered about. Clients paused, walking on, waiting. Here and there, a small group of queens held court, having arranged their clothes to look as much like drag as possible without trespassing into "masquerade," a man dressed to suggest a woman, which was then illegal.

There was an easy mingling among hustlers and queens here, a camaraderie absent in New York. As I strolled along the curved paths, one or another of the hustlers would greet me: "Howzit goin', man?" . . . "Just got in, huh, man?" A queen would squeal approval.

In a few days I had met Chuck, a sanguine, lazy cowboy; Skipper, once the most sought-after hustler in Hollywood; Buddy, a kid, just arrived, always a green, gullible kid; the fabulous Miss Destiny with her dreams of glory; tough, tattooed, dangerous Tiger; Trudi, the cutest queen in the world; Pauline, the ugliest—all those, and so many others among whom I would live and whose lives I would glimpse, sometimes only for fleeting moments.

But whom I would always remember.

The more I continued to explore the world I lived in, the harsher it was capable of looking at times, as if, in burrowing deeper into it, I was being forced to see more of it, more clearly. To experience its unique excitement, I had to experience its dangers. There was always a current of tension, tinged with possible violence in encounters among exiles and outlaws and those who sought them, and in the threat of arrest. That current found its voice in the growled words pouring out of jukeboxes, hard rock-and-roll moans in the hustling bars.

In that charged atmosphere, the world I had again moved into was making constant demands of allegiance, further initiations, powerful challenges, and commands to move closer to its edge, or to move out, a visitor.

At the Waldorf—the most hard core of the hustling bars in downtown Los Angeles, a bar where the harshest queens challenged any hostility as they perched on gutted stools next to restless hustlers, demanding instant connections once desire was established—I met a man, "in town to see the low life." As we stepped outside, he halted. "You're not queer, are you?"

The question did not surprise me. Even more assertively than along Times Square, where "straightness" was assumed without declaration, playing "straight"—"trade" for sale—was demanded of the hustlers. I had heard rigid variations from potential clients: "I don't want you to touch me, you understand?" . . . "You're not gay, right?" . . . "I'm not looking for a queer." It was a time that demanded deception.

I answered the man I was with: "No, man, shit, I'm not a fucking queer, man, shit."

"OK. Let's go."

At his hotel a couple of blocks away, he went down on me, insistently trying to keep me hard while restraining me from coming, until, finally, I became soft and gave up.

My cock soft in his mouth, he jerked himself off, quivering, shouting loudly. Then he lay back in his shorts, indifferently, yawning.

"I don't think I should pay you, you weren't any good, just lay there, didn't even come."

"I told you before we came here what was involved," I said.

"You tell yourself a lot of things, don't you, punk?" he said.

I dressed, stood over him. "Give me the money we agreed on, fucker," I said.

"You were the worst I've ever had," he taunted. "Here."

Half of what we had agreed on. "You owe me more," I said, snatching the money.

"Fuck you."

"I said pay me what we agreed to."

"And I said, fuck you."

"Listen, motherfucker," said a voice I recognized as my own. "If you don't give me what we agreed on, I'll take it." I grabbed his pants from the floor and went through his pockets to locate his wallet. For awful moments, it was as if I was viewing myself robbing this man, and I was trying to recognize myself.

The man sat up. I held onto his pants, pulling them away from his grasping hands.

"I left my wallet downstairs in the safe," he said, his voice losing some of its bravado. "Here, I kept the exact amount you asked for." He threw more money onto the bed.

I grabbed it. "I want more, motherfucker." Now the words were easy; my actions were easy.

"I told you—"

I went to the drawer next to the bed. I pulled everything out; I threw the few contents onto the floor, some underclothes, keys. No wallet there.

He lifted the telephone and spoke into it: "There's a guy up here, he's robbing me, threatening me, call the cops, send someone—"

I knew he wasn't talking to anyone; he would incriminate himself—and I saw his finger on the cradle.

I went through another drawer, throwing out the contents, a hotel Bible, some nonprescription medications. I went through the jacket he had hung in the closet, through the upper shelves.

He stood, dropping the lifeless telephone.

I replaced it on the cradle quickly—so the person at the desk would not inquire. The man's belongings were strewn all over the room.

"I swear to you, I swear I left my wallet downstairs. If you come to the desk with me, I'll get it, I promise."

I found the wallet. Shoved into a corner of the closet, under a suitcase. I opened it and took out all the money. I threw the wallet onto the floor.

Before I closed the door, I heard him shout: "You son of a bitch! You're not foolin' anyone, none of you guys are, you're all as queer as I am!"

As I left the building, I heard a gasp—my own. The person who had ransacked the man's room had earned credentials to be true to the streets, but he was now retreating. As I stepped into the lurid streets, I felt like crying. I thought, I'm me again.

Longing for another life that would not contain what I had done—to attempt to flush the incident out of my mind—I called my sister to ask whether I might come to dinner. "Of course, little brother, of course; I'll make something special—I've learned to cook."

She had. She made a scrumptious roast. Her husband helped her clear the table. My nephew played a piece he had just learned on his accordion; my niece spun about in what she thought was a grand ballet. I applauded extravagantly.

"Now everybody—out!" my sister said. "I want to catch up on news with my little brother!"

The children had left the television on. Senator Joseph McCarthy, scrunching before an open microphone, was pointing at a man off-camera testifying before the House Un-American Activities Committee.

"Asshole," my sister surprised me by saying when the camera focused on McCarthy; it surprised me not only because of the word she had used, but because I hadn't known she was aware of the dangerous political climate taking over the country. She clicked off the image of the scruffy man.

"Now!"

I settled to hear about the person I was sure she would be discussing—and to welcome the warmth of another life.

"Remember Alicia's cousin Lenchito?"

Vaguely, I did. He was a kid then, almost blind, his eyes washed with a bluish mist. Still, he was able to walk around briskly, re-markably well.

"He's eighteen now. The poor thing has to carry a blind cane to cross the street. A little saint, so kind."

The way she was propping her story meant it would be one of her best. It had always amused me to try to catch her in an inconsistency in her dramas, but I had never been able to.

"He's so moved that Tina can't get her own daughter to answer her letters—"

"Tina has Isabel's new address, sister?"

"The hired detective, remember?" my sister chastised me. "Tina's letters are returned—no such person here—"

"You said Tina gave up on her."

"How can a mother stop caring?" Having reasserted the unassailabilty of a mother's devotion, she went on: "Lenchito got a paid invitation to address some kind of blind people's convention in San Francisco, and he promised Tina he'd locate Alicia, no matter what; she's his aunt, you remember."

I didn't dare ask for more details about the blind people's convention; I was too eager to hear her news.

"So when he had finished his speech at the blind convention— he got an ovation—he took a cab to the address of that famous columnist. Oh, what Lenchito faced!"

My sister was becoming even better at building suspense. She was able to guess the ending of any episode of *Alfred Hitchcock Presents* on television, to everyone else's chagrin because she ruined the story.

"Lenchito got out of the cab and he made his way to the gate of the house." My sister was pacing her delivery as if to underscore Lenchito's weary journey to the gate. "A maid answered the buzzer. Lenchito identified himself as a nephew from El Paso. He told her he was blind, so that Alicia would be sure to know who he was. There was a long pause."

My sister paused, long. Then: "The maid came back: 'There is no one here by that name,' she told Lenchito."

"Maybe he asked for Alicia Gonzales."

"He used all her names," my sister snapped. "He's not dumb, you know. He was so angry he beat the gate with his cane."

I couldn't help it; I laughed. I imagined Lenchito beating at the gate with his blind cane, something like Morris pounding on the Heiress's door in the movie. "I'm sorry for laughing, Olga, but that sounds like the ending of *The Heiress*."

My sister was not fazed. "It does. I suppose Lenchito saw it—"

"Lenchito's blind, Olga."

"—or heard about it." She shook her head. "All I know is that Alicia refused to see her blind cousin and has the damn nerve to claim she isn't who she is."

Isabel Franklin was becoming legendary, a spectacular fraud.

The encounter with the man whose hotel room I had ransacked recurred in my mind. I justified it—he had insulted me, had backed off from our agreement. I stayed away from Main Street and Pershing Square.

Extending the pattern I had adopted in New York, I telephoned a temporary-help agency whose clients were attorneys, citing my "legal experience" in the army and asking for an interview. In an unfriendly tone, a woman told me that her agency no longer employed men.

I sensed that something was off; she had said "no longer." As curious as I was annoyed, I called again, determined to charm her—"You have a unique voice; you must have been an actress"—into granting me an interview. She did—"Let's talk."

I turned up at an office in a building downtown. A middle-aged man and a woman sat behind juxtaposed desks. Both were surprisingly friendly, asking me to sit down, to tell them more

about myself. I told them I had been in the 101st Airborne Infantry Division.

The woman turned to the man, her husband and partner in
the agency. "Yes?" she asked him.

"Yes," he echoed, smiling. "The 101st Infantry Division, eh?"
the man commended.

"We had to be sure," the woman explained, "that you weren't
one of those sissies flooding Los Angeles from Washington."

I knew what she meant. Senator McCarthy was extending his
hunt from "commies" in government to "perverts" in Washington.
There had followed an exodus of homosexuals to Los Angeles.

It pleased me to think that the woman's husband might be gay,
closeted even from her.

As I left with my first assignment—"with an important law
firm, one of our best clients," the man said, trying to impress me—
the woman called out in a most matter-of-fact tone, as if it didn't
matter at all, not at all, a cast-off remark: "Of course they will ask
us if you're homosexual . . ." She paused. I turned to face her.
". . . and we'll be able to assure them that—?"

"You can assure them I'm not," I said.

"Obviously not," the man seemed, mildly, to chastise the
woman for even asking. "He was in the 101st Airborne Infantry
Division."

In the following weeks, the agency sent me out to several offices,
whenever I wanted the work. The jobs paid well; I sent my mother
money steadily. I typed court reports, transcribed depositions, did
research on legal cases. I was well liked in the offices where I worked.
I flirted with the women and they flirted with me, finding me "really
cute." One maneuvered to keep me after hours with her. Sensing
what she intended, I told her I had a date.

No one in those offices, or at the agency, would suspect that, after work, at first sometimes and then fervently every night, I was going to Pershing Square and Main Street to hustle.

Some afternoons, in the building I lived in on Hope Street, I would go up to the roof to sunbathe in brief trunks. A side of the YMCA building faced the roof at a distance not too removed. Occasionally, I would look up toward the windows across the way and I would see someone signaling. If there were further signals of attraction, I would motion that I was going downstairs. In my room, I would put my pants on; then I would walk out to the front. There I would meet whoever had signaled. Often, it didn't work; those who had signaled were looking for a mutual connection, a mutual attraction. The few times it did work out as a hustle, I would ask the person to come up to my room.

Responding once to such a signal from a man at the window, I went downstairs to meet him.

"Hi," he said; he was good-looking, about thirty.

It wouldn't work out; he would be searching for a mutual unpaid connection. I wanted to defuse any anger the mistaken intentions would create, but he was already asking the usual question that preceded mutual casual sexual encounters:

"What do you do?"

"Uh, nothing, you know."

The smile faded. "You mean you're one of those guys that just lies back and expects—" I could tell he would now attempt to put me down. That was OK if it made him feel less rejected.

"Actually," I tried to do this tactfully, "I was on my way to Pershing Square—"

"To hustle?"

"Yeah."

"You go only for money, huh? And who the hell do you think would pay *you?* Well, let me give you some good advice: You just go on upstairs to your room, pay yourself, and fuck yourself."

Again, I immersed myself in the life of downtown Los Angeles.

Almost regularly, on my way to Pershing Square, I went to the public library a few blocks away. To assert a connection to my earlier life, I sat at one of the long wooden tables reading for hours. The old, impressive building, as solid as a stone temple and pervaded by the musty, oddly sweet smell of books, was a haven from the turbulence of the street life I would soon join, sometimes after only a few restless minutes, at other times during long lulling hours stretching into night.

I reread familiar books—Lorca, and I remembered Barbara (where was she now?) and Wilford, whose success I continued to follow in newspapers and magazines and whom I remembered with sad warmth. I discovered writers I had not read: Camus, Sartre, more of the metaphysical poets I had been introduced to by Dr. Sonnichsen—and Hart Crane, T. S. Eliot, more of Blake, reading pages of one, moving to another, returning, roaming back and forth trying to grasp all urgently, reading "newer" writers, Norman Mailer, Nabokov, Calder Willingham, Styron.

At first I would not check books out, because that meant I would have to carry them with me to Pershing Square and Main Street, and my pose of being only a street-smart hustler would be seriously compromised. When I eventually did check books out, I would do so in the morning, returning with them to leave in my hotel room. Walking back to my hotel room with two books I had checked out—having lingered at the library into early afternoon—I saw one of the hustlers I knew from Pershing Square walking toward me with a queen I also recognized. I dashed quickly across

the street before they could see me with the books that would os-
tracize me from my other world.

The night I pulled out of the library shelves the first volume
of *Remembrance of Things Past,* I didn't leave the library until the
guards began clearing it out for closing. The next day, I went to
the library when it opened in the morning, to spend the whole day
reading more of Proust, swept away by the images and rhythms,
the various lives flowing in and out of the pages—so moved that I
would stop reading, search out another writer in order to return
anew to this wondrous discovery, always returning to the passage
of magical recollection in the Overture:

"*And suddenly the memory returns . . .*"

Outside the 3-2-6, pushers loitered openly. That bar was a grayish
yellow, darkened into brown by cigarette smoke curling over gutted
booths, jukebox winking, leering at the sights, queens flirting with
hustlers, hustlers flirting back with them, considering them women.

Like a scared little boy, a queen would approach the entrance
to the bar. One step inside, in outcast-protected territory, she would
pause for a transformation. The collar of her "shirt" would be turned
up into a regal high collar; her fingers would dig into her hair,
fluffing it out into a corona; her hands would twist the tails of her
shirt into a knot, creating a midriff blouse; the tight pants became
toreador pants when squeezed and tucked at the waist. Attention
gained, the transformation accomplished, she strutted in proudly,
head tossed back.

I was sitting with Chuck the cowboy at the counter of Cooper's
Donuts on Main Street—a shabby after-hours hangout for queens,
hustlers, clients, and gay men just cruising—when two young
cops sauntered in. They paced the aisles, asking randomly for
identification, moving on without checking, harrassing, a favorite
cop pastime in gay turfs.

They paused at the door as if about to leave. Then they turned abruptly and pointed to the three people sitting nearest them at the counter: a lavish queen, Chuck, and me. "Come with us." Fear crept through my body. To object to the arbitrary order meant being handcuffed, with no chance of being released outside if the cops' game had played itself out by then. Chuck strutted to show he wasn't intimidated. I wanted to imitate him, but I felt afraid, cold, grasping the very real possibility of being jailed for nothing, charged with loitering, no visible means of support, resisting arrest.

A man sitting at the counter hooted drunkenly at the cops, daring them to come back and take him, motherfuckers. "Take us all, see if you can!" another taunted. The heckling spread. Emboldened, several men rose from their seats. Some moved out into the street, where we were being packed into the back of the squad car. The cops turned toward the growing group exiting the coffee shop.

Seizing the distraction—the queen shoving the cops away—Chuck and I scattered. As I ran into the cool night, I felt warmth returning, my breathing holding up. I passed the lavish queen. She had halted nearby, as if wondering why she was suddenly free.

Out of the doughnut shop, and, now, the closing bars, spilled more men—a dozen, more—flinging gathered trash at the cops, forcing them back into the squad car. Trapped, the cops called for backup. Defiance became almost festive. A queen danced around the isolated squad car; two men rocked it. Sirens wailing as if wounded, other squad cars entered the area, forcing men to dodge before them. Cops spilled out, grabbing at anyone they could grasp, letting go to grab someone else taunting them.

When it was over—quelled by shots fired in warning, the street barricaded, a smoggy morning dawning—the denizens of the area walked away like veterans who had survived a battle in preparation for war.

I had run away from it. I had watched the defiance from across the street, enraged but not joining—and I had barely escaped being busted.

25

I moved out of the building on Hope Street. I rented a larger room near MacArthur Park, a large room, with a private entrance, in the rear of an attractive house.

In Pershing Square a young man named Luke appeared one afternoon. He immediately stood out because of his sensational appearance.

The cute queen Roxy saw him first: "Oh, my dears, will you look at what just came in? Carry me away to die!"

He was one of the handsomest hustlers I had ever seen. He was neither tall nor short, with brown hair, slightly curly; sun-tinted strands licked his forehead over perfect features. In the bright light of the sun, his eyes were agate blue. Tight sinews and muscles, a gymnast's muscles, showed even through his loose T-shirt. His skin had absorbed the sun into a golden tan.

He approached a group of us loitering in the square: three hustlers, two queens. "I'm Luke McHenry," he announced his full name, surprising everyone; most in the area remained nameless, or provided only a first name, often a nickname. His wide smile friendly, he extended his hand warmly in introduction to each of us, shaking one after the other, a gesture so exceptional that everyone was surprised into responding.

"You're gorgeous, babe," said Roxy, rolling her eyes and pretending to swoon.

I felt a pang of resentment, which other hustlers there must also have felt—they shuffled about; one spat on the floor. The guy was too good-looking. A man who had been shifting his attention back and forth among our group fixed his gaze on Luke, who did not seem aware of the furor his presence had created. He sat down on the ledge with the rest of us, joining in conversation about nothing; he had a soft Southern twang.

I left the park soon after, going to the movies. I hoped that Luke would be only briefly on the scene.

The next night, he was just arriving at the park. With him was an older man. The two were parting; Luke, smiling, extending his hand out to the man he had just been with, perhaps agreeing to connect again—the man kept looking back at him, wistfully.

"Hi, guy," Luke said to me. "Remember me, from earlier? My name's Luke McHenry." Again, the warmly extended hand.

"Hi," I said, walking away. I saw another man eyeing him and I didn't want to see him making out while I remained waiting.

"Aw, cummon, guy, let's just talk," he coaxed.

On top of it all, he was too fucking likable: not conceited; he didn't swagger. Had I seen *The Incredible Shrinking Man*? he asked me. A favorite, I answered. Had he seen a ragged little movie that had held me captive, *The Little Shop of Horrors*?

"Guy, I most split a gut," he said. Then I did feel a warmth for him, a warmth perhaps unwelcome.

When I left the park to go to Main Street, I saw him talking spiritedly to another hustler, a hoody-looking one who was popular in the park.

"The fag tried to blow me, man; he ain't no hustler; he's a fuckin' queer." It was the hoody-looking hustler I had seen on the earlier night with Luke, the same one who had spat on the ground when

Luke had first appeared. The hustler was talking loudly, contemptuously, spitting between words to underscore his disgust. A group had already gathered: two other hustlers, a queen.

I knew that he was talking about Luke, and that the indignation spreading to the others was being aroused because the rigid stance of masculinity demanded of hustlers had been exposed through the handsome new guy in the park.

"Yeah, man," the hustler was continuing, "he took me to this pad he's staying at, with this old guy, and I thought we were gonna hustle the guy, but the old guy wasn't there; so he starts gropin' me, pulled out my dick and—"

By evening, the word had spread among queens and hustlers, and the clients, that Luke was queer.

I went to Harold's Bar on Main Street; a man bought me a drink—bourbon and water, "a man's drink, huh?" the man had approved. I didn't go with him, drawn back to the park.

Luke McHenry was sitting on a ledge, alone. Despite the pull that had brought me back, I prepared to turn away, walk away, not compromise my own status by association.

"Hey, guy—"

He looked up at me. I backed up. I sat next to him.

"You heard what they're saying about me, guy?"

"Yeah."

"I've been here all night, no one's talked to me. The guy I was staying with—he kicked me out, said his family's coming to visit."

I understood. He had been spat out, the victim of a rigid code that made us all, in varying degrees, liars, demanding we deny any trace of mutual desire.

"Can you believe it, guy?"

Yes, I believed it. That world of excitement easily turned brutal, as it did now when two breezy queens spotted Luke. "Oooo, Lukeeee," one cooed, "I always knew you were my sister, baby."

"Night, night, Lukey-girl," the other tossed at him.

They paused ahead, bristling with glee, peering back. I knew how quickly their darts could be aimed at me just for sitting here with Luke, ignoring their taunts.

Inhaling, as if dredging up all his courage for what he would ask next, Luke said, "Guy, you got a pad of your own I can crash in, just tonight?"

I inhaled, preparing the harsh answer: No.

"Sure," I said.

"You can sleep on the floor," I told him too anxiously when we were in my rented room. "I'll put blankets on the floor for you."

"Sure," he said, "sure, guy, sure, thanks."

I got an extra blanket off my bed; I helped him spread it on the floor.

I got into my bed, leaving my shorts on.

Luke lay on the floor, in his shorts.

I was aware, through light from a window, that he had sat up, his bare legs gathered before him. When he stood, I saw his body gleaming in the dim light, the whiteness of his shorts emphasizing his tan.

He was waiting.

For what?

To tell me he was queer, that it was true?

Or to deny it?

Waiting for me to say that I was queer, too, or for me to deny it?

He waited.

I waited.

I watched the moon-tinted outline of the lithe physique.

"Guy—" he barely whispered, and moved one more step toward me.

I pretended to be asleep, pretended not to know how close he was to me, pretended not to be aware of his almost naked body, so close now, and yet I felt isolated in that stifled room, and sad. Long ago, at that ranch in Balmorhea, I had felt this alone when I had walked out into the cactus garden. Then, the image of the kept woman had unexpectedly soothed me. I tried to invoke that image this time, only to keep away the awareness of Luke: *As if deciding not to complete the smile, or because the memory aroused had turned bitter* . . . but when the summoned image came this time, it only added to the sadness I was feeling.

Luke McHenry returned to the blanket on the floor.

In the morning he was gone.

After the encounter with Luke McHenry, Pershing Square became oppressive to me. I was not making out as easily as when I had first appeared on the scene. I shrugged that off—tried to shrug it off—as having resulted from my apparent down mood, a negative attitude that kept me distant. Some of the hustlers I had known were gone—nobody on the scene even wondered where. Others replaced them, new faces, new bodies. I shifted my turf to Hollywood Boulevard.

At the time, the boulevard—tawdry, already aging, past its legendary glory of stars and limousines—was taken over by factions largely oblivious of each other, workers from nearby offices on lunch break, idle residents from adjoining neighborhoods, shoppers from all over the city, tourists from everywhere, photographing everything.

Along the blocks, masculine homosexuals cruised each other for mutual encounters, pausing idly as if window-shopping; "butch" hustlers and queens—less bold than those downtown—shared an exile's camaraderie. Although the word was out to be cautious—a Hollywood newspaper was goading and trumpeting "roundups of queers" on the boulevard—activity thrived from early in the day to late at night.

During the day, at the Golden Cup coffee shop, young men played slot machines in back, while eyeing and being eyed by prospective customers. Others loitered near an outdoor newsstand that boldly sold "physique magazines," wrapped in sealed plastic, with photographs of attractive young men, like an advertisement for the hustlers nearby.

On that street, I met a natty little man whom I would remember as looking like a rabbit; he even nibbled at his rosy lips. On the way to his car, he proudly boasted that he had approached me without trepidation of any sort because he knew that everyone he desired could be bought. In the area where he hunted, that was probably true.

The man, whose name was Otis, lived in a large house atop a graceful hill, where he took me to a dinner served by an older woman, his maid. Probably to probe more deeply to affirm his fantasy with me, he asked me what I aspired to. Disliking him, and not caring whether any further connection would occur—he had already ostentatiously given me several bills that I deliberately did not count, asserting my own indifference—I told him I was a writer, although the typewriter in my rented room remained idle except for letters home.

"Oh, dear," he said, "and you look so butch."

Perhaps to taunt me further with comparisons—I had sensed a distinct cunning in his maneuvers—he showed me a home movie he had made, an eight-millimeter flick popular at the time.

There appeared, entirely nude, a young man doing calisthenics. The film lasted no more than five minutes.

"I paid him fifty cents," Otis said.

"What?"

"Fifty cents. It was the Depression."

Then he surprised me by inviting me—why?—to go with him the next day to meet a famous Hollywood director. Curious about his motives—and about the director—I met him at the arranged time.

After being buzzed in through a wrought-iron gate, we entered a courtyard squalid with flowers. A giant swimming pool reflected marble columns. In a rotunda draped with blood-red bougainvillea, a table had been set for dinner outside. Nearby was an outdoor bar. Behind the bar was a handsome man of about thirty, perhaps older, mixing drinks.

"Oh, George," Otis trilled. "This is John, from the streets."

There stood George Cukor, famous as a "woman's director." He was an unattractive tall man with a jagged face and glasses that he peered over, as if to focus more clearly on me. With a nod, he signaled to the man tending bar to bring him a drink, predetermined. The man brought the prepared drink over. The director hardly looked at him.

Otis leaned over to whisper to the director while eyeing the bartender.

The director said, louder than a whisper, "Of course, you can have him."

We sat at a glass table; the bartender had not said a word. A black woman served a watery stew, while the director informed us that tomorrow Vivien Leigh would be his guest. No stew tomorrow, I thought. Now the "women's director" announced that he was going to tell a "funny story."

At the time Lana Turner was involved in a scandal swirling about the murder of her sleezy lover, Johnny Stampanato, a petty crook and gigolo. Lana Turner was suspected of the murder, although it was her daughter, Cheryl, who would finally be accused.

". . . And on the stand, Miss Turner, all prissy and prim," the director was saying, imitating a woman wiping tears melodramatically from her eyes, "couldn't even open her mouth to speak. Who would have thought that she had made her way up by using that very mouth—so expertly?" He roared with laughter as he made a loud ugly sucking sound.

"John is going to be a writer of renown," Otis announced. That was the reason the cunning little bastard had invited me here, to taunt both me and the director with information that would set us at odds.

The director fixed his eyes on me over his thick glasses—he looked like a perched hawk. "Oh? The last time I talked to a writer, I ended up in *Confidential* magazine," he said.

"Perhaps this time you'll end up in a book." I said that only to trump his remark.

The dinner turned colder than the stew.

On the drive back, Otis congratulated me: "Oh, I loved that you put him in his place. Of course, he did seem—didn't he?—to dislike you," he said. He looked at me, shook his little head and said, "What a pity, my dear, you have a young man's body and an old man's mind."

"Better," I said, "than having an old man's body and a young man's mind."

"Hmmmmm."

Those incidents, and others I experienced—and often acted in— along with similar events I heard about, caused me at times to view the world of hustling as an undeclared war between two factions on the same battlefield: hustlers and their clients. Hustlers had youth, but it was terminal; some were through in a few short seasons, fading into lingering ghosts on the streets. Buyers would continue to want new young bodies, always available in a steady stream, and then in turn replaced; but too often, buyers longed for more, what was not possible from those they sought it in: love. That imbalance generated tension often heightened by mutual disdain—among the two interlocked factions.

And then there were the cops, another faction.

None of those considerations—quickly shoved aside—kept me from performing on that battlefield.

VICE SWEEP NETS 100S OF DEVIANTS

A scurrilous Hollywood newspaper trumpeted that. It described raids along the streets, in and outside gay bars. A successful raid, "netting dozens of deviants," it said, had occurred at a "hidden club" in Topanga Canyon. Men dancing with men were arrested for committing an illegal act. Lesbians were ignored; it was legal for two women to dance together.

As I approached Selma a few nights later, I saw two plain-clothes cops stealthily approaching a car where two men were sitting. The cops pulled the two men out roughly, knocking one down on the sidewalk. "What was your head doing down there?" one cop shouted at the man on the ground. Handcuffed, the two men were driven away in a waiting squad car. The resultant charge of such a claim, real or heatedly trumped up—spoken by rote when two men were seen sitting together in a car—carried the possibility of confinement in prison.

As the reign of Senator McCarthy raged on in Washington, more homosexuals fled to Los Angeles. Arrests increased. Entrapment was epidemic. Courts and juries believed any testimony presented by cops. Unmarked cars pursued men to their homes. The police charged in without a warrant to arrest men during a suspected sexual encounter; men caught having sex in private were charged with a felony that dictated imprisonment for up to five years.

That was the time, those were the times, of lost jobs, of threatened shock therapy, of gay men beaten and dragged bloody out of bars, exposed to rape by heterosexual inmates in jail "holding tanks"—a time of bashings, invisible years-long incarcerations, suicides, uninvestigated murders.

That was the time, those were the times, of denial, of subterfuge, of defensive lying. Even in gay bars, the accusation of being gay might be rebutted with anger by men cruising.

But nothing stopped the sex; nothing stopped the cruising. Life went on along with the violence and the denials.

Those were the times I lived in.

At the Carousel Bar at the very edge of Venice beach, queens dared to appear in drag—faces painted heavily as defiant masks. Tough hustlers, often tattooed, roamed shirtless, sometimes doubling as pushers. Among those who came to buy—or just to cruise each other from the beach—there were usually a few women, strident, incongruously elegantly dressed women considered "fag hags," slumming with wealthy homosexuals who were showing them "the lower depths of gay life." The Carousel was a loud, dim, crowded, seething, smoky bar pulsing and pounding with the rock music that overwhelmed the sound of waves lashing the coastline not far away.

I sat at a coarse wooden table with a man I had met on the beach earlier, a married man—or so a wedding band indicated. He had told me that this was his first venture into a world he had long wanted to explore. There was something sad about him, and I believed him.

A white cold light burst into the bar, freezing everything.

"This is the Los Angeles Police Department! All queers march out in a single file. Don't try to run, we've blocked all the exits," a harsh voice on a bullhorn blared from one of several squad cars suddenly parked outside—there had been the shrieks of halting brakes.

"A raid!" screeched a queen, jumping under a table.

Initiated patrons tried to scurry out, a few succeeding, others being thrust onto the sandy ground outside.

"What the hell is happening?" said the man I was with. He was already sweating, trembling.

"Just routine, man; just a hassle. Don't worry." But I did worry.

Goaded by two cops with prodding batons, everyone in the bar who hadn't managed to escape marched out, some slowly, defiant, blowing smoke from cigarettes into the faces of the cops standing in two flanking files outside. The cops flashed lights in everyone's face. The slumming women and their well-dressed escorts breezed by, waving airy greetings and farewells as they made their way unimpeded toward the beach nearby.

The cops were plucking a few people out of the ordered line, handcuffing them, to be taken away to jail—"for further investigation"—as examples. Some might be charged with "loitering" or "gathering in a known hangout for deviants" or having "no visible means of support."

"Identification!"

The men so singled by a cop's bark groped nervously in their pockets for identification, some spilling the contents of their wallets, then gathering them up urgently.

"OK, now, get the hell out of here."

"Identification!"

"I—"

"You! Put your hands behind your back—"

As we approached the inquisitory column, I was sure the cops would pull me out, or at least question me, as a hustler; I had seen them pull out three others, now handcuffed and inside one of the cars. Since the incident at Cooper's Donuts, I had begun to fear the mere presence of cops, although I tried to hide being afraid.

Now I wanted to separate from the man I had been sitting with so they would let him go—he was wearing a "respectable" sport jacket while I was wearing an open shirt and jeans. Apart, we stood a better chance of thwarting the cops' prepared accusations.

"What will they do to us?" the man asked me in what he intended to be a whisper, but it became a loud question when his voice cracked. I saw one cop, overhearing, look menacingly at us, as some men were allowed to leave, others were harassed, all were jeered at, and some were taken in. Objecting to being manhandled guaranteed being shoved into the squad car.

During a brief altercation, I whispered to the man, "My name is John Rechy. Tell me yours quick."

"No. Why?"

No time to answer.

"You with that guy?" the fat cop who had overheard the man's question earlier shoved the blinding light at him.

"Yes, yes," the man gave the wrong answer.

"You didn't just pick him up?"

"Oh, no, no, he's my friend, we came here together—"

"Then what's his name?"

"Uh, oh—uh—"

The cop turned away from him and faced me. "He says you're his friend, long time. So what's his name?" he demanded.

I shook my head, resigned.

"Soliciting for purposes of prostitution!" the cop raised his voice.

"You've got it all wrong, officer," the man I was with was pleading. "I didn't know what kind of place that was. I'm married. Look." He brandished his wedding band.

The cop shook his head mockingly, sneering. "Married, huh?—and pickin' up hustlers."

The man was about to cry; perspiration had turned his face bright under the scorching white light.

A hustler I had seen selling drugs, just behind us now in line, tried to run. The cop interrogating us rushed with his stick at him. I turned to the man I was with, "Run, run!"

He staggered away as the cops watched, laughing, allowing him to escape, their intent fulfilled.

I turned to run. A cop grabbed me.

"Come back here, queer!"

My face burning with accumulated rage, I heard myself say, "I'm not queer, man. I'm straight."

The cop who had grabbed me studied me. "OK, then get the fuck out of here."

I walked along the beach, the sea breeze cooling my face.

Again, I had lucked out, so close to being busted, freed only by sudden circumstance. But I didn't feel the vast relief I should have felt, that I wanted to feel.

I'm not queer, man, I'm straight.

A man with whom I had already made arrangements on Hollywood Boulevard took me to a cruising bar—"I want them to see me with you," he said. There, among attractive homosexuals seeking mutually responsive contacts, I saw, as out-of-place as I must have looked there, another hustler. He was easy to identify—the stance, the talk, the look—and he, too, was with an older man. We kept glancing at each other across the crowded bar, holding the stare, sending silent signals. We maneuvered to come closer within the bar, our companions not aware yet of the secret exchange. Keeping my eyes locked with the other hustler's stare, I went to the restroom, fully expecting that he would follow me. After a few seconds—during which I waited, pretending to be washing my hands, arranging myself in the mirror—he walked in.

"Hi, man."

"Hi, man."

"Let's make it," he said.

"OK," I shrugged, not regretting the easy acceptance.

In the bar, I told the man I was with that I had "suddenly remembered" I had to be elsewhere. It was the staple excuse to move away from someone already committed and now to be left. The man's eyes narrowed, as he saw the other hustler speaking to the man he was with.

"Sorry," I said.

"You're a son of a bitch, you know it, punk?" the man said. "You said you were a straight hustler, and now you and that other punk—" I moved away, feeling a mixture of emotions, sorry to hurt him, sorry to anger him, but feeling a more powerful draw, an entirely selfish pull.

I waited outside the bar, smoking. Again the monstrous insecurity. What if the guy in the restroom had merely set me up, to humiliate me, challenge my hustler pose, asserting his stronger one? What if—?

There he was. "I have a car, but no place," he said.

"I don't have a place," I lied.

We drove up somewhere into the Hollywood hills—beyond a scattering of houses, a sprinkling of lights. In an area of clustered trees in a field of bushes, he parked and we got out.

There, cautiously, nervously, each of us waited for the other to act first. Simultaneously—this had become essential—our hands roamed over each other's body, pulling down each other's pants and shorts, which gathered at our feet, our exposed cocks already aroused as we tugged at each other's shirts, to push them up, remove them, so that we were almost naked within slabs of light that filtered through the branches of the trees.

Our bodies pressed together, hard cock against hard cock, rubbed up and down, sideways, moist with sweat. He grabbed my cock as I grabbed his, and I felt the strange hardness in my hand, so hard, as he must have felt mine in his as we parted to look down at what was occurring between us. I put one hand on his shoulder, luring him down.

"Blow me, man," I said; a contest, a one-sided conquest.

For a moment, my words seemed to have ended any further contact—he pulled away, but then moved back again. "You blow me first, man," he said, lifting his chin at me, "and then I'll do it."

But it wouldn't happen; it had become too crucial a challenge, a draw, checkmate. Both understanding that, we pressed against each other, pulsing cock against pulsing cock, hips gyrating against each other's—and we came.

Self-consciously, we rubbed off our own come with our hands, as if to wipe away evidence of what had occurred between two hustlers who had posed at not being gay.

I laughed.

He laughed.

We drove back to Hollywood. "Shit, man, that's it," he said, "I just hadda make sure I'm not queer—and I did, I'm not."

"Me, too," I said. "The same with me."

26

I made friends with a very kind man named Dick who was from McAllen, Texas. We met at Schwab's lunch counter in Hollywood, the place where Lana Turner was supposedly discovered but wasn't really. Sitting next to me, he was so immediately friendly and warm that I dropped the hustler pose. He had been a chorus boy in Hollywood. During World War II he had choreographed shows for the USO, his highest accomplishment until he bought a barony from a pauper nobleman in Italy and became the baron de Mondar, knighted among Pasadena royalty in a ceremony that included a sword touched to his shoulder as he bowed. We got along so well—no talk about sex—that he invited me to a dinner party that weekend in his home on upper Hollywood Boulevard.

Velvet draperies, velvet furniture, velvet everywhere. The house was dominated by a painting lit from above by a single light, a glamorous Egyptian queen who looked amazingly like Joan Collins. "It was painted by Cleopatra," the baron told me—I was the first to arrive. "It would be worth a fortune except that she forgot to sign it." The painting had been given to him by his honored guest tonight, the famous performer Liberace.

In the winey predinner gathering on my friend's flowery lawn, Liberace focused his attention on me, to the chagrin of his two muscular companions. Assistants? Bodyguards? Current boyfriends sliding out of favor? A strange little old woman wearing a tiara was also there, responding, "Oh," to every comment she heard; I assumed she was a princess from Pasadena.

Liberace whispered something to the baron, and I was seated next to him at the dinner table. Conversation was light—mostly about antiques. Liberace had just opened a store for his many admirers, middle-aged female tourists. My mother had confessed to me that she enjoyed his performances terribly.

The meal had hardly progressed when I felt his hand under the table landing on my groin. I must have winced at the surprise, since the baron asked, "Are you all right, John?"

I removed Liberace's hand unobtrusively under the table, especially since his two burly companions were glaring at us—one had ducked quickly to peer under.

The evening was over. The three—the two companions sullen—left.

When I was alone with Dick and the frayed princess, who had passed out drunk, the telephone rang. It was Liberace. He wanted to talk to me. He was crying, lonely, depressed. "Please come, please. I need someone to talk to."

I felt sorry for him, the celebrated but isolated star. He had become mortified at what he had done under the table. He probably wanted to apologize.

The baron dropped me off at Liberace's mansion, atop a hill in West Hollywood; the house was bone-white even in the night, with marbly pillars.

Liberace led me in himself, holding a white poodle while three or four others tangled at his feet and yipped at me.

Inside, everything was black and white—including, I noticed now, the poodles skidding around, the black ones with a white ribbon, the white ones with a black ribbon. I felt dizzy, as if all colors had been drained out of my vision.

Liberace wasn't crying now. He was smiling his famous toothy smile. "Please sit down," he exhorted me with a slight lisp. He indicated a place next to him on the couch.

I sat on another couch. He jumped over. I stood up, annoyed. "You said you were lonely and wanted to talk." In my hustling activities, I was carving strict demarcations. If I was on the streets, clearly available, what was expected was allowed to happen, the proposition. When I was in another atmosphere—like the dinner party at the baron's home, and, I had thought, here—I could not slide into another mode, as a hustler.

"I am lonely, very lonely, and I do want to talk to you." His fleshy hands pulled me to him.

I pushed him away.

"Do you like jewelry?" He flashed rings that seemed to contribute the only dissonance within the black and white mausoleum of the room.

"No, I really don't," I said.

"I have a beautiful place in Palm Springs," he said. "Would you like to come with me?"

I walked down the hill to hitchhike back to my room.

Dick called me excitedly. "I have some gifts for your mother."

"What?"

"Yes, from Lee, Liberace. I told him what you told me, about your mother being such a fan. He sent her some beautiful goblets, and a replica of his piano. It actually plays a part of one of his favorite pieces."

I mailed the gifts to my mother. She was thrilled. "How wonderful to know such a great man and he, too, is a wonderful son," my mother wrote.

★   ★   ★

The temporary legal-help agency that sent me out on jobs called me about a job that would take me, all expenses paid, with a good salary, to San Francisco. The job was with the attorney general's office, representing the state of California in the ongoing, years-long litigation over water rights on the Colorado River.

When, at dinner, I told my sister that I was going to San Francisco, she asked me, "Will you look her up?"

I knew who she meant.

"I'm not sure."

If I did, would she pretend not to know me?

In San Francisco, I worked in a building whose windows faced Market Street. At its corner there was an arcade, where, I quickly noticed, hustlers hung out in the daytime. I avoided looking out at the thriving activity. I went to work at the office dressed more and more casually, finally in jeans. I thought that might sustain a needed feeling that I was only temporarily straddling two worlds, one in this office, the other just outside.

I became friendly with the office manager, an attractive red-haired woman named Nadine; she was in her midthirties. She often told me that I was "sexy," and I told her that she was very "sexy," too. Nothing more than that.

Often, for lunch, we went to a cafeteria next to the building where the office was located. Once, as we walked in, we caught sight, at the same time, of two effeminate middle-aged men. They were ahead of us in line. When we had gone through the serving line, the two men were already seated. As we passed them, one said something to the other, and they both stared at me, smiling.

"You've made quite an impression with those two," Nadine whispered.

Responding to the terrible cruelty that would jab at me un-expectedly, I said, loud enough for them to hear, and in a derisive tone, "Yeah, I know—those guys do like me." I had done that to confirm my posture of masculinity with Nadine, even though I had no inclination to extend my relationship with her.

During the next few days I looked for the two. One day they were there. Putting down my tray on a table Nadine had chosen, I walked over to them. As I approached, I saw a look on their faces that stamped itself on my mind: anger and hurt and, yes—although I would have preferred to reject this impression—a touch of fear, and that shook me the most.

"I want to apologize—" I said quickly, to try to assure them I intended no further hostility.

They looked at me, cold.

"I said something nasty a few days ago, about you, and—"

Their stare was even colder.

"It was hypocritical of me, and I want to apologize."

Their stare was unflinching.

Although I felt even more depressed about the incident than before the intended apology, I was glad they had reacted as they had, had not accepted my apology, had not released me from guilt, had ensured that it would remain festering.

Soon after, I was in the office on an idle day—the litigants were in court. I looked out the window. I saw a man approach a hustler at the arcade across the street. I stared. I could almost hear the transaction, echoing from all my own previous times—the asking about how much, the response, the qualifications. I stared out the window as the man, in a business suit, walked off with the young man, who was swaggering, sleeves chopped off his T-shirt, faded jeans. I felt a pull so powerful that I was almost dizzy with excite-ment at the prospect of returning to the world I had abandoned in this orderly office of laws. I gave notice that day to Nadine that I was not working there any more.

★   ★   ★

The Castro district had not yet become the gay haven it would turn into. It harbored a mixture of men and women, many young and seemingly free-spirited; they sat lazily on steps, often smoking marijuana—an illegal act they flaunted.

At a corner on Market, where the trolley that rode up and down Nob Hill filled with giddy tourists, one cool afternoon, a slender man picked me up. He looked like a businessman, in his forties. After preliminary arrangements—he was shy, nervous, looking about—he invited me to his home, "a few blocks up the hill," he said. He walked slightly ahead of me as if cautious that someone might recognize him and identify the situation.

In his apartment, he asked me to wait for him while he changed. I waited longer than I had estimated, and was almost ready to walk out of his fussily decorated apartment—delicate antiques everywhere—when I heard his footsteps, very loud, assertive. I turned to look at him.

Someone else was standing there. "Who the hell are you?" I backed away.

I then recognized him, the dainty man who had picked me up. He was now dressed in shiny leather. Almost every inch of him was covered; only patches of his face were visible under a low-slung biker's cap.

"Make me your slave, please, master," he said in a tremulous voice.

"I'm not into that, man," I said.

"Please." He held out a shiny belt toward me. "Punish me for wanting you."

He dropped to his knees, the leather creating a slicing sound like a sustained hiss. I did not welcome the sudden excitement I felt when he crawled toward me. "Master, I want to worship you. Punish me for wanting you."

To walk out on him now, at the height of his frenzy, to leave him on the floor like that, kneeling . . . To end this scene, I grasped his head and pulled it into my aroused groin, to stop his words, to end my own disturbing excitement.

He ground his head into my groin. He leaned back, looking up at me with pleading eyes. "You're a *man,* and I'm a filthy faggot! Punish me!" He gasped; his body contracted.

Exhausted, he got up, again the man who had brought me here, the same man but in an incongruous costume. Arranging an antique lamp that had tilted, he avoided looking at me.

Out on the street, I decided I would not attempt to see Isabel Franklin.

Every morning there was the promise of sun, and then, very soon, the wind would start whipping down the slanted streets, blowing cold into the city.

"Mardi Gras, man, that's where the real action is." The young hustler dug his hands into his pockets, thwarting the nightly chill of the city as we stood on a corner of Market. "That's where I'm headed, man." He eyed a man walking past us, pausing. "Just as soon as I hustle enough to get there, man, I'm splittin' for Mardi Gras, that's where it's *all* at, that's where it *all* happens."

27

That's where it all happens.

I arrived at the bus station in New Orleans on a day spattered with cold sunshine. In a rented locker at the bus station. I left my duffel bag and my typewriter, a judgment I nevertheless clung to. I had not slept on the bus, and I was tired. A large movie theater was showing *Witness for the Prosecution,* a movie that I had seen and liked, and that my sister Olga had ruined for me by blurting out the solution about halfway into the film.

"Are you sure you want to come in, sir?"

Only then did I notice the woman in the ticket booth. She was young, pretty, a Negro.

Although I was baffled by her question—had she reacted to my disheveled appearance?—I nodded, yes.

She didn't take my money, hesitating.

I pushed the money toward her.

"Sir," she said in a soft voice, "you are more than welcome to come in. It's a theater for Negroes—but you are welcome to come in."

I remembered the theater in Balmorhea that had challenged me. I remembered my reaction, the chafing sense of shame afterward when I had sat in the "white" section with Scott and Ross. "I'd like to see the movie, yes," I said.

She handed me the ticket.

I walked in. There were several people in the large theater, all Negroes, men and women. The film flickered in silver swaths, illuminating the faces of the audience; it seemed to me that everyone had turned to look at me as I walked along the aisle.

I sat down. Were they wondering whether I was there to create trouble? A man and a woman with a child rose to leave. Another woman and a man followed. Another man.

I walked out, feeling like a brazen invader.

I found a room at the YMCA, just as a man was checking out. "Probably the only room left in N'awrleans," the man at the desk said. "City's filled up for carnival."

"This far in advance, two weeks?"

"Sometimes months," he said.

As the seven days of carnival approached, the urgency in the city mounted. Streets, alleys, bars in the French Quarter were thronged by men and women of all ages, some already in costume. Bourbon Street became a raucous outdoor bar. People staggered about with bottles of beer, wine, and hurricane glasses filled with colored liquor. In Jackson Square across from St. Louis Cathedral, sleeping bodies were strewn like the first casualties of a war just beginning. Cathedral bells tolled lugubriously as if protesting against the cacophony of revelry. The police roamed into and out of bars, along crooked narrow streets, trying to expel vagrants before the carnival pitched the city out of control.

I felt the city vibrating with the call to anarchy I must have come to seek—*where it all happens*. Drums pounding in spontaneous parades asserted that call. These frenzied days of ceremonial orgy demanded to be seized fully before the mourning of Ash Wednesday ended them.

I flung myself into the mounting fever, drinking whatever drink was placed before me, swallowing any pill handed to me. "Uppers" and "downers" warred against each other, and, soon, it was as if I was dreaming awake, moving fast and slowly at the same time as I made my way from bar to bar, street to street, carried along by erupting laughter, the muffled beat of drums, forced euphoria, the agitated church bells—moving within currents of bodies crushed into masses of flesh, the city now existing within a timeless limbo of day and night, night and day, then night again, and sex again, sex in bars, sex in squashed rented rooms overlooking old Southern courtyards, sex in cramped alleys, pills and liquor, a sleepless time, a frantic dream.

Those days, those nights, through the haze of drugs and liquor, I encountered—at times clearly, at times like living ghosts—people I would remember forever, hustlers and queens and those who lived around them. Jocko, no longer on a circus trapeze, falling much more dangerously, the last carnival; Sylvia in her gay bar, looking for the son she had exiled, giving up; Chi-Chi, the giant queen with her readied upheld middle finger toasting the world; Kathy, the beautiful queen, dying, laughing at her death—and so many, many others. I felt I must now follow them to the very edge on which I saw them dancing on their own graves, having long abandoned the possibility of escape, even the desire to escape, not even a substitute for salvation left. I thought I heard, as I experienced their lives in brief spurts of drunken laughter and drunken tears, their extreme challenge, a demand for the last initiation, as if here in this old, profound city of cemeteries—*where it all happens*—I must enact a ritual of my own, finally, to be undone by the world they lived in, a world without exit, a world I had chosen; and that world allowed no short-term visitors, demanding total fealty. If I was not to judge myself a visitor, I must be undone, like the others. In those days of delirium it was as clear as that to me.

A heavy man and two others picked me up outside a bar. I rode with them, a dizzy drunken drive, out of the Quarter, to a motel. They took my clothes off, licking whatever of my flesh was exposed as soon as it was exposed, circling about me, pushing at their own clothes, drinking out of spilling bottles, liquor dripping down my body and licked, as I stood unsteadily, bathed by thirsty tongues, grasped by hands.

When it was over, they lay back on the floor, dozy. The fogginess of liquor, the heightened awareness of pills, made me reckless, alert, excited, compelled.

I went through the sleeping men's pants; I found their wallets, I took out most of their money. I lay back on the single bed.

When they woke, I asked them to drive me back to the Quarter.

In the moving car, one checked his wallet. "My money's gone," he said. Another one searched his own wallet anxiously, then the third of them. "So's mine." "Mine, too."

"You were so drunk you don't remember spending," I said coolly in a voice I was used to. "Yeah, and you haven't paid me."

When I stepped out of the car, swilling from the bottle of liquor I took from one man, I waited until one of them fumbled in his wallet to pay me from what I hadn't taken. The blast of cold sun made me reel, dormant pills and new liquor ganging up, pulling me harshly into more shifting currents of flesh in the Quarter.

On the streets . . .

Floats sailed along Bourbon Street mounted by teary clowns and laughing angels throwing out glass beads, mummers marching along spectrally, hordes of people somersaulting to grasp tossed beads; slaves decked in chains joining kings and queens and acrobats and gladiators and Tarzan and Jane.

I jumped to catch a spinning star, a trinket tossed by a clown turned angel. It fell to the ground, where others battled for it.

"Mardi Gras!"

The carnival had begun. I tried to make my way along cramped aisles of masked revellers, staring at faces that looked like masks, masks that looked like faces. Time hopped, then was spliced like strips of film. I was in a bar and someone was blowing me. I was in an alley, as masked revelers invaded, dancing. Others pushed, shouted, screamed, wept, rushed, fell, recovered. I was in a bar drinking among almost naked bodies of men groping, shouting, going down, pressed against each other, fucking.

Outside . . .

I stared down at the ground where someone's mask had fallen, an abandoned face.

"Who are you?"

"Cinderella!"

"What?" I had only overheard those words, not asked of me.

Someone, male or female, in a twinkly gauzy dress, had flitted by like a lost butterfly, and was now fluttering away, repeating in answer to a tourist's question, "I'm Cinderella, I'm Cinderella."

I wove along the streets and into bars, out, into other bars, the streets, back into bars, laughing, drinking, smoking, drinking, surrendering to hands, surrendering to mouths, laughing, drinking out of giant hurricane glasses, liquor reddish like thinned blood. I was now in a bar, and a clown fell to his knees and removed his mask. The painted face pasted against me smeared me with colors.

"What a gorgeous mask!"

"What?"

"I said, what a gorgeous mask!"

A man stood before me; he *was* addressing me. I touched my face—had I put on the discarded mask?

The man touched my face, with one finger.

"It's not a mask," I said.

"I know, I just meant that you're gorgeous!"

I opened my mouth, seized by a strong desire to laugh, but no sound came, or rather sound came but not from me, from the crowds, from the clowns and angels and harem women, and ballet dancers, and smiling skeletons.

And more pills, liquor, sex, sex, pills, liquor, sex . . .

I have to leave, I thought. *You can't!* I will, I'll fly out of this city now, I'm out of control—*where it all happens.* I'll leave before I'm trapped—*in what?* Can't get out—*of what?* No exit *where it all happens.* Land's end.

I looked toward where the bells were tolling.

On the steps of the cathedral—I had made my way there—a woman apart stood smoking, surveying the masked debauchery, and—

. . . *she completed an intricately graceful choreography of slight movements as she withdrew the cigarette from her lips . . . and she looked up, and she smiled, definitely smiled, this time*—

At me.

Only when I woke up—wakened because the cathedral bells had stopped tolling or I couldn't hear them—did I realize that I had made my way into a dank hot night movie theater. On the screen, cartoon figures were jumping, cackling, spastic bodies out of control. I was leaning back groggily on the seat where I had fallen asleep, still half asleep. I felt a gnawing at my groin. Looking down, I saw a man blowing me. Illuminated by the flashing color of the cartoon, a cockroach skittered away along my chest; my shirt was pulled open.

I sat up, pushing the crouching man away. All the money I had stuffed into my pockets, now turned inside out, was gone, taken as I slept a dark, terrifying sleep, maybe stolen by the man while he was blowing me. I checked my back pocket: my wallet was still there, secured by the weight of my body as I slept.

Rushing out—running, it seemed a long distance and into the cold dawn—had the tides of people heated the streets or had I not noticed the cold within the frenzied pace? I found my way back to the apartment where I had been staying—oh, yes, I now remembered I had moved out of the Y into someone's apartment. The groggy man there, blinking, didn't seem to recognize me. I walked past him and retrieved my duffel bag and the case with my typewriter.

The sun was washing over the debris of the carnival; glittery trinkets winked among the trash now being collected by giant trucks. On the morning streets, people walked about reverentially with ashes on their foreheads. Drunken revelers who remained slept along streets and alleys like living debris. Lent had begun.

In the stark light of a winter sun, in an old, old city, on the day of Lenten mourning, I stood on a street strewn with fake beads and trash. I had become the person I had only played at being. I made my way to the Delta Airlines ticket office.

"I have to leave New Orleans," I said to the young woman behind the counter. I looked into my wallet; only the few bills that I had put there instead of in my pockets remained. I placed the bills on the counter. "I need to go to El Paso."

The attendant counted the money. She frowned.

"It's not enough?" I asked her.

"I'll furnish what you need," she said.

Did I seem that desperate?

I thanked her, walking away.

"You'll need money for a cab," she said, and gave it to me.

At the door I noticed how very pretty she was. I asked her name.

"Miss Wingfield," she answered.

I flew back to El Paso, to my mother's love. I surrendered to her embrace. She was still in the projects, my promise to her still unkept, remote.

"*M'ijo,* you don't look well. What's happened to you?"

I had become gaunt, my eyes hollow.

During the days that extended there, and as before, my mother slept in the bedroom. My brother Robert, separated from his new wife, slept on a bed couch in the living room. I slept in the same room on a roll-out bed.

Rather, I tried to sleep. Sleep wouldn't come. When it did, it brought nightmares, of masks, leering angels, weeping clowns.

As a child, I was often overwhelmed by a feeling of devastating sorrow for everyone, for everything. At those times, I would stand on the ragged porch of our house on Wyoming Street in El Paso and I would pray into the black sky: "Please help everyone." Years later, after long sex-hunting on the streets, that feeling of isolated horror, infinite sadness, would recur. Black, black depression would pull me down, lower and lower, until I felt that I was drowning in darkness.

Now, in El Paso, during those sleepless nights, I felt the accumulation of those black times, felt it so powerfully that I could not breathe; I had to go outside, even late at night, till dawn, to breathe again. I would sit on the small step in front of the unit, smoking, smoking a lot, muffling my crying so my mother wouldn't hear.

Paralyzed days passed like that.

Then one day I needed to convey what had led me to feel the inevitability of my own self-destruction. I would write to Wilford. No, that seemed unfair after the last sad encounter with him. In El Paso, he had introduced me to a soldier whom he had run into in the library, a very tall, very thin man. The soldier had known Wilford in Urbana and then reconnected with him at Fort Bliss. Wilford gave me the man's permanent address as a definite connection to him if our paths separated. I had retained that address throughout the years in a drawer at home. Illogically, I decided to write to him.

My cherished portable typewriter that my father had given me was gone, left at the New Orleans airport when I was racing to catch my flight out of the city. No, I would not attempt to recover it. It seemed appropriate that the memory of the time my father had given me the typewriter would have an ending, a cherished completed memory now.

I rented a typewriter. I placed it on a table in my mother's bedroom. I wrote a long letter to that man who was a stranger, a long letter about the anarchy of sex and liquor and pills and thieving, and nights without mornings, nights that extended from New York to Los Angeles, nights that had culminated in New Orleans.

I did not need to send the letter; I had written it to myself.

Days later—this surprised me because I thought I had torn it up—I found the letter and read it. I revised it slightly; I gave it a title—"Mardi Gras." I mailed it as a story to *Evergreen Review,* an adventurous literary magazine of the time, and to the New Directions Anthology.

I received a letter from Mr. Laughlin, the publisher at New Directions. Yes, he would publish "Mardi Gras," but it would not appear for another year, the new collection having just been issued. Almost simultaneously, I received a letter from Don Allen, the senior editor at Grove Press, publishers of *Evergreen Review.* He and the staff were considering the "story" for publication, he wrote. Was it perhaps part of a novel?

It was not. I had no intention of writing about the world I had lived in; "Mardi Gras" would remain a letter, only that. To write more would betray that world. Allow the stories of the people I had lived among, and remembered so keenly, to provide my own escape when there was none for them? Thinking that the publication of the letter would encourage the publication of *Pablo!* I quickly wrote to Don Allen claiming that "Mardi Gras" was part of a novel—"almost completed."

I waited in El Paso, having dinner nightly with my mother and my brother, my mother cooking my favorite dishes, asking me to join her in nightly prayers, which I recited by rote, granting them no power, other than the power of her hopes.

Days stretched out with no commitment from Don Allen. I was becoming restless in El Paso, doing nothing, going for long aimless drives, watching television on a set my brother Robert had bought my mother, on which she watched cherished Mexican serials that I shared with her—serials full of anguish and demands and, finally, redemption for the good, banishment for the bad. I began to think that the miraculous opening into my life as a writer was closing, again feeling a resurgence of the dark paralysis. I had to move.

I told my mother I was going back to Los Angeles. I longed for my sister's old sustaining camaraderie, her gossip. There, I would get a job, order my life, resist the pull of anarchy. I returned the rented typewriter.

Without even asking whether I needed it, my brother Robert gave me $100 to take with me.

"No, Robert."

"Johnny, you can give it back when you can," he said.

Another good-bye between me and my mother, still in the projects, a good-bye never less painful, never less sad. Yet another in the long good-bye that life was turning into.

28

"Beautiful sister!"

"Little brother!"

How I had missed her, her smile.

"Is there a letter forwarded from El Paso for me?" Still no word from Grove Press.

No letter.

I stayed a few days with my sister, enjoying her and the company of my brother-in-law; his marriage to my sister was idyllic, it seemed to me, especially given the conflicts it had created in El Paso.

I took my nephew and niece, an energetic and good-looking boy and a pretty, flouncy girl, to a nearby playground. I whirled them on the merry-go-round, pushed them on swings, bought them ice cream, enjoying myself and them.

"Uncle Johnny!"

"Don't call me uncle, you hear?"

At night we all watched television, my sister always ahead of whatever movie was being shown. "It's so clear that the sister is the one who . . ."

This time my sister had no news about Isabel Franklin.

★ ★ ★

I moved back downtown, to another hotel on Hope Street. I contacted the agency I had worked for earlier, at temporary jobs with attorneys. The man and woman at the agency were glad to have me back. They immediately sent me out on a job in a glitzy law firm on Wilshire Boulevard, miles away from Pershing Square and the bars on Main Street.

Forwarded from El Paso to my sister Olga and delivered to me when I rushed to her house to receive it, a letter arrived from Don Allen. "Mardi Gras" would be published in the next issue.

Not soon enough to quell my anxiety but actually not long after hearing from Don Allen, my letter appeared as a story in *Evergreen Review*. The few lines about "Mardi Gras" identified it as "the first published story by a new American writer" and indicated that it was part of a novel in progress.

I began to receive letters forwarded by Grove Press from readers, touching letters from men, from women, empathizing with the feelings detected in it. On another rented typewriter, I answered each.

While reminding me that he was waiting to see the rest of the novel that I had told him was "almost finished," Don Allen suggested I write some shorter pieces—perhaps something about my hometown, El Paso.

Excited by the request, I wrote an impressionistic view of my hometown: the incomparable sky; the infinite desert; memories resurrected from early years; the mountain I had climbed; gaudy flashes of Juárez, across the border; loving memories of my mother; and memories, rendered as tender as I could, about my father.

Published as "El Paso del Norte," it drew more mail.

I continued working. I sent my mother money regularly. I haunted the public library. With amusement and sadness, I reread the section of Freud's *Interpretation of Dreams* that I had read before the troops at the insistence of Acting Corporal Bailey.

Don Allen suggested another short essay. I wrote an impressionistic view of Los Angeles, which I had come to see as a Technicolor city of lost angels, perhaps the metaphorical place of exile for the rebellious angels cast out by God. I celebrated its overt narcissism, the display of physicality on the last horizon, the last stop before the sun disappeared each night into the ocean. Titled, "The City of Lost Angels" it drew more mail.

Carey MacWilliams, the great editor of the *Nation,* asked me to write for the magazine. I wrote about discrimination against Mexicans, in the interior of Texas—remembering Miz Crawford. I wrote about a juvenile detention center in El Paso where minority teenagers were being treated like war captives. I wrote about a kid I had known in the projects who had committed suicide in an isolation ward of Huntsville; he was twenty-one. Those articles drew more letters, and more suggestions for material from other magazines; I wrote for the *Texas Observer, Nugget,* the *Saturday Review.*

Eager to send it to Grove, I continued to revise *Pablo!*—certain of its publication now that I was making a reputation, if the many letters were to be believed, and I did believe them, gladly.

I still had no intention of writing about the hustling world. I guarded, intimately, the memories of the people encountered throughout those cities of night. I had conveyed only a glimpse of that world in "Mardi Gras," a letter. But betray the streets and bars, betray the times of unique excitement?, the highs of outlawed exile? Expose those times, those people to possible judgment by a world that had rendered them invisible? No.

But what if I wrote about them with the compassion I felt, the closeness of exile? If I didn't, would those lives I now sheltered disappear entirely, just as the actual denizens disappeared invisibly— and where?—along the last stops of skid row?—into the artificial surcease of drugs and liquor? Perhaps—I thought of Jocko in New Orleans—to suicide.

In the rented room on Hope Street, I began to set down an account of my encounter with the flaming drag queen who called herself "Miss Destiny." Once, in a bar, both of us high on booze and pills, she had told me about her longing for a white wedding; she, a bride, would sweep down a spiral staircase to join her husband, a hustler who would love her faithfully forever.

With growing enthusiasm that tempered the sadness even in memories that were often funny, I wrote about her, about Main Street, Pershing Square, about her and some of the others—Trudi, Buddy, Chuck, Skipper, those whose faces at times seemed to float over my typewriter, my memories. I titled the story "The Fabulous Wedding of Miss Destiny."

I awaited Don's response to it.

The response came; he admired it, he wanted to publish it in *Evergreen*. Others on the staff were still reading it.

Further news came: Barney Rosset—the daring publisher of Grove Press and editor in chief of *Evergreen Review,* the man who was tearing down censorship in America by publishing Henry Miller and D. H. Lawrence—had rejected it. No reason was conveyed to me.

My betrayal of the world I had begun to reveal in that story had been confirmed. I had exposed those lives to more rejection.

Guiltily, I felt a strong pull back to the streets. Like a repentant lover, I returned to Pershing Square and the hustling bars on Main Street.

Might I revise "The Fabulous Wedding of Miss Destiny" Don Allen wrote to ask me. I had no idea how I could change it. I had set it down as closely as I could evoke the actual events, almost compulsively so; wincing at any temptation to alter a single detail that I remembered. When I changed the color of a dress Miss Destiny had worn, I felt immediate remorse. Hadn't *she* chosen that color?

It was a rare, starry night. I went up to the roof of the four-story building I lived in and I lit a marijuana cigarette. The bells of a nearby church began to toll the evening's time. I looked in the direction of Pershing Square. In the haze of the marijuana, I remembered a game of statues I had played with my sister Olga and other children. Spun around in turns, we had to freeze in the position we fell in. That image drifted into my mind along with the impression, in a wispy cloud that floated in the dark distance, of an angel.

I returned to my rented room. I incorporated both impressions—angels and stilled statues—into a passage of epiphany in the story of Miss Destiny. I sent it to Don.

Don admired it even more. Barney Rosset rejected it.

Now my response was anger. How dare those lives of exiles, of outlaws, be thrust aside even in literature, doubly exiled? I knew of no other publication where my story would be accepted. I hustled even more feverishly, early afternoons, late nights.

Don Allen wrote to me about a literary quarterly that had spun off the *Chicago Review* in a controversy over the editors' having printed sections of William Burroughs's *Naked Lunch* and Allen Ginsberg's *Howl*. In reaction, the editors had formed a new quarterly, *Big Table*. Don encouraged me to send "The Fabulous Wedding of Miss Destiny" there. I had his permission to convey his own admiration and the fact that he had recommended it be sent there.

It was accepted—no payment involved—and published in the third issue of *Big Table* as "'The Fabulous Wedding of Miss Destiny,' a section from a novel in progress." Letters from readers multiplied. I received solicitations from agents offering to represent the announced novel, and letters from several publishers asking to see the novel: Jason Epstein at Random House, editors from

Macmillan, Dial Press. I heard from Norman Mailer, James Baldwin, Ken Kesey.

Don wrote that he was coming to Los Angeles and wanted to talk to me about my writing—and, he added, "to see the scene."

A few days later he was in the city. He called to make plans to meet. When he repeated that he wanted to see "the scene," I mentioned a few popular clubs on Sunset Strip. He said, too quickly, "Oh, then your writing isn't authentic."

Jesus Christ! He wanted to see the bars and streets I had written about, not what I had inferred for a sophisticated New York editor. His doubt shook me. Was the world I was writing about so hidden that even the editor who had championed my stories was ready to doubt its existence?

I borrowed a car from a man I saw regularly, whom I had met in a bar. I did not tell him the reason I needed the car, since it would have destroyed the image he had of me as a street-smart hustler. I offered to get him some "dynamite dope"—he loved to feel that he was slumming—but, I said in my most concerned voice, I didn't want to expose him to danger, since it would involve some tricky maneuvers. He believed it and lent me his car.

I met Don at a classy hotel. A tall man, very distinguished— I thought he was English—with a swipe of graying, silvery hair, an aura of supreme sophistication, a bearing like John Barrymore's, and the movie actor's classic features. I imagined him with an elegant wife, sipping a Dubonnet before dinner, like John D. Rockefeller.

I was dressed in my usual hustling "drag"—I had come to call it that, in amusement: fitted Levi's, engineer boots, shirt open three buttons down, and a motorcycle jacket slung over one shoulder if it was early in the warm evening.

"Oh," he said, and smiled as if I had fulfilled his expectations of what I would look like—and, I hoped, how I would dress.

Apprehensive because of the incident with Taub in New York—although Don Allen had already proved his interest in my writing—I was glad that there was no hint of his being homosexual. I had become an expert in detecting nuances, signals—I saw none. Now, once I had verified that I knew "the scene," we would be able to talk about me as a writer. I would mention *Pablo!*—and Wilford's enthusiasm.

In the car as we drove to Hollywood for dinner, we conversed easily, about Los Angeles, about my time in New York. Several times I conveyed my gratitude for his interest, to which he merely nodded graciously. When he approached the matter of the novel I wasn't writing, I veered away.

"How much is written now?"

"More than half."

"I would like to see it."

"I'm not ready to show it."

We went to dinner at Musso and Frank's, the Hollywood restaurant that was frequented by Faulkner and Fitzgerald. We sat in a booth and talked about *Evergreen Review.* I asked him why Barney Rosset hadn't wanted to publish "The Fabulous Wedding of Miss Destiny." He shrugged. "He's brave and unpredictable."

"You still want to see the 'scene'?" I changed the offending subject. I had deliberately used his quaint word.

"Yes."

OK, then, that's what I would show the elegantly dressed classy gentleman-editor from New York.

I took him to ChiChi's, the toughest bar in downtown Los Angeles. It was as if, for him, it had prepared to display itself in all its tawdry splendor amid intimations of dangers. Ratty pushers lingered outside, tough queens cursed and shoved their way in, rough hustlers gathered in tight conspiratorial groups.

They all seemed to spot Don at the same time. Everything and everyone froze.

Don, too, froze. "I think it's perhaps too noisy," he said, already heading back to the car.

I kept myself from laughing because I liked this man, very much, already, and I respected him. He, singly, had been responsible for everything I had published.

When I left him at the hotel, he asked me to come up tomorrow so we could talk more about my "pending work."

Pablo! Yes, I would tell him about *Pablo!*

I arrived at the hotel—no more car. I had to hitchhike, as punishment for my not having provided the owner of the car with the "dynamite dope" I had promised him. I took the elevator up to Don Allen's room. He opened the door with an amber drink in his hand.

"Would you like—?"

I shook my head, no. I needed a clear head when we discussed my complex novel about Maya legends, the sun and the moon, the narcissistic boy and the girl he meets in the jungle, the—

"Please . . . sit down." His speech was slightly slurred; his eyes were drowsy.

I sat on a couch. He sat next to me. I didn't move. He edged over toward me.

He said, "Give us a kiss?" Only a slight inflection had converted his words into a question. He reached out for me, coaxing me toward him.

I stood up, feeling disoriented, harshly remembering Taub in New York. "I have to leave; I have to return my friend's car," I lied.

He stood up, very formal again, but unsteady. "I'll call you before I leave, John."

"Great."

It was over, I thought, when I was back in my room. The interest in my writing, certainly genuine at first, had been compromised.

Or was it possible that my material had aroused more than literary interest when it had first been read by him? I didn't want to believe that. He had helped me so much, so much.

When I returned from the Main Street bars the next night, there were two telephone messages at the desk for me, both from Don Allen, only one hour apart. Please call him to arrange getting together for dinner the next day. I considered not answering. Yet what if—?

He took a cab and met me in a restaurant nearby.

I greeted him awkwardly; he greeted me as graciously as before yesterday's incident.

When we had ordered, he handed me a contract from Grove Press for a book I had not even yet begun, the book I had claimed was more than half finished. With the contract was a check sent through Western Union to him for me, an advance of $2,500 for the novel.

I felt saved.

"Thank you, Don, thank you very much."

The vague incident in the hotel seemed to have disappeared, perhaps carried away by—initiated in—a blur of liquor. In the long professional, and friendly, relationship that would extend for years between me and Don Allen—who would emerge as one of the most important people in my life, to whom I would owe so much, so very, very much—nothing of the sort ever occurred again, not a word of solicitation, not a gesture of invitation. Along with Wilford Leach, he became the main champion of my work.

This was all I was sure of: my writing was all that would allow me to move my mother out of the government projects into her own home. Now, I sent almost all of the advance money to her.

29

"You're John Rechy, aren't you?"

I was bewildered by the question that an attractive muscular man, in his upper thirties or early forties, had asked me, intercepting me as I left Harold's bar. If he hadn't thrown me off balance, I would have lied and said no. I was determined to remain anonymous, separate from my identity as a writer. "Yeah, why?"

"Damn, man," he said, "you are one fabulous guy. Your story, 'Mardi Gras'—wow, man—and that Miss Destiny, the Fabulous Wedding. Great! You're telling it, man; goddamn, man, you're the only one really *telling* it!"

As wonderful as that was to hear, it also scared me. If the few pieces I had published were identifying me, what about later? Would I be able to continue to live my anonymous life if my street identity was canceled?

The man—he identified himself amiably as "Smiley"—asked me to have dinner with him in a nearby cafeteria. I was glad it wasn't the cheap Green Rose Cafeteria across the street, where customers often took hustlers but I never went: or Clifton's, the crazy "Jesus oriented" one a block away, where, in a shady "grotto of meditation" downstairs, a life-size statue of Jesus knelt before a running stream. No, we went to the "expensive" cafeteria, Clinton's.

As we ate, Smiley told me that a group of friends "in the canyon" were very excited by what I was writing, especially "Miss Destiny."

"When will the novel be out, man?—can't wait."

"Soon," I said.

He had come to downtown Los Angeles, roamed the bars and Pershing Square looking for me, he said, taking his lead from the locales I had described in "The Fabulous Wedding of Miss Destiny." He would pause intermittently—look at me, shaking his head as if he couldn't believe it—and say, "You're telling it, man, you're the only one really *telling* it."

"How did you recognize me?" I asked nervously.

"I knew that when I saw you, I'd know it was you," he said, "and I did, right away." Then he smiled. "I have to admit, you're not the first hustler I've asked if he's you."

I laughed. Smiley approaching Chuck the cowboy hustler in Pershing Square and asking him if he was a writer was something I wish I had observed. Always ready to fulfill anybody's fantasy, Chuck would lazily have pushed his wide hat back and said, "Well, uh, man, if you want me to be, uh, yeah, sure—"

"Have you heard of a writer named Christopher Isherwood, man?"

I had, but I had not read anything by him. "He wrote *I Am a Camera,* didn't he?" I was gradually dropping the hustler pose, then resurrecting it, then dropping more. To be addressed as a writer excited me at the same time it continued to make me uncomfortable. In the "costume" of a hustler, I was talking like a writer.

"When you meet him, don't tell him that. That pisses him off. John van Druten wrote *I Am a Camera* from Christopher's stories. He gets bugged by people who recognize him through a play he didn't write."

"I don't think I'll be running into him," I said.

"Listen, where can I reach you? I'll arrange for my friends to meet you—Isherwood and a couple of others, a film director, Jim Bridges, and Gavin Lambert—"

Which role would I be expected to fill, the hustler in the stories, or the writer who had written about hustling? I shook my head, no.

"Come on, they'll dig you, come on," he said.

Knowing that I wouldn't go but feeling flattered by the invitation, and to test it, I gave him the telephone number of the hotel where I was staying.

"Oh, and, uh, would you like to make it together?"

He had approached me as a writer; now he was propositioning me. That was now arousing particular anxiety. Be who? I prepared an excuse for not going with him.

He didn't press the matter. "I'll call you."

I went back to Main Street, my identity there secure.

Back in my room and evaluating the encounter with Smiley— and startling myself because the sudden awareness made me realize that the memory had receded for some time but had now returned with even greater clarity—I thought of the kept woman of Augusto de Leon as . . . *the hand with the cigarette drifted away from her face, was lowered, and she touched the tip of the cigarette so lightly to an ashtray that the ashes vanished, merely vanished.*

Smiley called. His friends were having a "small gathering." "I can pick you up at your pad," he said in his typical jive talk. Surprising myself, I said yes.

At the upstairs apartment we went to—I didn't know whose it was—there were about half a dozen people, all men, all drinking. When we came in, they all looked at me—stared at me. I felt on display.

Smiley introduced me to them all.

"This is Christopher Isherwood." He was a smallish man in his fifties, quite British, nattily dressed. "Oh, I'm delighted."

"Don Bachardy." He was Isherwood's young—very young-looking—longtime companion. Too pretty to be handsome. He seemed to want to be a replica of Isherwood, bouncing on his feet back and forth as he talked, affecting a British accent, although, I would learn, he was from Long Beach.

"William." No last name; he was a handsome married man. He referred immediately to his wife's absence—"My wife couldn't come, had to stay with our kid"—although there were no women there; he was nearly drunk.

"Tom Wright." Another writer, a friendly man from the South—he had a sweet Southern stutter; I liked him immediately.

The evening proceeded smoothly, with small talk about books, a gracious remark now and then about my writing. "It is very good," Christopher said.

Tom asked me, "Wh-wh-when is the novel c-c-coming ou-out?"

I had never heard anyone stutter so engagingly. I dismissed the question: "I'm still working on it."

Another man came in with a young companion. The first man was somewhat dumpy with ordinary features. Smiley whispered with obvious amusement: "He's Zsa-Zsa Gabor's chauffeur." The younger man was identified as—"a reporter from the *Times*." He was handsome in a hustlery way. Both had already been drinking.

There was immediate tension between me and the younger man.

"Oh, yeah, uh, you're the guy who's writin' about hustlers, huh? How do ya know so much about it?"

The married man, drunker, joined the baiting: "Hey, hustler John," he slurred at me, "how about you and me driving down to Long Beach and picking up a couple of sailors to blow?"—challenging my rigid role as conveyed in what they had read.

Christopher's kind questions pulled me away from the antagonists. He touched my arm briefly—"and do call me Chris"—leading me to one side, where we might talk. I wanted to impress him, a famous writer. In horror the moment my own words registered, I heard myself say, "Mr. Isherwood"—I couldn't call him Chris, not yet—"wouldn't you agree that, after all, we are *all* cameras?"

Smiley doubled over with smothered laughter; Tom tried to hide his smile. Don Bachardy looked at me, aghast, as if he would demand that I leave. William raised his glass of liquor in a toast to my gaffe. Zsa-Zsa's chauffeur and his friend were arguing loudly and hadn't heard.

Not only had I done what I had been warned against, confusing Christopher with van Druten, but I had sounded childishly pretentious. I put my drink against my cheek to cool the embarrassment.

Isherwood swayed back and forth on the balls of his feet, "Well, uh, yes, yes, of course, John," he said; "yes, we are all cameras."

In my room a few days later, the telephone rang. It was Christopher Isherwood, inviting me to dinner at his canyon home that weekend; he would pick me up. I said yes. I had impressed the famous writer.

I went to the public library to familiarize myself more with him. I had known only that he was famous. I was glad to find out he was much more than that. I found several of his books, including *The Berlin Stories*; I read the stories on which the play was based. I had time to read all of *Prater Violet*. His impeccable prose excited me; I thought he was a brilliant writer. By the time he picked me up for dinner with himself and Don Bachardy, I would be able to talk intelligently about his work—and mine, my own fascination with literary structure, already manifested, perhaps not yet seen, in my own "The Fabulous Wedding of Miss Destiny."

I was armed for an exciting literary evening. I dressed in khaki slacks, shoes—not the usual boots—and a regular shirt. With this famous celebrated writer, I would drop my stance as hustler. I would be a writer.

Isherwood picked me up in his small car, a Volkswagen. We drove to his home. It perched atop one of the canyons of Santa Monica, a sensational setting—flowers growing up and down the roads, budding hills, trees bursting with flowers, lofty palm trees, the ocean just a steep decline away.

Inside, a large window welcomed a view of the ocean, foamy crests against the land.

Don Bachardy was in London, Christopher explained; he was in art school for a time. He had left soon after I had met them.

We went out to dinner, walking down a series of steps along a craggy path that led to a short block of small buildings—a gay bar, a restaurant, an antique shop. Across the street, the swirling ocean tinged the air with a salty smell.

At the restaurant, cooled by night gathering mistily, we had dinner. A waitress asked Chris if I was "another son," a nasty tone in her question. "This is John Rechy, a writer friend," he said.

When we returned to his home, he lit the fireplace in the living room. He fixed drinks; we sat before the flickering flames— orange, blue, blue. We talked and drank and talked and talked—about writers, writing, literature. I even talked about the novel he and his friends—and Don Allen and the people at Grove—were anticipating, the novel not written. Perhaps because of the liquor, I became spirited in discussing it as if it really existed, indicating that I was shaping it as a series of encounters, like the experiences themselves. That might have been the first time that I actually considered, if only briefly and vaguely, writing it. I was enjoying, with heady excitement, this literary evening fueled by friendly liquor in the company of a famous writer.

Before that memorable fireplace, time passed. It was two o'clock in the morning—"too late to drive." I easily accepted Christopher's invitation to spend the night in his guest room.

"Thank you, yes."

He showed me to an ample room, well furnished, with a large bed. Here, too, a window faced the cresting ocean, waves crashing, receding.

"Good night, Chris," I said, "I've had a terrific time. I'll see you in the morning." I began to take off my pants as a signal that I wanted to go to sleep now, very tired, just a bit woozy.

He sat down beside me. I sat up, startled.

"It's a big bed," he said.

"It is," I said. My pants now off, I tried to slip under the covers, but in trying to do so hurriedly, I caught my feet on the sheets.

He was on me, on top of me. I pushed him away.

"What's the matter?"

"Look, Chris," I said, facing what was happening and trying to cope with it without severing what I now considered my friendship with him, "I can't sleep with anyone else, I never have—" If what I thought was happening, then who had I been all night?

He grabbed me, drew me to him. I pulled myself away, to the very edge of the bed. "You offered me the guest room . . . Chris."

"Well, this is my bedroom," he snapped. He rose, grumbling. "Oh, then, come on," he said testily.

Grabbing my pants and shoes, I followed him to another room, a smaller room, a smaller bed. "Good night, Chris. I really—"

I slipped into the bed.

Here he was again, pushing, shoving, poking.

I stood up angrily. "I have to leave, Christopher."

"I won't drive you," he said.

"You picked me up."

"I'll drive you in the morning; you'll have to stay."

If I stayed, he wouldn't leave me alone. Yet I was miles away from downtown Los Angeles.

"Let's have some coffee, and then you can drive me," I said. He walked away from me.

"Drive me back!" I followed him to the door of his bedroom.

On his bed, he grumbled—"You can stay or you can leave"—and turned over.

I walked out, into the night—soothed by the fragrance of flowers drifting into the light fog. I walked down the long, long road of the canyon, walked down, down, down, toward the edge of the ocean, to Pacific Coast Highway, to hitchhike my way back to downtown Los Angeles, miles away. Son of a bitch, I kept repeating, what a lousy son of a bitch that Isherwood guy is. Now that the cold ocean air was hitting me I realized how drunk we had both been. I was glad he hadn't driven me back.

After a chilly half hour or so of shivering—I had opened my shirt nearly to my waist and had rolled up my sleeves—I was picked up by a man who drove us to the shadows of a closed gas station. He gave me the money I bargained for. I knew who I was then, with this man: I was hustling, period, no ambiguity.

Don Allen wrote to me that it was important for me to continue publishing sections of the book. Anticipation was growing, he told me. Whether he meant at Grove or elsewhere, I wasn't sure.

I sat at the typewriter in my room. Write what? Tell what? Chuck . . . Skipper . . . Mr. Klein . . . Chi-Chi in New Orleans . . . Jocko . . . Seize how much of their lives? Dare to presume that I understood them? Try to convey the exhilaration of hustling: the extreme highs, the unbearable lows, why being paid for sex without

reciprocation on my part—over and over and over, never enough—
held me so powerfully even though it might spill over into despera-
tion? How to explore that? How much to remember?

I pushed the typewriter away, tore up the paper on which I
had managed to type a few desultory sentences, and went to the
Waldorf bar on Main Street, the sounds from the jukebox blasting
into my ears, bursts of laughter erupting. Wounded laughter?—did
a particular shrill laughter so often heard in exile bars stumble, right
in the middle, as if on a bruise? No, it was joyful laughter, the laughter of free exile. Was I hearing all that clearly for the first time?

I managed to write more "chapters" that were quickly published in *Big Table* and *Evergreen Review*: one about Pete, a young
hustler with whom I had once hustled a wistful, sad little man who
wanted us to pretend he was our mother watching over us "sleeping" in bed naked; another about Chuck, longing for a vanished
frontier; and another about . . . Mr. Klein, resurrected as Mr. King,
and so, now, frozen in a story, left waiting between two lions.

Hitchhiking on lower Wilshire Boulevard one night to eventually reach Hollywood Boulevard, I met a man named Bob. He
had seen me hitchhiking on the corner, in that section not known
for pickups, certainly not known as a hustling or cruising area. He
had driven around Wilshire quickly, thinking someone else would
pick me up.

Despite the ambiguity of the street on which he had picked
me up, I played the hustler role I had perfected, although at first I
didn't think he was gay—hitchhiking always pitched me into that
role. In easy conversation, he guessed that I was eighteen, and I let
him believe that. He was in his upper thirties, slender, tall, good-
looking in an undramatic way . . . like an engineer, which he was.

I spent the night with him, in a modern house in Pasadena,
all glass windows, several of which slid open onto a pool entirely
calm in the breathless night. In trunks too large for me—his—I sat
at the edge of the pool with him, talking. He mentioned foods he

liked, making conversation. I mentioned that I liked filet mignon, perhaps risking an edge of my street hustler's image by that much knowledgeability.

In the consecutive days I spent with him—three—we had filet mignon for breakfast, for lunch, for dinner. Conversation was easy with him, although my stance restricted the range of subjects. About movies, I joined him. Other times, never in condescension, he seemed to want to convey information about subjects he felt would benefit me, perhaps to teach me: about politics—he was a professed liberal—and about his travels to other countries. Often he would stop himself and say earnestly, "Now tell me everything about yourself, Johnny." Then I would edit details of my life that would sustain the view I knew he had of me, instinctively bright, not too many years of school. It no longer surprised me how easily I could become that other person. Sexually, he fed my need to be desired.

I would not move in with him, as he suggested—offering me my own room. I kept my room in the hotel on Hope Street.

I saw him week after week, often daily, staying over at his home on weekends. He gave me money frequently, generously, never just before or after sex, usually when he drove me to my hotel room. He would announce different reasons for giving what he did—for rent—"probably due"—for clothes—"you can always stand another pair of jeans although you look great in faded ones." I spent more and more time with him. I did not write, even as the contractual date for the novel to be delivered to Grove Press came.

And went.

We were at the beach in Santa Monica. I lay on the sand, tanning, knowing he was admiring my body. He rubbed it with oil, lingering, smoothing the liquid even under my trunks, so that I had become aroused.

"Will you please?" he asked me.

I hadn't heard what he had asked. "What?"

"Will you rub some sun lotion on my back?"

I pretended I hadn't heard him. The thought of touching him that intimately, especially publicly, on the beach, impeded me; it would amount to a compromise about who I was at that moment. I lay back on the sand and closed my eyes, not wanting to see whether he had been hurt, whether he had understood my hesitation. When I opened my eyes, he was looking at me in a way I could not identify —perhaps did not want to identify. Bewilderment? Hurt?

Dressed, we lingered on the beach, walking along the cooling sand barefoot. I saw some men moving toward the underside of the piers, into growing shadows. They disappeared into the dark maw. I wondered whether Bob was aware of them, that they were cruising, that as the day darkened, sex would occur within the light-slashed darkness.

Bob stopped along the cresting line of the ocean. He was looking out, beyond the water, where the sun was fading into a bluish dusky haze, not yet the day's total surrender, a brief limbo before night.

"Do you know what this time of day is called?" he asked me.

"No."

"The blue hour. It's a light that creates contrary perceptions, the time of day, just a few moments between dusk and night when everything is at once clearest and most unclear; distance disappears, objects seem sharp." He laughed. "I'm sorry, Johnny, I didn't mean to bore you."

I had followed what he meant as the blue moments disappeared, swallowed by the night. I didn't tell him I understood. It was at such times that I felt burdened by the identity I assumed.

On a radiant Sunday, when the ocean, so calm, gleamed like a blue mirror, we drove to a restaurant in Malibu to have a late breakfast. Sitting at a table that overlooked the ocean, which spilled in crests against the craggy rocks where the restaurant was perched, he was silent for a long time, a quiet moodiness I had grown familiar with.

"I'm concerned about you, Johnny," he said.

"About—?"

"You're just a kid, but what about later—I mean, what will you do with the rest of your life?"

I felt fraudulent. Tell him I had a college degree, that I had a contract to write a book, that I could easily get jobs?

"I just don't think about that kind of stuff," I said—Johnny said.

"You should go back to school," he said.

I didn't remember whether I had told him I hadn't finished high school; perhaps he had only assumed it from my street posture and the age he still believed me to be.

"I don't mean necessarily high school, unless that's what you want," he went on, "but maybe some specialized school, where you can learn something that will give you a good life."

The imposture, too perfect, had created a trap, springing now, with someone I truly felt close to.

"I've written off for some catalogs. They're at home. If you want, I'll go through them with you. I'll pay your tuition."

I held my breath, wanting to tell him I was sorry, sorry that I had duped him so successfully.

"Think about it," he said.

We finished breakfast; the conversation returned to what it had been before, about nothing now.

He drove me back to the hotel on Hope Street. I asked him to wait for me in the car. I rushed in and retrieved a copy of *Big Table,* with my story of "The Fabulous Wedding of Miss Destiny." I in-

scribed it to him: "To my wonderful friend Bob. Always—Johnny."
I ran out, someone else ran out, someone else I would now allow
him to see.

He looked at the book, he looked at the story, he looked at
the inscription. He looked at me.

"Little Johnny," he said. "Congratulations."

30

In my room, I sat smoking—I smoked a lot now when I was upset. I had darkened the room, wanting to create night, intending to fall into the comfort of sleep, sure that it was all over between me and Bob; but light slipped through partings in the blinds, and I was unable even to doze. I felt miserable, knowing I had hurt a very good man, a very good friend who cared for me a lot. The knowledge that I had hurt myself, by losing his friendship, did not assuage my guilt.

I lit another cigarette and—

A slender streak of smoke arose, and with it came the memory of the kept woman as—

—*the smoke lingered about her, and she completed an intricately graceful choreography of slight movements as she withdrew the cigarette from her lips, extending a moment of suspense.*

I watched the smoke from my own cigarette. More and more I pieced together the smallest details of my brief interlude with Marisa Guzman. What was eluding me about that distant interlude that rose up so assertively, so unexpectedly?

As I often did in times of emotional turbulence, grateful that she was now living in Los Angeles, I sought out my sister Olga, not to share with her the source of my anxieties but simply to be soothed by her stories, her dramatized gossip about family matters and, invariably, as I expected and counted on, about Isabel Franklin. In learning of others' entanglements I would, at least momentarily, forget mine.

"Look!" my sister said when we were alone after a late breakfast and her husband and children were gone. She was plump again, yes, always beautiful, as sassy as ever. She pushed a magazine into my hands, open to a certain page.

It was a glossy magazine, like *Vanity Fair,* slick, determinedly chic. The article was illustrated with many photographs. In the largest one, a lovely, elegant woman sat on an elegant couch in an elegant room. Behind her, steps swirled into a second level of the house.

"It's Marisa Guzman," I said, startled and pleased that the memorable kept woman of Augusto de Leon was being awarded such lavish attention in an American magazine.

"Look closely," my sister said.

I did.

"It's Alicia Gonzales," my sister said.

Yes, there sat Isabel Franklin in her home on Nob Hill in San Francisco. Other photographs, smaller, showed her roaming her "fabulous home," as the writer of the article described it. Only one photograph, the smallest one, was shared, with a man past middle age, her husband, the famous columnist.

There it all was, my sister's stories and conjectures verified.

Alicia Gonzales of El Paso, who had become Isabel Franklin of New Orleans, was now Mrs. Bert Schwartz of San Francisco and a doyen of the city's society—or, as the writer of the article implied, a certain faction of it.

"Read it," my sister said, laughing. "Read it aloud to me and tell me it's possible."

The gushy writer of the article gave the woman's name as the former Isabel Franklin, recently from New Orleans. Her parents were from Spain, where she had returned to bury them, one month apart. She was a mixture of French and Spanish heritages—"some nobility somewhere there in the background," the reporter quoted her as having said, "without pretension, just dismissing what is generally known." "Her home in Nob Hill," I read on, "is a show-place, to which artists and other celebrities regularly seek an invi-tation. She has a reputation as a great hostess."

My sister was poking at me, laughing, coaxing me to share the details of the article with her, delighting in it—"Read that again."

"A recent guest," I read on aloud, "was—"

"The midget writer," my sister anticipated.

"Truman Capote," I read aloud, "with whom she laughed and shared sophisticated, witty stories about their memories of New Orleans." I continued reading, fascinated: Invitations to her home were coveted by actors, politicians, everyone who was anyone. Toward the end of the fawning article, the writer tossed off a con-cealed gibe: "Although some in old San Francisco society consider her somewhat 'nouveau arrivée' and have not opened their arms to her—yet, she has established herself as a woman of substance and grace, staples of her noble ancestry."

"The gall!" my sister gasped. "A poor Mexican girl from El Paso!"

I was wrong in believing that the relationship between me and Bob was over.

He telephoned me to join him for dinner, as I had done be-fore almost regularly. He seemed unchanged toward me. He did not even indicate what had to be obvious now, especially if he had read my story, that I was not the wayward young man I had pre-tended to be—replete with street talk and gestures, the boy he wanted to send to school. After my own awkward embarrassment at first, I welcomed the development. We now talked about writers that he liked, that I liked. To my surprise, sex remained as it had been before, as if, at those times, I became again the same object of desire he had originally pursued.

Still, my need to prowl the streets swept over me. I had to return, as if to prove that I could not be drawn away from the enticing world of anonymous desire by my feelings toward one person, toward Bob. With him, I was restless now. I became moody and did not tell him why. I went hustling—liberated again!—and met Bob afterward for dinner.

"I had to," I told him. "It didn't mean anything, not like with you."

"I understand, Johnny," he said. "I do understand."

Again, the unexpected reaction—like his easy acceptance of the fact that I had been lying to him about who, what, I was. There was, again, no anger, no accusation, and that thrust me into what I had been prepared to resist, guilt: guilt not for what I had done—there was no guilt there—but for its having hurt someone, despite his disclaimer, who, like Wilford, I had come to love as an intimate friend.

"Johnny, that book you're writing—"

It was the first time he had mentioned that. Of course, he had read the note in *Big Table* about the almost completed novel. I had written hardly anything more. The new deadline I had promised Grove had also passed. Each time I conceived of setting down what was expected, what I had indicated I would write, each such time, I was whipped into a frenzy of doubt and guilt—and self-recrimination—doubt that I could recapture those unique times, which I was still living; guilt that if I did, I would be plundering real lives, sealing them into a book while the actual lives would go on beyond our shared experiences, far beyond me, without me, secure in a new life.

"What about that book, Bob?" I asked him.

"Are you working on it?"

"No. I can't write here." That hadn't occurred to me until I had spoken it, that writing about the life I was still living was a factor in not being able to transform the experiences.

"What if you returned to El Paso?"

El Paso! The isolation, the ancient memories, the wind . . . El Paso.

"I'll send you money regularly," he said, "if that will help."

I returned to El Paso. There, in the government projects where my mother still lived, I began to write and eventually to finish the novel that I would title *City of Night*.

I wrote frantically, every day, sometimes into night, from early morning, typing on a rented Underwood typewriter that I set up on a table in my mother's bedroom, the house kept quiet by her beyond the closed door, opened only when I came out to dinner, and at night when she went to bed. My divorced brother Robert and I once again shared the living room at night, he on the couch, I on a roll-out bed. The bedroom door was also opened during the day when I came out now and then to translate into Spanish and read to my mother a passage I thought appropriate.

"You're writing a beautiful novel, *m'ijo*," she told me proudly.

How to bring order to a world that thrived on anarchy? I chose a prose that might convey the dissonance of rock and roll versus the formal strains of classical music that my father had loved. I listened to Chuck Berry, Fats Domino, Elvis Presley, Beethoven, Tchaikovsky, Bizet, Bartók—lots of Bartók.

Often, from the window of the projects would emerge the sounds of Verdi's *Requiem,* a favorite. That music would soar into the sounds of our neighbors' radios, sad Mexican laments, a beautiful cacophony.

The structure of my novel was emerging: Each main chapter was a "portrait." That would impart the actual series of encounters, mostly fleeting. I wrote out of sequence—the ending of the book first, adapted from the letter that had become "Mardi Gras." I wrestled with the order of my memories. Who had appeared first in Pershing Square—the fabulous Miss Destiny or Chuck the cowboy? A portrait titled "The Professor" dealt with an older, brilliant man laid up, longing for impossible love from the "angels" he paid. I had met him in Los Angeles, but did his story fit better in wintry New York? Would that shift falsify? How much could I interject into what I had seen, only seen, heard, only heard, in order, from a distance, to attempt to find meaning where I had, then, detected none? How "truthful" was it possible to be, while relying on the total unreliability of memory? I decided this: The sequence of my novel would be determined by the sequence of recollection. Adjusted memories might even yield what wasn't clearly there in order to illuminate what was.

Individual chapters found their own structure. In a chapter titled "White Sheets," I evoked my fascination with mathematics for its structure. Just as the answer to a graphed algebraic problem is found in the intersection of two lines, so the protagonists in that chapter found the possibility of connection only at midpoint—and then they separate, like the diverging lines of such a graph. I saw in the fall from near stardom of a man I called "Lance O'Hara" a suggestion of Greek tragedy, the bruitings of the furies heard in bar gossip predicting his downfall.

So it went; and always with the recurring sense—kept dormant only for intervals—that I was betraying the secret lives I had shared.

Bob called daily, encouraging me, reassuring me. I told him that I was writing an ending chapter that would deal with our relationship. "I want you to promise me that you won't do that, won't write about that. Don't, John!" That was the first time he was abrupt with me, the first time he had called me "John." "I promise." I veiled much of what had occurred between us into a last chapter titled "White Sheets."

After rummaging through several titles—"It Begins in the Wind," "Masquerade," "The Fabulous Wedding," several of those announced with excerpts in *Evergreen Review*—I chose, at Don Allen's suggestion, *City of Night,* which had, from the beginning, been the title of the chapters that occurred between the portraits.

"Johnny!" My brother Robert unexpectedly opened the door I kept closed while I worked. It was Sunday and he was not at work; my mother was at Mass.

"Robert?" Seldom did my brother annoy me.

"Your movie star is dead."

He hadn't forgotten her name. He had wanted to soften the news that I immediately grasped about my beloved movie star.

Marilyn Monroe was dead.

A suicide?

Had she ever finally believed that she, at first a plainly pretty young girl, had remade herself into the world's most desired movie star? If she had killed herself, who had she wanted to kill?

One day my book was finished. My mother, my brother Robert, and I wound about the kitchen table collating the original typescript and three carbon copies of the almost 800-page novel.

★   ★   ★

I was on my way to return the rented Underwood typewriter. I could not. I bought it for fifty dollars, knowing that I would keep it forever.

Galley proofs arrived. The book was all wrong! I panicked. With a pencil, I began making small changes in the margins of the proofs, then bigger ones—and then I found myself revising long passages, typing them on pages I pasted over the galleys. By the time I had finished reading the proofs, I had rewritten, in pencil, ink, and on the typewriter, at least one-third of the novel. The announced publication date had to be postponed while the expensive changes—backed strongly by Don Allen—were made.

It was then, when I faced the fact that this book would definitely appear for anyone—anyone!—to read, it was then that I was jarred to realize that I had betrayed the street world I had lived in, in yet another way than by exposing it: In writing about that world, I had in effect hidden it again, pushed it all, all those lives, into the limbo of fiction. Wasn't that dishonesty, a license to conceal? I had tried to inject meaning where I had seen none. Major dishonesty— to order chaos.

Not only in writing about the night world of Times Square and Pershing Square had I used the out of fiction. In writing about my father—the intimate moments when I sat on his lap, on the laps of his laughing friends—I had blurred it all. Don Allen had detected that in the first finished version, had insisted I deal with those moments clearly. Instead, impulsively, I removed the incident entirely—and, finally, at Don's insistence, I restored it, toned down, and that's how it appeared.

But wasn't greater honesty also possible in fiction, to relegate to invention what can't be faced otherwise? If, throughout interludes in my street life when I was playing the roles I chose, I had been dishonest, wasn't I, in fiction, being truthful?

Those confusions, contradictions, festered as the time for the publication of *City of Night* approached, a time I dreaded and anticipated.

Would I ever be able to write about my life without the scrim of fiction?

City of Night was published in 1963 while I was still in El Paso. It was greeted at first with strident reviews. The first of many was shrill, appearing in the *New York Review of Books*; it was titled "Fruit Salad." The reviewer questioned my existence, suggesting that Grove Press had concocted the book in its offices. It was clear to me that the reviewer, notoriously disturbed, was trying to wish away the authenticity of my book, was threatened by it; he was well known for hiring "dumb hustlers," an identity contradicted by me and my novel.

Still, his shrill review set off a wave of speculation about the "real identity" of the author, speculation fueled by the fact that I refused to promote the novel, chose to remain apart from it. Articles in newspapers, magazines, and tabloids purported to identify me. Impostors claimed to be me and made news in columns. One imposter drunkenly proclaimed his assumed identity in New York's gay bars. Another was in Fire Island, the guest of a rich man. Another appeared in Paris. By keeping my identity private, I was making it possible for others to claim it.

For years I battled with Barbara Epstein, the editor of the *New York Review of Books,* to grant me space to respond to the venomous review. That space was finally granted, thirty years after the bitchy review had appeared.

There were more reviews, hundreds. Almost daily I would receive a batch from Grove. Soon, the reviews turned to praise.

★ ★ ★

In my hometown, my novel was sold under the counter in some bookstores, kept in a private collection at the public library I had frequented so often. Few people in the city knew I was in El Paso.

The guilt I had tried to keep in abeyance while writing about lives I was now leaving far behind resurged once the book was published. That awareness reverberated throughout the day, at night.

And yet, I told myself—

Pete, the shrewd Times Square hustler, would be always young and desirable in my novel. (*But how old was he now, how quickly aging, where now?*) Miss Destiny would always be yearning for her wedding in my recounting of her impossible hope. (*But how soon would she weary, give up, surrender?*) Skipper, Jocko—in my novel they would always be left on the edge, surviving. (*But how soon after that did the inevitable falling occur?*) . . . All those lives lived frantically would go on beyond what I had written about them. Yes, I had been true to the exhilaration allowed only to those exiles, those outlaws, an excitement I would substitute for nothing else.

But I had escaped—I hated that word. I had survived—I hated that word, too . . . I had escaped the final dangers of that world only through the accident of talent. Guilt at times became so suffocating that I gasped aloud, with anger at myself, with sorrow for the lives abandoned.

My novel became a top best seller, going into printing after printing, published in foreign countries. Yet I was broke. No royalties would be payable for months. Soon, I would have to ask Bob to stop sending me money; the book was finished, the goal met.

I had to buy my mother a house of her own.

I applied to a local bank for a loan against future royalties. As "security" I took copies of best-seller lists on which my novel rode high. The loan was refused.

I wrote to Don Allen about getting an advance. He consulted Barney Rosset. I was advanced $5,000, a sizable amount at the time.

Joyfully, my mother and my sister Blanca went hunting with realtors for a house. They found one that my mother loved, a white duplex with a rose garden, nothing ostentatious, no, not yet; it was an attractive house in a good neighborhood—away from the projects.

I did not want to see it until everything was in order, with new furniture that the advance would cover. I wanted to see my mother in it.

That day arrived. The house was furnished, freshly painted. On the day she was moving in, my mother hugged me, tightly; I held her. "Thank you, *m'ijo,* thank you for my house."

She paused on the step before the government unit she would now be leaving. She looked about at the other units, where the Mexican women who had turned to her for advice, for solace, lived and would remain.

"I'll miss my friends," my mother sighed, "but they can come and visit me in my new house." She moved away to my brother's car to be driven to her new home.

Now I would see it. I drove there in an old 1954 Studebaker I had bought for $150.

My mother greeted me at the door. She smiled her most radiant smile as she took my hand and led me outside to her garden, a rose garden now in bloom. I felt I had truly succeeded.

In the house with her—she furnished the living room and her bedroom not unlike a doll's house—I felt a happiness I had not felt before.

I remained in El Paso, in my mother's house. I converted a handsome wood-paneled den with a wall-size window into my study. I

took my mother out to lunch, dinner. I hired a woman to help her
with the household chores.

I heard from Bob less and less. I supposed he finally had faced
the fact that I had never been the person he had picked up hitchhiking. In my lasting affection, he joined Wilford.

Time passed.

Intending to leave "next month," I stayed in El Paso. I took
long rides out into the desert. I climbed Mount Cristo Rey, up the
steep incline, clasping rocks, to the very top, as I had done years
ago when I had seen the family of Mexicans ensnared by the border patrol.

I delighted in the fact that my mother was able to invite her
friends from the projects for visits, and to watch the wondrous
color television, extravagant for the time, that I had bought her.
She would serve sweet wine for her guests, having baked a cake
to accompany it.

President John Kennedy was murdered in Dallas. With my mother
and my brother Robert, I watched the developing drama. My
mother held her rosary steady in her hand, whispering prayers for
the slain president.

I went with her to a Mass held for him, a man beloved among
Mexicans. The church was crammed; people knelt outside, unable to find a place inside. Sobs punctuated the Mass recited by
a cadre of priests. Throughout, El Paso was somber, in personal
mourning.

The vicious aunts came over to watch the funeral on my
mother's color television. Both wept constantly, making sure they
were heard. Their weeping was interrupted once:

"That wife of his isn't crying!" one of the aunts announced
in shock when Jackie Kennedy went by.

"Imagine!" the other aunt said. "She should be fainting from sorrow after every step of the way to the grave."

Weeks later they returned to our house, the malicious aunts. I was in my study, reworking *Pablo!* to finally show Don Allen. In the living room, my mother was serving the aunts coffee and cake.

I heard my mother say, "My son made all this possible for me, this house."

One of the aunts raised her voice, so that I would be sure to hear:

"Yes, and do you know what he wrote about?—to get you this house, your son?"

"God save us for the lengths we travel," said the second aunt.

I headed for the closed door, to confront them; but I paused, hearing my mother say:

"Yes, I do know what he wrote. He wrote a beautiful book. He's read parts of it to me. And, Maria, Adela," she addressed them pointedly, "I know there are envious people smarting at his success. I know this, too—Maria, Adela—he can go in through the front entrance of places that wouldn't allow you in through the kitchen."

I never again felt I had to come to her defense with regard to me.

The reaction from the rest of my family was different. My beloved brother Robert, leafing through a copy of *Big Table* that contained "The Fabulous Wedding of Miss Destiny," had pushed it away from wordlessly as I watched. It was the only time in my life I would feel betrayed by him. After *City of Night* was published, he and my brother Yvan and my sister Blanca followed my literary success proudly—congratulating me abundantly, bragging about me to everyone, giving a family party for me—but until many, many years later, they would not, and this included my sister Olga, discuss the subject of my books. Never would there be any reference to my having lived the life I had written about—almost as if they disbelieved it.

And I preferred it that way, never distrusting their unconditional love.

In El Paso, I took up bodybuilding, partitioning a section of my study to serve as a gym. I could not much longer be a slender "young man." But I could be a muscular man, another figure of desire. Muscles came easily. Although I continued to extend my time in El Paso, my chosen isolation—long, longer—I was, I suppose, preparing for my return to the arena that was, daily, luring me back, its summons increasingly strong.

With more royalties coming in, I bought a classy Mustang, tan with a black top and with a wooden steering wheel. I saw it as a projection of myself.

31

Los Angeles was on fire.

In Watts, on a day of steamy heat, a black woman was stopped for a routine traffic violation claimed by barking white cops. Anger during years of outrage waiting only for the flicker of a match. A car was overturned, a white-owned shop was set ablaze—and six days of riots flared, leaving many dead, mostly black people, and thousands wounded. Smoke drenched the city and went far into the ocean, even into mansions in Bel Air.

My sister Olga had lived in the far periphery of Watts, among friendly neighbors who included Negro families. When the riots occurred, the black families had distanced themselves from her and her children, ignoring her expressions of sympathy about the conditions that had ignited the rage, evoking some of the outrages she knew about against Mexicans in Texas. But every seemingly white face had become the enemy. My sister's husband was fired at, a shot he managed to dodge.

We traveled, my mother and I, to Los Angeles to visit my sister Olga, staying overnight in a suite in the gaudiest, most expensive motel I could find in Phoenix—so that my mother would not tire from the long drive. More than a year had passed since the riots, soothing fears for now. The open wounds were turning into deep scars.

My mother stayed with my sister and her family in a small rented house in Torrance, miles from the conflagration; I rented a room in a nearby motel with a pool.

The first two days in Los Angeles, I spent with my sister and my mother, driving around with them to see the beautiful city of palm trees and flowers.

Now I was ready to return, anonymous and with full allegiance, to the world that I would prove to myself I had not betrayed, had not left.

As soon as I drove up to Selma Avenue, I saw that the hustling scene had changed. Some of the hustlers looked even younger than when I had first turned up. A few were effeminate. Before I had left, street hustlers were masculine—and, yes, those were still there.

I parked on a side street, so that I could scout the altered territory. What if time had thrust me out of this arena? I waited about half an hour for twilight, gathering my courage to test myself in an arena whose raw cruelties I had witnessed, had contributed to.

Undoing yet another button of my denim shirt, to open it almost to the top edge of my Levi's, my new dark boots shiny, I got out of the car. I paused. I took a few steps toward the main stretch of hustling, more steps, quickening. I saw several young men on a corner. They looked so young! I halted. Terror gripped me. I turned back. I ran. I fled to my car. Before I had reached it, a man walking toward Selma stopped before me.

"Wow," he said, studying me.

I was back, someone else, a muscular man—not the lithe young man I had first been on these streets.

In the evenings, I joined my mother and my sister Olga and her family for dinner; warm gatherings I welcomed, although I had not yet been alone with my sister to hear all her news. Earlier, at the motel, I lay by the pool, tanning, preparing. Later, each night, I returned to Selma to hustle.

But now hustling wasn't enough. There were long empty days and a vast craving to fill.

Years ago, hustling, I had heard gay men talking about all the sexual encounters they had had during an afternoon in a territory for sex-hunting known by almost everyone who cruised the city. It was a miles-long field of sexual anarchy in Griffith Park, a vast park, acres and acres, in the midst of the city. There was no hustling in the gay areas, just mutual cruising.

I found the area by entering the park and following a car whose driver had looked over at me in a way I understood.

It was a warm summer day in the luxuriant park, which had fields of green and bramble spotted by wildflowers. Driving up the paved two-lane road that wound and curved about hills, I had seen hundreds of gay men sex hunting, many good-looking, athletic, sensual. I saw many, variously slipping down the slopes onto many paths. I knew immediately: Sex occurred in coves formed by overhanging branches and clusters of trees.

Shirtless, my torso oiled, I parked my Mustang on the side of a sandy islet off the main road and stood there waiting.

Soon, a car parked nearby, just as I counted on. Instinctively joining the rhythm of the hunt, I slipped down an incline into the bushes, knowing I would be followed. I was. The man went down on me. I pulled back before coming. Another man had slipped down the decline to join us. I turned to him—and then to a third man. When I left, they turned to each other.

Three! Three sexual contacts in less than one hour.

Leaving the park at dusk to visit my mother at my sister's, leaving again after dinner to hustle on Selma, returning to the motel room to sleep, I went to the park day after day, increasingly early, as early as before noon.

I found a spot that I preferred. It formed a kind of proscenium, a "stage" shaped by trees whose branches clustered into an arc.

In this arena saturated with the lure of sex, my need to be desired intensified. Encounter after encounter; I began to number each. As the numbers grew, so did the craving—like a geometrical progression that keeps on multiplying; a demand, a command for more and more unreciprocated contacts, making up now, surpassing, what I might have abdicated during the reclusive years in El Paso. Although I mutually desired many of the good-looking men who approached me, I still refused to allow myself to respond to them, as if that would compromise the posture I still asserted when, later, I went hustling on Selma.

Another evening with my family. No further gossip about Isabel Franklin, my sister drew me aside to tell me, somewhat desolately.

Another night hustling.

Another afternoon in the park.

More numbers: thirty in one week.

★   ★   ★

My mother was eager to return to her home; I had promised her we would be away only ten days, and she had counted them strictly. When I suggested extending our stay, she grew tired, sad.

As we drove into the desert back to El Paso in my tan Mustang, I looked in my rearview mirror and I saw a reflection of the city of lost angels enshrouded within a gray cloud of fog and smog, like an enshrined biblical city in which I had performed a sexual ritual. Right then, on a tablet of paper my mother held steady on the console between us, as I drove back to Texas, I began writing in pencil my second novel, *Numbers*.

In El Paso, trying to match in the prose the franticness of the sexual hunt I had embarked on, I finished that novel in exactly ninety days, on the same Underwood typewriter that I had rented, now mine. It was a novel about Johnny Rio, an ex-hustler, who, returning to Los Angeles, begins numbering sexual encounters in Griffith Park. I located the character modeled after myself in a trap from which he can't escape, the "numbers" being finite. Perhaps I was still trying to assuage my guilt for having an out from a world that trapped so many others. I conceived of this novel as being about the attempt to stave off time, to stave off death with sex. As the book progressed, the imagery turned increasingly dark; the beautiful park became almost sinister, a presence—"the Park" spelled with a capital P in the latter part of the book—warring with Johnny Rio.

Like *City of Night,* that book became a scandal and a best seller. The fact that the cover had featured a photograph of me, leaning against a wall in what was said to be a "suggestive" pose, a photograph reproduced hazily enough so that I would not generally be recognized from it, created even more criticism. The book's somber meaning and structure were overlooked; the criticism focused on the graphic sexual encounters.

In El Paso, I remained reclusive. I drove into the desert, climbing the familiar mountain, not taking the easy cleared path; clinging to sliding rocks to reach the top.

El Paso was stifling me, the craving for the sexual anarchy of Los Angeles was commanding, summoning. I had to return—this time alone, my mother increasingly unhappy at the prospect of being away.

I rented a motel room in Hollywood. To extend the anticipation of returning to Griffith Park, and because I was eager to see her, always missing her, I called my sister and she invited me to dinner.

When she instructed the rest of her family to leave us alone, I knew she had delicious information to convey. "Now, sister Olga, tell me what you're so eager to tell me. I'm sure it's about Isabel—"

"Alicia," she insisted on correcting, "and about the midget writer's famous party!"

Of course, she was referring to Truman Capote's famous black and white masquerade party. Tabloids, newspapers, magazines, all thrived on its details and the caravan of famous guests, including Jackie Kennedy, and—I was sorry to learn—Norman Mailer, whom I would expect to have stayed away. Capote's so-called "nonfiction novel"—how, I wondered, was that different from fiction, and how, then, was it a "new literary form"?—had brought him a fortune, and with what I considered blood money made from the doomed lives he had ransacked, the lives of the killers and their victims, he had given what was called "the party of the century," inviting "everyone who matters"—along with some of the people involved in the murder trial, including the prosecutor. For me, that party was a cruel celebration of the murders and the executions. The simpering of the writer and the giddy responses of the invited added to my reaction of disgust. All of that confirmed my decision not to publicize my novels; I rejected requests for interviews and stories (until, much later, when it became necessary to call attention to the fact that my books were facing censorship). I saw my separation as a way to respect lives "borrowed"—arrogated.

"Tina's friend in San Francisco read about it in a newspaper. It said 'everyone who is anyone' was invited to that party." My sister held her breath dramatically: "And so was Alicia—"

"Isabel," I insisted.

"Can you believe that the airline sent her bag to the wrong hotel—with her gown? She claimed the maids in her hotel were all praying that it be found in time for the ball. I bet if it hadn't been found just in time, she would have gone naked rather than not go and be seen there with all those famous people."

My sister inhaled, long, her eyes closed, as if to be able to tolerate what clearly disgusted her. "Can't you just hear her screaming at the Mexican maids and preening like a princess?" She threw up her hands. "I've given up wondering how she continues to pull it off, even with that snobbish midget writer."

"Well, you have to admit, sister, that she *has* pulled it off." Yes, the Mexican girl I had dated—who had nervously dropped a cigarette on the floor of my rich uncle's Cadillac—had duped them all, including Capote's famous troops.

I stood on a sandy indentation off the main road in Griffith Park. A man drove by, U-turned swiftly. He parked near my car and got out.

"Did you know that someone wrote a book about you?"

"Who wrote a book about me?" I asked, disoriented.

"I don't know the author's real name. No one would write a book like that under his own name."

"I don't know what you're talking about," I said, wanting to choke off this encounter. I walked to my car and opened the door to get in.

The man called out:

"Good-bye, Johnny Rio."

He had assumed I was the character in *Numbers*. I had become my own character. I had become Johnny Rio.

But he had not recognized me as the author. I was still anonymous. I rejoined the cruising ballet.

Hustling on Selma that same night:

A young man stopped. "Hey, I heard you're real famous."

How the hell could he know? I prepared to deny being the writer I was sure he was going to refer to. Earlier, in the park, I had suspected the same, and had been reprieved.

"Someone said you'd been a famous model once, man," he said.

Being a "model" on the streets then meant being a "physique model" in the proliferating gay magazines of the time, glossy magazines that featured nude males; to be a "physique model" was a cherished goal among hustlers. This young man had pushed the fancied accomplishment of mine into the past. It didn't reassure me to see that he was no more than eighteen years old.

"But, hey, you still look good, man," he said. "Still good enough to be hustling, huh? I hope when I'm your age—"

I hurried away from him, forcing myself not to hear what he was adding. He had whipped up my doubts, doubts that now could be exorcised only by more sex, multiple manifestations of my desirability to fill the deep emptiness exposed.

Those times, I plunged into the anarchy of new territories I was discovering, quick unpaid contacts in darkened alleys, infamous garages, street underpasses, small parks that thrived at night, streets of nighttime cruising, encounters in parked cars.

Then there were the deadly times when nothing worked out, when no connection succeeded, when rejection smashed at my stomach like a brutal fist. I would rationalize. I told myself I was conveying an urgency that made those who wanted to approach me flee from me instead—anything rather than feel undesired. I would force myself to continue the hunt, demanding that I be wanted.

Those monstrous times, I would drive from one sex-hunting area to another. I would get out, cruise among hunting strangers, and, then, no one would solicit me—or someone would, and the encounter would dissipate. Deep in the night, I would still be hunting in known alleys, seeking out whatever light there was from whatever source—a mothy distant light from a nearby street—so that I would not become only a body, any body.

Those times, the franticness would send me to hustle back at Selma, where I had been earlier; but on the fatal nights, it would all be as if the world I had thrived in was conspiring against me. As I waited on the streets where I had been so popular—perhaps only last night!—cars would glide by, a man would peer at me, and then would drive away, leaving me wounded, grasping for reasons why that had occurred. If that same person then moved on to someone else on the streets, I would bleed doubly—and I would extend the hunt, demanding to succeed, not allowing myself the deadly questions: Was I through? Had time left me behind? Was I finally looking my age? Could I no longer pull it off? I flexed my muscles, touched them, rubbed them, reassuring myself that my body was intact, still challenging time.

Without surcease I would drive back and forth to the places that thrived past midnight, underpasses, garages, dark streets. Still, no connection, many approaches, no connection. The raging need pushed me on. Even if it was chilly—cold—I would remove my shirt, rub my body with fresh oil, demanding attention. Nothing. Why? I must look dangerous—anything but undesirable.

The deadly accusatory tint of smoggy dawn would augur the day, the end of the monstrous night, and I would still be cruising, from street to street, alley to alley, underpasses that turned into hunting turfs, where bodies of men pressed against concrete walls, and now I was standing alone on a deserted turf, the sun glaring down.

Exhausted, sweating, I returned to my rented room, but the horror of having been denied all night would send me out again, to shatter the nightmarish sense of defeat, the hunt without connection.

I would drive back to Griffith Park. Then, as if the world I had pursued had lifted its deadly curse, its punishment for all the past conquests—its payback for all the triumphant exhilaration of the sex hunt—everything would change. I was desired, again counting contacts, one after another after another, to make up for the depths I had plunged into. More. More.

I counted twenty-seven sexual contacts in the park in one day, twenty-seven without once coming.

Why? I had asked that question before, but I preferred not to ponder it—what had carved this insatiable need in me, this unfillable demand to be, not really wanted, not loved, no, no, only to be desired? How easy it would be to invoke my father, the childhood game he had asked me to play, sitting on his lap—"Give me a thousand"— in exchange for a few pennies. How easy to extend that to the gray men (they existed only as shadows now) to whom he passed me around for more pennies. Too obvious, too easy. Because there was this: the violent unreliability of memory, the vicious tricks it plays, the camouflages it creates, one terrible imagined memory substituted for an even more horrifying one, thrust back, away. What could that be, the camouflaged origin of the driven sex hunt? There were mysteries that existed only as mysteries, and that, to me, was one.

32

Gerard Malanga came calling.

Don Allen had written me that the poet-actor-writer-performer was coming to Los Angeles and wanted to meet with me, to discuss a possible association. I knew about Malanga; he was supposedly Warhol's "lover," although in actuality he was not. Purportedly heterosexual, he was one of the original members of Warhol's factory. He recently had been traveling with a kind of S&M-ish dance show in which he brandished some whips. I had seen him in the film *Chelsea Girls*.

I agreed to see him, and he turned up. He was not as handsome as I had feared, not as handsome as he photographed, although certainly a handsome man of about thirty-plus years. He was shorter than he appeared in the movie I'd seen. He was beyond glamorous, with flowing brown hair, a classic face, lips that seemed eternally between a sneer and a seductive smile. He wore a jacket with glittery decorations, tight suede pants, low-rise boots. He seemed to be prepared to be photographed at every moment, and the resultant photographs reproduced—widely.

I liked him. I felt no competition with him, as I had feared. We were quite different beings. There was no sexual tension that I detected.

What he came to propose was a collaboration, a book about his association with Warhol. He would describe wondrous adventures—including a time when Mrs. Warhol and Mrs. Malanga despaired of the fact that their sons were leaving the East for perverted California. The fear of abject perversion was indeed justified—they were going to Disneyland. Getting into the spirit of the matter, as if we were playing a clever game—I did not welcome the thought of collaboration with anyone—I suggested a title: "Narcissism, Madness, Suicide: The World of Andy Warhol as Experienced by Gerard Malanga and Re-Created through John Rechy."

I thought he would swoon with delight.

After he left my apartment that day, we agreed to meet again, in a few days. The prospect intrigued me increasingly. After all, I would be the only writer involved in the venture; Gerard would simply tell me stories I would then dramatize. Too, Warhol was a fantastic creation, existing simultaneously in several guises—at times sending out impostors to fulfill his contractual appearances; he was an enigma who often acted like a petulant child—mouthing one-word answers to complicated questions during interviews, and doing so in a breathy voice.

On one of the rare times that I attended a "Hollywood party" during a period of surcease from the streets, I had met one of his earliest "superstars"—Tom Baker, purported to be the first actor to be photographed frontally naked in a nonpornographic movie, as he had been in *I, a Man*. A very handsome, masculine man, with a reputation as a compulsive heterosexual seducer, he gravitated toward me that evening when I had separated myself from the others there—actors and writers. Laughing, at times mirthlessly—mostly rambling as if he were on speed—he told me something that fascinated me about Warhol: The artist controlled the beautiful narcissists around him by withholding desire, depriving them of their main—often only—strength, the power of their desirability. "After that movie I made," he said, "nothing more happened, nothing, man; no more roles, nothing, no one calling; it was like we couldn't exist without him." Only a few weeks later, I learned that Tom Baker had died from an overdose, perhaps a suicide.

By the time Gerard was to return to discuss the proposed book, I had become excited about doing it.

Looking even more glamorous in a Studio 54 way, he turned up wearing a man's fur coat—it was a chilly afternoon, but not chilly enough for fur. He set up the tape recorder he had brought. I sat on a chair facing him as he lounged on a couch not unlike Truman Capote in the famous photograph of him lying on a hammock. We began. Rather he began:

"Who is Gerard Malanga?" he asked in dramatic despair. "Poet? Artist? Actor?"

"I think we should start with when you met Warhol, Gerard."

"Of course . . . When I met him as a poet? When I met him as an artist? When I met him as an actor?"

So it went. All about himself. After a few minutes, I suggested we continue at another time, having decided that there would be no further "collaboration."

Very serious now, dramatic, he asked whether he might ask a favor of me.

"Of course, Gerard. What?"

"Will you take me to the Griffith Park you described in your book *Numbers*?"

"Aren't you supposed to be heterosexual?" His suggestion annoyed me.

"I am—or whatever. I don't want to go there to cruise. I just would like to be able to be there with you, the author of that book, in the actual setting."

"I'm not a tourist guide, Gerard," I said. "If you want to go there, go there by yourself, but not like a visitor."

He was unfazed. When we parted, he gave me a tight hug and a kiss on each cheek.

As if the mere suggestion that I might take anyone to "see" the park had questioned my allegiance to it, I drove to the park early the next day.

I had already had sex with three men by just past noon. Now I waited at my car, again, on a sandy islet adjacent to a long path leading down to several coves of entangled branches. I never parked where other cars were in the immediate area; that signaled several hunters already in the foresty coves. Shirtless and oiled, the top button of my Levi's unhooked, I preferred to wait alone by my Mustang for others to approach me.

A handsome young man walking by stopped, glanced at me, and nodded as a signal. Moving past him, I entered the wooded area, down a familiar path and into a branchy secluded hollow, like a cave. I waited.

The young man entered the cove. He slipped onto his knees. His fingers reached to open my fly.

Footsteps, hurrying, uncommon in the area.

He stood up.

I started to move away along the declining path.

"Los Angeles vice officers! You're both under arrest!"

Two cops in plainclothes, looking like typical sex hunters, were on us, their handcuffs ready.

"Arrested for what?" I said.

"That guy was going down on you," the dark cop barked.

"That's a lie." In their urgency to arrest, they had stopped what this cop was claiming. He wrested my hands behind me and handcuffed me. He shoved me along the path, back to the main road, past other startled sex hunters who went scurrying away.

Ahead of us, the other cop was leading the young man I had been with, now also handcuffed—I thought I heard him sobbing—to a waiting unmarked car. I was pushed into another.

Shirtless, I was driven to the downtown jail, a large fortress of a building, gray, dark. There, the cop led me still handcuffed into a metallic elevator that scraped as it moved up, and it opened into a large room, the color of piss.

Several cops milled about before a desk. I was led past them, into another room where I was fingerprinted and photographed. I felt frozen. These men, in the guarded seclusion of windowless rooms, had absolute power; they could claim whatever they wanted. Behind what looked like a cage, a cop took inventory of my belongings to be taken from me, my wallet, keys. I could keep some change and a slip of paper on which I had written the telephone number of a bondsman given to me by someone in the park with whom I had sex on an earlier day—"The park is hot with vice, man, watch out"—a number I had forgotten about till now.

I was led farther into the innards of the rancid building—there was the smell of incarceration—where several cops, coming off duty, loitered. I kept searching for the young man arrested with me. He would be somewhere invisible within this maze of a fortress.

"Strip."

I turned the humiliation and fear into a desperate triumph. Sitting on a bare bench, I removed my boots and pants. Then I stood up. I flexed, exhibiting my body. Several cops turned quickly away. A few stared.

I took a shower as demanded. I dressed. I was led into a dank cell, by myself, along a row of other cells, all of which looked vacant.

I told the cop who was locking the cell that I wanted to make the allowed phone call.

"We'll let you know when," he said. With an echoing clang, he shut the jail gate. The cell was dark, with one cot and a bare toilet, streaked.

"What they bust ya for?" came a voice from the cell across from me. A slim young man seemed to have awakened, rubbing his eyes and sitting up on a bare cot.

"Nothing," I said.

"Me, too—for nothing," he said. "That's why everyone's in here. For nothing." He laughed.

A hot and cold encroaching fear ran through my body as I realized—in flushed waves—what had occurred, where I was, what was possible. Someone could disappear here and no one would know. My body erupted into cold sweat. I called out, "Officer"—hating the word, "officer!"—to demand using the telephone.

No one came.

"They'll come whenever they want to," the man in the cell across from mine drawled. "Just relax, buddy. Whatever is gonna happen is gonna happen."

It had already started to happen, I thought—as a new wave of realization swept over me that I was behind bars, that my freedom had been snatched away—and for nothing, because of a lie, the interrupted act; and even if otherwise, what fucking crime?

"Rechy!" a voice boomed out.

"Here!" The unwelcome urgency in my voice echoed along the halls.

I was led outside the cell to a phone on the wall in a corridor. I dialed the number the man in the park had given me. Please, let him answer, I kept saying as the phone rang and rang.

"Gibson bonds."

I clasped the phone. I was connected to the outside world, the world I had been wrenched from, and this was now my only link, a voice on the other end of the line.

"My name is John Rechy," I said. "I'm a writer." That was, as far as I remembered, the first time I had spoken those words to a stranger, my full correct name, my identification as a writer. Whatever was necessary to escape this trap.

"I'll be there," said the voice.

I was led back to the iron-barred cell.

"Got your call, huh?" came the voice from across the hall.

"Yeah."

Time passed, minutes that were hours.

"Rechy!"

I was led to a small counter, two seats faced each other, separated by thick glass through which we would speak through individual phones. I looked at the man on the other side of the glass, the bail bondsman. He was smiling. I knew instantly that he was gay. I was glad that I was shirtless.

His look on me reassured me. "You'll be out in a few minutes," he said.

I was out, in the bondsman's car, moving along through the night in downtown Los Angeles. A dark rebirth, because I knew that the trap I had fallen into was allowing only a partial opening, that it was poised to spring even more viciously.

"Is your car in the park?"

"Yes—but they close the park at night," I said.

"I know a back way we can use."

It was the first time I had seen the park in the dark, without the presence of the sex hunters who roamed the glens and coves. So quiet, so placid in the warm darkness.

There, ahead, was my car, its isolation in the dark shadows a blunt reminder of what had occurred.

"You need a drink," the bondsman said.

Yes, and to be with someone who would reassure me that things would be right. There was no use pretending that I wasn't afraid.

In my retrieved Mustang—I felt so warm in it—I followed the man to his small house in Silver Lake.

Inside, jiggling some ice, carrying a bottle of liquor, he said, "It's very serious."

"Getting busted in the park?" The words, spoken, made the situation even less real.

"Yes, it's a felony. Oral copulation, both parties. He handed me the drink and sat down on the couch next to me. "Punishable with up to five years in prison."

Hot sweat froze. "What?" I took the drink, holding it as if it was an anchor within a violently shifting reality. "It didn't happen," I said. "The fucking cops interrupted it."

"Don't worry," he assured me. "I'll put you in touch with the best lawyer."

He put his drink on a table. He stood up; he sat next to me; his hand cupped my groin.

Although his advantageous advance made me angry, in a weary impotent way, I would do nothing to sever the connection that indicated the possibility of escape from the yawning trap. I lay back and closed my eyes. He bent over my limp cock and took it in his mouth, trying futilely to arouse me.

When he had jerked himself off, and I was ready to leave, he said, "By the way, I read your book *City of Night*. It's terrific."

I called my sister to cancel our planned dinner that evening.

"Is something wrong, little brother? You sound strange."

"Nothing, sister. I'm just tired."

There were times when I felt that my sister could read unspoken signals from me, the way she figured out mysteries in the movies or on television.

"Are you sure you're OK, little brother?"

"I'm sure, beautiful sister."

The attorney recommended by the bondsman told me there were several preliminary steps I could take in our defense. He had the arrest report. The cop had designated his exact location, several feet away from where he had busted me and the young man whose name I learned only now—Sam. I was familiar with the area described. From the distance claimed, the verdure made it impossible for anyone to see what the cop alleged. The attorney suggested I hire a photographer to make a film of the locale to indicate that impossibility, and an investigator to draw a map of the area.

For once since the nightmare had begun, I felt relief. The attorney had Sam's telephone number; he was being represented by another attorney.

I met with Sam in his apartment, after I had called him. A sweet good-looking young man—he resembled a high school tennis player—he was as frightened as I had been at first. He had been put into the tank in jail, with dozens of others, dangerous men. He had cowered there, trying to hide, until his attorney got him out. He did not want to be in the film we were to make in the park to present in court. As I left, he told me that he had been arrested before, on the same charge, and that he had been convicted, a matter that would affect our trial.

An overriding vanity, which I grasped as another element of re-assurance that everything was going to be all right, overtook me the afternoon I went to the park with the photographer to film the area of the arrest. The day of the bust, I had not worn a shirt.

I had considered being filmed that way, "for authenticity." Instead, I wore a tight flesh-colored T-shirt that would convey a similar impression. Trial or not, I wanted to look good. As I was being filmed walking down the path—counting steps to indicate the distance between the place of arrest and the claimed location of the cop—I smiled. That would bring Johnny Rio, intact, into the courtroom.

I remembered Marisa Guzman as she lifted her veil from her face. For her incursion into the territory her father had forbidden her to enter, she had ensured that she looked beautiful.

Now, as I stood being filmed at the vantage the cop had described, my fear eased further. All the cop could have seen were entangled branches.

"You may need some publicity photos for your next book," the photographer told me. "Why don't we go to my studio?"

The familiarity with which I was referred to as a writer still startled me.

In his studio, I felt good as he photographed me—in jeans, boots, a cut-off denim vest, and no shirt, with a cigarette dangling, a scowly look. He clicked and clicked.

After one particular photograph he labeled "Terrific!" he set his camera down. "You are one hot dude," he said. Kneeling, he opened my pants and slipped down before Johnny Rio.

The trial was set, not a jury trial. Our attorneys opted for a trial with a judge. They were confident. They had seen the film we had taken, photographs of the park, the drawn map. The cop who had arrested Sam had not made a statement. There was no way that the single cop's testimony would hold up.

Before the proceeding began, I met with Sam in the hallway. He seemed to be distant, cold.

"What's the matter, Sam?"

"My attorney said that this was dragging out because you want material for a new book."

"Jesus Christ!" I felt the anguish of the past months wrenching inside me with added disgust. I wanted to shout at him, If you hadn't been caught before, then we wouldn't have to deal with that, too. But this would indicate that I was being contaminated by the false charges.

The judge, a man over sixty, looked stern. Sam and his attorney, my attorney and I, and the district attorney entered the pale courtroom. Both cops were already there. A court recorder waited to take down testimony. I breathed in relief that no one else was there. Beyond the immediate proceeding, my anonymity had survived. My new fame as a writer had not intruded.

When the cop who had arrested me was on the stand, my attorney showed the map drawn of the terrain—without the brush or the lush trees or the entangled branches indicated. The cop located himself along the open path. From here, he said, he had witnessed me with my pants down to my ankles; he had witnessed Sam squatting before me—and he had witnessed "a full act of fellatio" before he and his partner moved in to arrest. He was asked whether the details in his arrest report were accurate as to location.

"Yes, of course."

The other cop did not testify.

I was asked to show the movie of the park on a rented projector. The courtroom was darkened. I said that the camera had been placed exactly where the officer had indicated he was standing; at the same distance he had designated, in feet, in his arrest report and had reasserted just now. The film began. I saw myself on the screen swaggering along the path, appearing shirtless, smiling, looking as if I was auditioning for another kind of movie. I closed my eyes, regretting my stupidity in the display. Still, the point had been made. The distance claimed by the cop and recorded in the film belied his report.

"There is only one way to gauge this matter," the judge said coldly, "and that is by going to the site in the park. The court is adjourned to reconvene in the area in question. The officers will designate the site of the arrest there."

Even the prosecutor, who seemed not to be interested at all in the matter—he looked friendly to me—was startled by the extreme shift of the court to the park. "Your honor—?"

"We will reconvene in the park, counsel," the judge said sternly.

It was just past noon, one of the busiest times in the park for sex. I saw the look of apprehension on Sam's face, and the smiling contempt on the face of the cop who had arrested me—of course, he knew what would be occurring there when the court arrived.

By a fast route I had discovered on the freeway, I sped there, dreading that I would be stopped for speeding. I drove into the park, up the familiar road, to the familiar site.

I had beaten the others there.

But, goddamnit, there were at least ten cars parked at the side of the road there. That meant that there would be at least that many people on the terrain; more, including those walking. Men might be having sex in the very same cove where the arrest had occurred.

I ran into the heart of the cruising arena. I shouted: "A trial judge is coming!" My words shattered the pervasive silence of the sex hunt. There was rustling all around, of men scurrying out.

"A vice trial is coming!" I shouted into the usually traumatized mood of the park. Hurrying about the paths, I came on two men in a grotto of trees. They were fucking. "A trial is coming," I softened my voice. The two men continued frantically, finishing, before they ran away. More men slipped out of coves, some running deeper into the park.

I heard cars parking. I rushed to stand by my Mustang, as if I had just arrived.

The judge drove up in a Rolls Royce as the lawyers, the two cops, Sam, the two attorneys, and the court recorder parked their cars.

"Show me where you were standing, officer," the judge asked the cop who had testified.

In a jagged file, we walked into the area of the sex hunt, deep, deeper.

"I was here," The cop planted himself firmly in the position where he had indicated, on the map and in the arrest report, that he had stood, the place the film had identified.

My attorney asked me to start walking toward where we had been arrested. Sam was to follow. We walked down the path, moving farther and farther from where the cop and the others waited. We were out of their sight even before we reached the designated cove.

"I was *here!*" I heard the cop say loudly. He strode down the path, placing his location much closer to the cove.

Inside the cove now with Sam, I looked back. I could not see the cop, even at the closer range he was claiming.

"You still have no view of the defendants from here," Sam's attorney said, catching up with the cop. The judge followed.

The cop took several more anxious steps. "I stood here!"

In the cove, I could still not see him. Neither would the others be able to see me or Sam.

The cop stalked down the path, down, along the path, into the cove. He put his hand roughly on Sam's shoulder, forcing him down. "Kneel, like when you were blowing that guy!" He shoved Sam's head against my groin and pushed me against him.

"Take your fuckin' hands off us!" I shouted at him.

He raised his hand as if to hit me. I raised both my hands to ward him off, and then realized that I had hit him, hard. Fists clenched, he came at me.

The attorneys were there, placating us. The judge remained behind.

As we moved out of the territory, back to our cars, two men scurried out of the bushes, adjusting their clothes.

"I've seen enough," the judge said as he went back to his Rolls Royce.

On the side of the road, I stood with my beaming attorney. The prosecuting attorney walked over. "Congratulations," he said with a wry smile, as if to indicate that he was satisfied with the obvious outcome in our favor. "I've read your book *City of Night,*" he told me; "it's very good."

The next day, in the hall outside the courtroom, our attorneys gave me and Sam the news that the judge had already found us guilty. Sentencing was set for a few weeks from now, pending reports from the probation officers we would be assigned to.

Time crawled. I called my mother daily; I was terrified to think what would happen to her if I was sent to prison. I avoided seeing my sister, but I called her often, to hear her calming voice. "I sense it; something's wrong. What is it, little brother?"

"Nothing, sister. I just have some business I'm tending to, about my books." That was all I could think to tell her. How could I tell her that I was waiting to be sentenced, and that the charge carried a possible sentence of five years in prison?

★　★　★

Again, this time at the sentencing, the attorneys met me and Sam in the hall outside the courtroom. The judge had agreed that the evidence was flimsy, and so he was finding us guilty of a misdemeanor, not the serious felony. There would be no jail time. There would be probation of two years, and, for me, a fine of $1,000; for Sam $500.

I wanted to laugh—even then, even there—when I learned what the judge had chosen to convict me of, a charge usually reserved for hustling.

"Because of who you are and what he knew about you," my lawyer confirmed.

As I walked out of the monstrous courthouse, I realized that I had been arrested as Johnny Rio, but it was John Rechy, the writer, who had managed to avoid incarceration.

I drove straight to the park. I left my Mustang in the same place where it had been that fateful day. I took off my shirt. I walked down the same path where the cop claimed he had seen me and Sam. I waited in the same alcove where the arrest had occurred.

A handsome young man walked into the cove. We neared each other.

Footsteps, crunching on the ground, dried leaves.

Fear gripped me. What if . . . ?

I shoved the fear away.

The contact charged by the cop had not been completed—now it would be, in this same grove—and it was, in mutual desire for the first time.

We had got off easy—I never saw Sam again—in that time when arrests, automatic convictions, and severe prison sentences were routine. Vice cops, rubbing their groins, arrested whoever solicited them. Accused falsely, many gay men pleaded guilty so that their lives would not be ground down by the courts. Gay men faced punishment by public exposure, registration for life as sex offenders, and being ordered to appear in lineups with heterosexual suspects involved in child molestation. Gay men netted in cruising areas were, notoriously beaten after being handcuffed; often they were kept in jail at the cops' whim for forty-eight hours without charges, released, then charged again, and kept incommunicado for another forty-eight hours. In the aftermath of salacious news reports about "perverts," bashings soared. Even murder might be justified if the killer claimed to have been enraged at being solicited for sex by a gay man.

Anger at those outrages was ignited during a New Year's eve party in a bar called the New Faces in downtown Los Angeles. Men in costume, several in drag, cavorted there till almost midnight. The tide of revelers rollicked across the street to a new bar, the Black Cat, which had planned an extravagant New Year's celebration.

At midnight, with a group named Rhythm Queens leading the gathered men in singing "Auld Lang Syne" and as multicolored balloons were sent aloft and men kissed each other randomly, vice cops raided the bar. Flailing batons, brandishing handcuffs, using pool cues, the cops beat scores of gay men and arrested them on various charges, smearing the street outside with blood.

As the resultant trials extended with deadly rancor and slowness, rage flared, and less than two months later, more than two hundred gay men and women protested on the street, waving signs and shouting, "No more abuse." Police cars and unmarked vehicles responded, and watched, frozen, from the sidelines at this troubling new development: queers protesting, intimating violence—and violence did erupt, sporadically at first with improvised missiles hurled at the stunned cops, and then much more forcefully. Men rushed at the cops, smashing the windows of squad cars, hurling rocks at the astonished fleet.

The riot was given tiny notice in the city newspapers, which cited a "street disturbance."

That occurred in Los Angeles in 1967. I was not there. I had already returned to El Paso.

And so time passed, times of turbulence in the world, the devastation in Vietnam, of massive protests, of the rise of violent "flower children" preparing to be led by Charles Manson, of drugs and acid dreams and nightmares, of spurious celebrations of love.

In those years I joined the turbulence and the celebrations. Aroused by my detestation of war, I joined GIs for Peace. We met for strategy sessions in my home, and invaded Fort Bliss with fliers opposing the war.

And I welcomed the destructiveness of drugs hoping they might assuage but they only deepened the depthless endless sorrow at my mother's death, which, even now, many years later, I cannot entirely face.

33

By 1977, I had written five books. The most recent one, *The Sexual Outlaw: A Documentary,* threatened to surpass the original outrage created by *City of Night.* Bookstores were returning it. A television station in San Francisco had rejected an advertisement for it. A reporter had offered to do a story about this incident in San Francisco, along with an interview with me. Grove Press coaxed me to accept. I agreed, certain that I could control whatever would compromise my cherished private identity.

By then, the Castro district in San Francisco had become a gay haven. On warm afternoons, hundreds of gay men lolled about, many shirtless, but many in leather despite the warmth. There was a mood of euphoria on those streets, a strange euphoria, a forced confidence asserting that times had changed for gay men.

I tried to identify it as I moved from turf to turf. It was a desperate euphoria, which seemed to me to contain a sense that it might not last, that it must be seized, must be sustained on the highest level, at a pitch that could not endure.

Cruising those streets, and the more intimate areas where sex occurred openly at night, I would hear—emanating from a bar or a cluster of men walking along the streets, and even, at rare times, held only for moments, breaking the heavy silence of somber orgy rooms of ritual punishment—a mirthless laughter, laughter that belonged to the euphoria, a terminal euphoria, laughter that began as a gasp, stumbled as if on a wound, and then rose, rose into a shriek, throttled.

Don Allen invited me to lunch to meet some people who, he said, "are eager to meet you." I met them at a fancy Chinese restaurant.

Don introduced me to Michael McClure, the glamorous poet and playwright; an effeminate fashion photographer; and Allen Ginsberg.

Bluntly, but not sounding hostile—as if he was really only amused—Ginsberg said to me: "So! You still don't get fucked?"

The fashion photographer tittered; Michael McClure adjusted his long blond hair; Don Allen said, "Hmmm"; and I was taken aback—my face felt flushed. "That's none of—" I started to say.

In that curiously friendly tone, Ginsberg went on, while showing off his facility with chopsticks: "I suppose, umm, that you believe your stance makes you, umm, the powerful one in sex." He laughed; his beard jiggled. With a swipe of his tongue, he ascertained the presence of a piece of something Chinese that had nested in his beard. I knew that he was performing, showing off his bravado, his lack of inhibition. "Man," he said, in an altered, jivey tone, "when I'm blowing someone or I'm getting fucked, I *know* I'm the one who has power; I'm the one who's drawing out the come into me."

I liked that his philosophy assigned power to both performances in sex; it was a sexual democracy. "Fine with me," I said. "Equals, both feeling powerful." It amused me to think of him as the exalted guru he was becoming, had become, because he continued to talk relentlessly dirty at the table, while Don kept saying, "Oh, Allen," and McClure languished handsomely in the red-leather booth, and the fashion photographer looked around as if scouting for locations.

"What about when your body grows old and you can no longer attract your numbers?" Ginsberg extended his oddly friendly interrogation.

"It will never happen," I said firmly.

"How will you stop it?"

"It will never happen," I said.

When lunch ended—despite his bravado at my expense, I liked him—Ginsberg invited me to visit longer with him. ("Uh-hmmmm," said the fashion photographer. Don Allen said, "Oh, Allen." Michael McClure, recognized, signed an autograph graciously.) Ginsberg was staying at Lawrence Ferlinghetti's "pad." Would I join him?

"Sure." I accepted a visit with the legendary poet.

In a ratty part of North Beach, I walked up what seemed to be a hundred steps to a nondescript apartment, where, inside—amid hardly any furniture, only books—Ginsberg sat on the floor in what I imagined was the manner of a guru. He was wearing something flowing that looked like a muumuu, white, muslin. He indicated a cushion for me to sit on.

"Relax; take your clothes off," he said, again in a pleasant tone.

"No," I said. The conversation would not turn literary if I sat there naked. Maybe this was part of his mystical approach to detect visitors' auras—and enjoy their nudity. I asked, "Why?"

"Because you said you'd never grow undesirable. I hope that is true, really. For now, I want to see your body when I know it's beautiful—and then it will be so forever in my memory."

What a rap, I thought, laughing, but the implication of his words had stung me, challenged me, aroused the demon of losing desirability.

"I'm comfortable as I am," I said.

"Too bad; I really would like to see you naked." He reached over to something on the floor that looked to me like a lyre. He began playing the instrument and singing—I recognized the words—from Blake's *Songs of Innocence* or *Songs of Experience*.

The phone rang. Ginsberg answered. "You know who's here with me?" he said to whoever was calling. "John Rechy . . . Yes, him. Yes, he is very . . ." He extended the telephone toward me. "It's Peter," he said, "he'd like to talk to you."

I knew he meant his supposed "lover," Peter Orlovsky. Rumors were already afoot that they were nothing of the kind; like Andy Warhol and Gerard Malanga, they were said to be just posing.

"Hi."

"Man, Allen says you're in terrific shape."

Orlovsky must have asked him if I was in good shape when Ginsberg had answered yes. "Yes, he is very . . ."

"You work out, man?"

"Yes."

"How much do you press?"

"Take off your clothes," Ginsberg was whispering in my ear.

Soon after, I had lunch in a pretty restaurant with another writer who had learned I was in San Francisco and contacted me through Don Allen. Albert Stern, a friendly man who seemed to want to know everything about everything, and everything about everyone, had written an article praising *City of Night,* and I thanked him for it. I admired his books, and told him so.

We chatted amicably about writing, his, mine—what was he writing next; what was I writing next?

" . . . an item in Bert Schwartz's column; everybody reads him."

He was suggesting that this would help me in the campaign to overcome the barriers developing against *The Sexual Outlaw.*

I agreed: "But I don't know Bert Schwartz."

"The best approach to him would be to contact his wife; she loves to have famous writers at her gatherings, and you might—"

My words came automatically, the way one remembers a friend evoked by another: "I do know her. I dated her once in El Paso, years ago."

Albert's fork, poised to bring a piece of chicken salad to his lips, was held there for seconds before he brought it down on his plate, leaving the intended action incomplete, putting the fork down with what sounded to me—when I thought about it later—like a clang!

"You knew Isabel in El Paso?" He seemed to have abandoned eating.

Only then did I realize the significance of what I had said. I retreated, trying to erase my clumsy words. "I take it back; I don't know her. I saw a picture of Mrs. Schwartz in a magazine once, and I remember thinking she looked like the girl I knew." Why was I so adamantly guarding Isabel's identity?

"I'm sure she is someone else," Albert seemed to allow. "Isabel's from New Orleans, by way of Spain—Castilian, I think."

I needed to end this emphatically. "The woman I knew was Alicia Gonzales, and she was Mexican." To divert his interest further from Isabel to me, I added, "Like me."

"I didn't know you were Mexican—Mexican-American—John."

"I've never seen the need to announce it," I said, more testily than I wanted. "I assume people know, and, if not, it's irrelevant."

"Yes," Albert said. "Of course."

I ran into Albert a few days later at a book fair in the Convention Center. "About Isabel Schwartz," he said.

I held my breath. "Yes?"

"She isn't the person you thought she was."

He had pursued the matter, still sniffing gossip; he had not believed my dismissal. "But I told you she wasn't."

"I saw her at the opera last weekend. She was waiting for Bert to join her. I said I'd had lunch with someone she might recognize, John Rechy—you know, trying to help you get that item in Bert's column."

I felt a trap opening. "I *told* you I don't know her." I checked my impatience; I didn't want to block the information he clearly wanted to give me.

"She said, 'I don't know anybody by that name.'"

I was stung. Claiming no knowledge of me even as a writer! More than that—much more—how dare the fucking bitch say she didn't know me? Fine, then, I would blurt out the whole truth about her. She'd given me the perfect opening, the perfect reason to do it, and so easily, with such a reliable messenger.

Albert was waiting expectantly.

"There you are, Albert; you found out what I had told you. I don't know her and she doesn't know me." How quickly my anger at her had dissipated. She had *had* to deny knowing me if she was to sustain her claimed identity, and I had chosen to be her ally in upholding her camouflage.

"She did turn white when I mentioned your name, and she walked away," Albert added.

Back in Los Angeles, I waited, regretting my inadvertent part in any scandal that might occur. But I heard nothing further about the matter—and surely my sister Olga would know of any dramatic development. I had finally convinced Albert—or he had convinced himself—that there was no connection between Isabel and the girl I had known. I was relieved.

What did I feel about Isabel Franklin-Schwartz? I could detect no tinge of lingering romance toward the girl I had dated. There was, of course, the fascination that her camouflage evoked. That was not enough. I could not find an answer for my strong feelings about her, my enduring interest in her. All I knew was that with Albert I had felt a sense of protectiveness toward her.

34

More time passed.

I left El Paso permanently, painfully selling my mother's home. I moved to Los Angeles. I was still determined to remain anonymous. I hunted sex in the shady glens of Griffith Park. Challenging time, at times terrified, I hustled on the new turf along Santa Monica Boulevard. My body survived, kept firm and muscular by rigorous workouts. Every time of conquest affirmed this, and denied that age had encroached.

Once again I was in San Francisco. The paperback edition of *The Sexual Outlaw* was also facing problems of censorship. In England a suit was threatened immediately after the publisher announced its publication. Australian customs had confiscated copies. In America, books ordered were returned after complaints from customers. I had stayed in touch with the reporter in San Francisco —she had written a good and sympathetic article about the earlier conflicts over the book. Now she offered to deal, in a further article, with the present circumstances.

We met at the Fleur de Lis restaurant, an expensive favorite in San Francisco. The decor seemed to have been inspired by an elaborate circus. A heavy awning—perhaps velvet—hovered like a tent over the barely lit dining room.

Soon after we had been fussily seated, the reporter, a chic, smart, pretty woman, startled me by saying, casually:

"There's Schwartz and his Spanish wife." A devoted San Franciscan, she had told me during our earlier encounter that it amused her to keep up with talk about the various—"often shaky"—levels of society in San Francisco.

There she was, Alicia Gonzales, Isabel Franklin, Isabel Franklin-Schwartz.

And she floated in like a queen into her court, removing a cape that an attendant took just as it was being allowed to slip down from her shoulders; her husband, the San Francisco icon, was at her side, a rotund man wearing expensive clothes that he did not look entirely comfortable in.

The restaurant staff was at attention. Around the room, sophisticated diners avoided glancing at the famous couple. The maître d', bowing periodically, was leading them to their table.

As she passed us, Isabel nodded at the woman I was with.

Then her eyes glanced over to me.

She halted.

Her head turned toward the entrance, as if she was considering leaving.

She looked away from me.

She placed her hand—as if for reassurance—on her husband's arm, causing him to pause, too.

Following the maître d', who had hesitated during the bewildered moments, they walked ahead.

The maître d' led them to a desirable table within view of ours. Extending the ceremonial seating, he pulled out a regal chair for her, a chair that would face our table. With a nod, she indicated her preference for another seat, one where she would have her back to me.

If I had had any doubt that she had recognized me, it was now gone. She was avoiding me, perhaps even hoping—even trying to believe—that I had not recognized her after so many, many years, so many identities assumed and discarded.

Wait. What was happening?

She was leaning over to whisper to her husband, who signaled the maître d', who swooped back to their table. Words were exchanged; the seating was once again ordered to be rearranged. Now she sat facing me, in full view of me—and I was in full view of her. Our eyes connected.

She was challenging me.

But what was the challenge? Surely she didn't think that I—in this arrogant restaurant with everyone aware of everyone else, and especially of her and her husband, and I with a woman well known in San Francisco—surely, no, she wouldn't believe that I might be considering intruding on her and her alerted husband and, by her boldness, her fixed stare, was keeping me in check? No, that wasn't it. What challenge, then, was there for me to accept, especially in a setting she had managed so carefully to choreograph?

Then—

She asked for a cigarette—I saw her husband extending a shimmering case to her. From it she took a cigarette, as carefully as if she was choosing a precious jewel from a box. Although an attendant materialized to light it for her, her husband had already half-risen from his seat to do the honor.

My concentration was fixed so intently on her that my friend nudged me back to attention—"John, you're staring. I'm sure she loves that." My eyes remained fixed on Isabel Franklin-Schwartz.

With the chosen cigarette in her hand, her lips tilted; there was an inception of a smile—*I knew this without actually seeing it from the distance where I watched.* As if deciding not to complete the smile, her lips parted to receive the cigarette. She held it there at the verge of brushing her lips before she allowed it to touch in a movement that occurred without transition.

She inhaled, the barest rise and fall of her breasts, the only indication—*I saw that clearly; and . . .*

A slender streak of smoke arose, lingered about her before it evaporated. The cigarette remained touching her lips as if reluctant to separate. Then her free hand rose—*I knew this was next*—and rested lightly on the elbow of the arm whose fingers held the cigarette, and she completed an intricately graceful choreography of movements that extended as she withdrew the cigarette from her lips but kept it close, as if deciding whether to inhale from it again, extending a moment of suspense. Her motions reversed, she rested the cigarette on the edge of an ashtray.

Now—*I knew*—she would complete the attempt that had once been foiled in my uncle's Cadillac, her attempt to imitate the grand kept woman of Augusto de Leon, whom we had both studied, if only for seconds, both in awe, each superbly elegant motion captured in our minds—*I knew that, too*—as she smoked an ordinary cigarette. I had been the only witness to the failure of the woman I now faced in this ornately luxurious restaurant, the only witness when, years ago, at the Oasis Drive-In, her hands, trembling, had exposed her insecurity and she had dropped the courted cigarette, a catastrophic failure in the test she had set for herself, a failure that must have aroused doubts of her ever leaving behind the poor Mexican girl who was Alicia Gonzales from El Paso, Texas; doubts of ever becoming as grand as the grand kept woman she had attempted unsuccessfully to emulate. Now, from the only person who had witnessed that failure, she could supplant it with her perfect performance.

She reached for the cigarette that had rested on the ashtray, and, holding my look, demanding that I watch the next graceful move—no demand was necessary—she brought the cigarette to her lips, allowed it to remain there poised. Then the hand with the cigarette drifted away from her face, was lowered, and she touched the tip of the cigarette so lightly to an ashtray that—*I was sure of this without being able to see it*—the ashes vanished, merely vanished.

After moments, she reached again for the cigarette on the ashtray and looked up, and she smiled, definitely smiled this time, at me, for me to confirm the triumph of her borrowed identity, its powerful inspiration.

And I did confirm it, with admiration. I nodded and smiled.

Suddenly her elbow, as if pulled down by some force beyond her—or, yes, within her—connected with the very edge of the table, and her body swayed clumsily to one side, thrusting the lit cigarette onto her lap.

With a muffled sob, she pushed it away, onto the floor. The maître d' uttered a cry that mixed with not-quite smothered giggles about the restaurant. In a flurry, every attendant was rushing to snatch away from the floor the existence of the fatal cigarette.

I looked away from the tiny, major disaster, this major failure of Alicia Gonzales to be someone she was not.

In the following days, the memory of that incident persisted, often with sadness. It was as if on that evening in a restaurant with mesmerized candlelight, I had shared Isabel's humiliation, her symbolic failure—as if I had been her.

35

Months passed. My life remained the same. Clinging to my cherished anonymity that allowed me to continue to exist in the sexual arenas—turning away from anyone I thought recognized me as a writer and so compromising my street identity—I cruised for numbers in the park during the day, and I hustled for sex-money at night, constantly reassuring myself of my desirability, and then, for long intervals, writing furiously as if the two "worlds" were at war.

In my apartment on Los Feliz in Los Angeles, I was working out when the phone rang. A determinedly cheerful voice announced itself to be that of the famous columnist in San Francisco. I assumed he wanted to interview me for an item he would propose.

After a few moments, not many, of pleasantries exchanged between people who don't know each other but suspect that one wants something from the other, he said, casually:

"I understand you knew my wife in El Paso."

My instant surprise was not that he would not have known that, or believed it until now, but that it had taken Albert so long to tell him about the conversation I regretted.

"Who is your wife?" I asked. I wanted to mark time, to discover his real reason for his calling me now.

"Her name was Isabel Franklin before we married, but it might have been another name when you knew her."

I was being ambushed by this startling call and the reason for it. I needed to be careful of what I said. I needed to hear more.

"My wife—" He was proceeding cautiously, as if he, too, wanted as much unqualified information from me as I now wanted from him. "When I met her—she claimed—she said—she told me she was from New Orleans, her family was from Spain, she was Castilian."

Then it was true that he—specializing in gossip—had not known for years that those were lies. Out of the mixture of emotions this irony stirred in me, I laughed. "I'm sorry, I—"

"But it is funny," he said. "My wife's real name is the one you mentioned to Albert—Alicia Gonzales?—and she's Mexican. I wouldn't have cared about who she really is or what her background was. I care only that she lied, and now I want to put an end to her lies."

"You're divorcing her." I understood.

"Yes."

Was this what the call was about? Grounds for a favorable divorce? Considerations of alimony, property? Was he trying to engage me as a witness to the layers of fraudulence he had believed for years and would now use against her?

"I feel sorry for her," he said quickly into the telephone. "She doesn't know who she is."

She doesn't know who she is! I needed no rehearsal for what I said:

"When I spoke to Albert, I told him I wasn't sure we were talking about the same woman. And, Mr. Schwartz, I *am* sure now that we were not. I confused her with a photograph I saw, only that." My words would not convince him—there were too many links to the easily available evidence he needed about Alicia Gonzales. That didn't matter to me. Only this mattered:

I *needed* to protect her.

★　★　★

She doesn't know who she is.

I had heard those words before. No, I had heard words like them. *Do you know who—?* Where? When? Why did the memory of the kept woman of Augusto de Leon sweep into my mind with the insistence of something more, much more, nudging the familiar memory? *As if deciding not to complete the smile, or because the memory aroused had turned bitter, her scarlet lips parted . . .* I had felt that insistence before, of something more pushing at the cherished memorized details—*an intricately graceful choreography of slight movements . . . a moment of suspense.* Yes, I had been aware of the edge of another memory insinuating itself. *Aren't you ashamed?* Of what? When? But those times, that hint of something more—*Who do you think—?* had withdrawn at the point when, in the memory, I had become aware of Isabel Franklin staring at the object of fascination at which I, too, stared in awe, that time when I, when we—I knew this for both of us—when we had clasped within our memories what we saw as a perfect creation, Marisa Guzman, who had escaped the drabness of the life we must have foreseen as our own; and she had brought, if only briefly into our unhappy lives, moments of beauty and possibility, and more, much more, to be discovered only later, much later. Isabel—no, she had been Alicia Gonzales then—Alicia and I had become allied, an allegiance that had extended, if only in our memories, through the years. In defending her, I had been defending myself.

And suddenly there it was, the full memory of that day, which had lain dormant until now, sprung awake by Schwartz's words echoing other words, similar words, entirely different words, words always there, waiting to spring at the proper moment.

That day of my sister's wedding the spell of the kept woman had been shattered as she sat on the drab couch she transformed into a throne. A harsh, square woman invaded the room, too brashly to have stumbled into it by chance. Like an authoritative guard, she held her hands over her ample bosom as she glowered sternly at the seated regal woman.

"*Tú, mujer! No te da vergüenza que te vean aquí? Pos, quién te cres? Sabes quién eres?*"

For moments, the poised woman seemed neither to see nor to hear the hostile woman who had demanded: "You, woman! Aren't you ashamed to be seen here? Who do you think you are? Do you know who you are?"

The kept woman rose from the faded couch. She smoothed her dress, running her hands down it to banish any wrinkle that might linger. She stood. She lifted her hat's veil entirely from her face. And she said—

Words that I heard and pushed away, words I wasn't sure I heard, words I know I heard, words carried away by the sounds of the wedding party in the adjoining room, words kept away in my mind, words returning only now, allowed with the full force of their implied judgment on Alicia Gonzales—and on me—for all our subterfuges and masquerades, words that would now reverberate with full meaning in my own life.

"I am," she answered the agitated woman, "Marisa Guzman. You probably know me as the kept woman of Augusto de Leon. No, I am not ashamed of who I am."